Water and Fire

Melinda McDonald

WATER AND FIRE

Copyright

© 2008 by Melinda McDonald.

All rights reserved.

Cover design by Kelvin Owens

To my husband, Ron

Thanks to

Kathy Liesman, Sandy Baksys, Rachel Ommen,
Classie Murray, Joe Sturm, Kathryn Harris,
my daughters Emily and Chelsea,
and the members of the Cherry Hills Baptist Church small group
for their support and encouragement.

"When thou passest through the waters, I will be with thee; and
through the rivers, they shall not overflow thee:
when thou walkest through the fire, thou shalt not be burned;
neither shall the flame kindle upon thee."

Isaiah 43:2
The Holy Bible
King James Version

"There is no grievance
that is a fit object of redress by mob law."

Abraham Lincoln
Address Before the Young Men's Lyceum
Springfield, Illinois
January 27, 1838

Springfield, Illinois. August 14, 1908.

The sound of shattering glass woke Sheba. She lay in her thin nightgown, facing the clapboard wall of her sleeping room, perspiring under the coarse cotton sheet. Above her cot hung a gilt-framed print of Jesus, blue-eyed and bearded, knocking at a closed door. A corner of the frame glowed in the gaslight from the streetlamp outside the second-story window.

She rolled over and sighed with relief when she saw that the window was still intact. Before she went to bed, she had cracked it open to catch any breeze wafting through on that stifling August night, and now she could hear the crowd in the street below. "Curse the day Lincoln freed the niggers," a woman cried shrilly. Shouts of assent followed. "Yeah, let's get 'em." A bottle broke on the pavement and the crowd cheered. Red torchlight danced on the room's walls.

They must not find her. Sheba sat up, grabbing for her clothes, draped over the chair next to her bed. Pressing against the back wall of the room, she pulled her red calico dress over her nightgown, fearful that someone in the crowd on the street would see her dark figure. As she tied her undergarments and hairbrush into a shawl, the shouts and crashes of the mob faded.

She paused and listened before descending the steps from her sleeping room to the dressmaking shop below. It was hers, at least it had been. Sheba could hear the crowd in the distance. Shots were still being fired, but only light from the streetlamps streamed through the high transom window above the street-level door.

She pulled the door open slowly, so as not to jingle the bell on the knob: the street outside was littered with bottles, shreds of cloth, bricks and rocks. She slipped through the opening, and then closed the door behind her, pulling until it clicked shut. She was struck by the futility of this action as she turned to gaze through the shattered window of her dressmaking shop, shards of glass glinting across the wooden floor. She fought the urge to go rescue her unfinished garments and yard goods, but she knew the crowd might reappear at any moment. If they did, she was as good as dead. Instead she turned and crept through the streets of the ravaged downtown, scuttling from shadow to shadow, toward the only refuge she knew: the Lawrence House.

August 1906. Crossing the Tracks.

On a stifling summer day in the brightness of the morning, a young colored girl stood at the entrance to a very strange house. She pressed the black button for the doorbell, then took a step back and contemplated the arched front door and the tapered bricks that canopied it. Sweat beaded up at the nape of her neck, then slid down the back of her white, high-necked blouse.

As she waited for the door to be answered, sixteen-year-old Sheba Tully swayed gently, cardboard suitcase banging on the back of her legs. All during the long walk from the Lincoln Colored Home on the east side of the railroad tracks, Sheba had prayed for courage, stealing sidelong glances at the deep lawns shaded by overhanging trees, the towering white houses with empty, encircling porches.

In her short life, Sheba had never crossed the railroad tracks that bisected Springfield, neatly separating black from white. To the east were the Badlands, postage-stamp sized yards populated with chickens and children belonging to the tiny wooden houses where the Negroes of Springfield lived. Scott Burton, a Negro, ran a hugely profitable barber shop here and the Lincoln Colored Home, so named for the city's most famous resident, stood to the north of this large area. West of the tracks, the wide, well-shaded streets of the city stretched and, with very few exceptions, only white residents lived here.

Sheba hadn't expected to feel so overwhelmed, so dirty and unfit, as she picked her way along the sidewalk. After all, colored girls were hired as servants in all the best homes, or so Ruby Burton, Scott's wife, said. All of a sudden, she heard female voices and without thinking she stepped into the gutter to give the two white ladies the sidewalk. As they bustled by, she heard, "You'd think Susan would have something better to do with her money…," then the women turned down Fourth Street and disappeared.

When she first saw the Lawrence House, her stomach had turned. She'd known then that there was no turning back to the safety of the east side. The structure sprawled out over half a block, flanked with porches, balconies and oddly patterned windows of colored glass. Sunlight gleamed from the red tile roof, playing on the upturned tips of the eaves. A patterned greenish design crawled around the top of the wall, near the gutter. The unbroken lines of the roof made the house look as though it followed the lines of the earth it was built on, unlike its neighbors, which thrust upwards, into the green branches of the trees.

"What you want?" She started from her reverie as a colored woman of indeterminate age opened the wooden door and thrust her head out. Bits of gray hair poked out from under the kerchief wrapped around the woman's head and she scowled at Sheba.

The girl almost sighed with relief. Another colored woman, a friend, an ally. "I come lookin' for maid work 'n I thought you might be needin' somebody." She hated to waste her only weapon with a servant, but she had to get in the door, so she pulled out a tattered white calling card, her most precious possession. Given to her by the mother of the mistress of this house, the card represented what she felt was a promise, a promise of employment. "See, I got this here card t'show from old Miz Lawrence recommendin' me for a job."

The servant shook her white-wrapped head. "Don' mean nothin'. That ol' lady, she dead." She began to close the door, muttering, "You girls come dime-a-dozen wantin' t'work at this here fancy house."

This wasn't going well, so Sheba decided to take more decisive action. She stepped forward and raised her voice. "I got qualifications. Why I done maid work and sewin' for Mr. Scott Burton, the colored barber, I reckon you heard a him." The door stayed where it was, almost closed, but not quite. Sheba couldn't tell if the woman was listening or not.

Before the maid could answer, Sheba heard a throaty, feminine voice, coming from an upper level. "Hattie, I'm back." The door pulled shut. Sheba stared at it for a minute, then gathered her courage and rang the bell again. This time a different person opened it, a middle-aged white lady with faded brown hair stringing down from a bun. Flour speckled the woman's apron: a cook by the look of her.

Determined to be more forthright with this woman, Sheba pushed the card into her face and said, "Is the missus needin' a maid? Jus' listen. I got this here card from her ma." In desperation, Sheba handed the card to the servant, who regarded it with suspicion.

"Well, suppose you step in here and wait while I show this card to Mrs. Dana." The cook swung the door wide to admit Sheba into a small entry hall. She was inside at least and this encouraged her. The hall was bathed in light diffused by glass the color of amber and forest green and gold. Turning as the woman closed the door, Sheba glimpsed a pattern of angular butterflies in the glass over the door.

The cook vanished and Sheba's anxiety returned, fear that the mistress of the house might not like her. She looked around the entryway and saw that a statue presided over it. Almost as tall as a child, the statue depicted a lady with plain, center-parted hair wearing what looked like a nightdress. Something moved behind it and Sheba realized that she could look past the figure to a level slightly higher than her breast and see an entire room, with an arched brick fireplace that resembled the front door. At that moment, a woman swept past the fireplace, then reappeared on the stairs to the left where the servant had disappeared.

"So you're here about a maid's job." The woman stood on the bottom step, eye to eye with Sheba, who was taller by several inches. Her dress, a filmy affair made of what looked like handkerchiefs, wafted behind her. She glanced at Sheba, then at the card in her hand. "I see you have Mama's card by way of recommendation." The woman looked up at the girl, then her thin lips relaxed into a smile, revealing enviable white teeth. "Well, if that doesn't take the cake. I remember you from that day at the Lincoln Colored Home. Mama took a liking to you, said you reminded her of someone in the Bible. What's your name girl?"

"Sheba Tully, ma'am." Tongue-tied, she stared at the woman, who appeared to be in early middle age, with ash-blonde hair curling around her strong, regular features. Sheba felt a pang of relief. The calling card appeared to have done its work, opening the door of this house and setting her apart from the other job-seekers.

The woman continued talking as Sheba followed her up the stairs. "I am Mrs. Dana and you come at an opportune time. We usually employ two live-in maids and one has just left to go to East St. Louis to be married." They entered the area that Sheba had seen earlier from the entryway, and Mrs. Dana took a seat before the fireplace on an angular settee. Sheba remained standing, remembering Ruby's advice never to sit in the presence of a white person.

"Now then, I need to find out a few things about you. Do you have any experience with house cleaning work and sewing?"

Sheba squeezed the handle of her cardboard suitcase with nervousness. "Yes'm. I done house cleanin' and sewin' for Miz Burton for 'bout two years. An' Miz Burton she taught me to sew too on a real sewin' machine."

"Well, I'll want to check your references, but I'm inclined to give you a chance, just for Mama's dear sake." Mrs. Dana paused, and then said, "We need you to start right away. Hattie isn't as young as she used to be and we're having a dinner party tonight."

Sheba said nothing, but her stomached flopped again. She had no experience with the kind of fancy dinner parties she was sure Mrs. Dana hosted. But she hadn't spent every Sunday for the past five years at the Pleasant Grove Baptist Church for naught and now she entreated God to come to her aid as she followed her new mistress into the kitchen.

Instead of the heavenly host, there were two servants in the kitchen. The women who had answered the front door were working, one at the sink and the other kneading bread on a wooden table. Mrs. Dana addressed the colored woman at the sink. "Hattie, this is Sheba, our new maid. Please show her where to put her things. I want her to start immediately." Then she turned to speak to the cook about dinner.

Hattie sighed as she dried her hands on her apron. "C'mon upstairs." Sheba tried to catch her glance, but Hattie refused to acknowledge her. Instead, she lumbered through another door, leading Sheba into a small pantry, then up some narrow winding stairs to the house's second story. As they climbed, Sheba

4

could hear Mrs. Dana in the kitchen talking with the white cook. "She'll do fine for a house nigger. She's not real dark and she knows how to sew."

Sheba stopped and stared at Hattie's back. She had heard the slur before: it was a hurtful term, surely not something a lady would say.

"You comin' girl?" Without turning, Hattie shouted down from the top of the curved, narrow stairs and Sheba continued her climb. Shaking a little, she forced herself to remember that just this morning she had left the Lincoln Colored Home, just another colored girl with no prospects. Now, less than a day later, she was starting a new situation at the home of the richest lady in Springfield. Surely God was on her side.

A Thrilling Story

Elliott Loper was the sole occupant of the newsroom of the *Springfield Record*. The next morning's edition had been put to bed at seven o'clock, and now the newsroom was populated only by dark desks, each topped with an unlit lamp and a typewriter. He surveyed the empty room, the breeze from the open window hitting his face, imagining himself interviewing the Governor or in the midst of the wreckage of a tornado – anything that might result in a story that would get him off this abysmal graveyard shift. He ran his fingers through his curly, pale hair, then put his hands behind his head, leaning his wiry frame back in the chair and closing his eyes, the better to think about how to accomplish this.

Abruptly a siren whined next to the open newsroom window and the young man startled awake. This might be his chance, one never knew. Elliott leapt to his feet, grabbed a notepad and bounded down the stairs as the hand-cranked siren grew louder. He could hear it fine, since it was coming from the station next door, a proximity that was alternately a blessing and a curse.

Emerging from the newspaper building's shadowy entryway into the pale light of the streetlamp, Elliott fell into step with a policeman, whose silver badge shone on his blue uniform. He addressed the officer, hoping that he was showing the appropriate respect. "Heard the siren, and I assumed there'd been a hold-up." He skipped a little as he tried to keep up with the policeman, who broke into a trot and was headed toward the next block, where an Interurban car was stopped on the tracks, lights blazing. Through the open sides of the car, he could see that it was packed with passengers, all colored.

"Something like that, son." The officer's hand went to his belt where his firearm was holstered. "Stay behind me and don't get in the way." He sprinted up the steps to the car with Elliott on his heels. As Elliott gained the top of the stairs, he saw that the attention of the passengers was fixed on a man who swayed in the aisle near the front of the car waving a large revolver.

"Don't nobody move," the man cried, his speech slurred. Nobody did, including Elliott, whose gaze was riveted on the back of the Negro, as he stood, legs planted wide in the aisle, brandishing the gun. The passengers hunched on the wooden benches on either side of the streetcar, many of them clutching picnic baskets.

"Drop that gun immediately." The policeman's voice boomed. The man spun to face them, then lost his balance, stumbled, dropped the revolver, and fell to his knees in the aisle. The fall seemed to have unnerved him. "Oh please, Off'cer, don't shoot. I ain't gonna hurt nobody. Why that gun ain't even loaded." The policeman grabbed the man's wrists and pulled him to his feet, fastening handcuffs and binding his arms in front of him.

Glancing over his shoulder at Elliott, who was scribbling notes as if his life depended on it, the policeman shouted, "Son, grab that weapon for me and bring it along to the stationhouse." Then he turned and pushed the man down the aisle and into the streets, kicking him for good measure. "Don't you folks worry none. I got this one taken care of."

Elliott picked up the gun by its barrel and rushed down into the street. As the Interurban clanged and departed, he followed the policeman who dragged the staggering Negro into the stationhouse. They entered the brightly lit police station and Elliott experienced a slight thrill of civic pride. He had played a role in capturing a drunken man who was threatening passengers on the Interurban streetcar. As the officer pushed the man into a cell, Elliott glanced down at the revolver in his hands, turning it over and feeling its weight. It was heavy, but elegant and he wondered if it might belong to a woman. He grasped the gun's pearl handle, then glimpsed something unusual. There above the round "Colt" emblem the initials "KH" were scratched deep in the silver metal. He wiped the gun with his thumb, but the initials remained.

The officer returned to the room. "Well, thanks for the help son. The man's drunk and can't even walk right. He gave those folks a turn, that's for sure." The man's voice indicated a smile that did not appear on his face, and he held out his hand for the weapon.

Elliott pointed to the initials. "That's a little unusual, these initials here on the gun. What do you think this means?" As he passed the gun over, he met the man's tired eyes.

"Well, sure, there's a good possibility it don't belong to this drunken fellow, at least from what he says."

"What d'you mean?" Elliott pulled his notepad from his pocket and began to write.

The policeman scratched his head and yawned. "He was yammering 'bout how that gun wasn't even his and to please let him go. I reckon he stole it, but we'll find out when he sobers up."

Elliott poked his hair with his pencil. "Well, I guess the owner's initials are 'KH'. Got any idea who that might be?"

The policeman sank into a wooden chair behind the desk. "I got no idea. No idea." He stared at Elliott in silence.

"Well, I better go. This story's first-rate copy for our morning edition. Any other information I should know for the story?" Elliott moved toward the door.

The officer was writing now and didn't look up. "That Interurban car was comin' from Irwins' Park, a big Negro jamboree out there I guess. Oh, and we did get the fellow's name out of him, least the name he says he has. Craig. Joe Craig."

"Much obliged, sir." Elliott nodded as he left the room, the policeman busily writing his report.

Back at the newsroom, Elliott threaded a piece of paper into the typewriter. The wall clock's round face glowed in the streetlight. It was nearly midnight. He had time to write the story, file it with the night desk editor, and still get a few hours of sleep before the next day's obituaries were due. The clock was ticking, drumming the two o'clock deadline into Elliott's brain.

He began to type. Headline: *Joe Craig, alleged to have made threats on Interurban Car*. He pushed the carriage return and began the story: *While returning from a negro picnic at Irwins' park Wednesday night, Joe Craig is said to have threatened passengers on an interurban car with a big revolver which he flourished in a frightening manner.* The staccato pounding of the typewriter echoed in the empty newsroom.

The Privileged Ones

The five Lawrence House servants were gathered in the kitchen, covertly scrutinizing the new maid and devouring an early dinner. It was five o'clock, about an hour before they usually sat down together; however, this evening there was to be a dinner party and the servants would be needed.

The help sat in silence around the kitchen table, ready to partake of the simple meal of cornbread and greens. Assuming that they were waiting, Sheba bowed her head to say a prayer. "Father, bless this food to our use and us to thy service. Amen." She looked around the table, and guessed that the group never offered thanks before their meals. A young colored man with a tan complexion and teasing smile who had been introduced as Thomas spoke, his mouth full of cornbread. "So where you come from, Miss New Maid?"

Hattie tittered, while Maud and her husband exchanged glances. "Why I come from the Lincoln Colored Home and from Mr. Scott Burton's." It was nervy for him to request such personal information and Sheba concentrated on buttering her cornbread.

Thomas persisted. "Oh, so you from the Badlands. Well Scott he's a fine gentleman, but the Colored Home ain't so grand. Guess you must be an orphan." The young man took a swig of milk from his metal cup.

Sheba decided the truth would come out at some point, but she balked at telling the whole sordid story of her past. Surely God would not begrudge her withholding the fact that her mother was working in a brothel in the worst section of Springfield, the Levee. "My daddy he got killed at the mine and my mama, well she kinda' disappeared -- so Mr. Scott and his wife Miss Ruby, they took me in. But then they had a new little 'un and there warn't 'nuff room, so's I had to go to the Colored Home." She observed the blank faces around the table but couldn't resist adding, "But you know, I b'liev God He done had it figur'd out, 'cause He sent Miz Dana and her mama to me there."

At the mention of the departed Mrs. Lawrence, Hattie look up from the mountain of greens she was shoveling into her mouth. "Oh that sainted woman Miz Lawrence. She so good to us colored folks. I like to cried my eyes out when she passed, so far 'way and all." Consumed with emotion, Hattie put down her fork.

No one had enlightened Sheba on the circumstances of Mrs. Lawrence's demise. "What happened to Miz Lawrence 'for she passed?"

Hattie wiped her eyes on the tablecloth. "Oh, that so sad. Miz Lawrence and Miz Susan, they went on a long trip, oh all over creation, to the West Indies and Florida and I don't know where all. And when they be on the train comin' back, why Miz. Lawrence up and died. And here Miz Susan just built this nice big house with a special bedroom and all, so's her poor mama wouldn't have to climb stairs. I done worked for that lady for fifteen years." Hattie seemed overcome with her memories.

Maud, who had been chewing her greens, swallowed, then said, "Here's what I think, I think the mistress is cursed or somethin'. First her babies died – that happened to me and it's pretty bad." She glanced at Sheba, "Then her husband passed, and her daddy and old Miz Lawrence. Now all she's got left is that dried up cousin of hers." Maud's husband, a sallow man in overalls, nodded agreement as he reached for more greens.

Hattie stood and picked up her plate. "Best hurry up -- they be needin' the kitchen for that fancy party." At this moment, a young white woman in a black dress and white apron came through the kitchen door from the garden carrying a large covered platter. "See here's that caterin' girl already."

The caterer's girl shoved the platter on the table, and the servants scattered from the dinner table. She looked from face to face while Maud opened lower cupboard doors under the counter to reveal what looked like radiators turned sideways. As she turned a knob at the side, Sheba could hear the slow hiss of steam filling the pipes. "Good, the tenderloin'll keep warm in here," said Maud as she put the platter on the metal and closed the doors.

Hattie turned to Sheba, who was still staring at the cabinet doors. "You better go upstairs and comb your hair. That doorbell'll start ringin' 'for you know it. And that's your job, least part of it. You gotta' answer the door for all those high-brow folks comin' tonight."

It was a little scary but more exciting, thinking about all those fine folks she'd get to see now that she was working for Mrs. Dana. Sheba rushed upstairs and patted her hair down, washed her face, then started as the doorbell for the main door rang. She dashed down the back stairs and made her way to the front hallway. Mrs. Dana was nowhere to be seen, but the lights were lit and sonorous music drifted down from above, where a hired musician was pumping a player organ on one of the balconies. Sheba opened the door and drew in her breath as she faced a gentleman in top hat and black and white evening clothes and a woman who sparkled with pink jewels. She smiled and pulled the door wide.

The couple swished into the entryway and the gentleman removed his top hat and handed it to Sheba, who stared at it, then realized she was being rude. "Please tell Mrs. Dana that Mr. and Mrs. A.J. Kimber have arrived."

She placed his hat on one of the stands in the entry, then mounted the stairs to announce the pair. But before she reached the top, she saw Mrs. Dana, gowned in shimmering white satin, advancing through the reception area. Her mistress saw the pair in the entryway and called, "Alvin, Marie – how good of

10

you to come." As she beckoned the couple up the stairs, the doorbell rang again and Sheba opened the door to the next glittering pair.

Soon all eight guests had arrived and were seated around the long dining table, dimly lit by the butterfly glass chandeliers in each corner of the long room. Mrs. Dana nodded and laughed, her lustrous skin glowing. Miss Florence Lawrence presided at the foot of the table making no attempt to converse with the other guests. Sheba had been introduced to Miss Lawrence late in the afternoon, when she visited the kitchen to give orders to the servants. Miss Flora, as the servants referred to her behind her back, was a fortyish maiden cousin who lived with Mrs. Dana. Tonight she wore a high-collared grey embroidered gown and had her brown hair swept high, but unadorned in sharp contrast to the elaborately garbed guests seated between the two cousins. Since it was summer, the ladies were dressed in pale colors, their filmy dresses ornamented with lace and loaded with jewelry. Their intricate hair arrangements were accented with tiaras, jeweled combs, or feathers. The men were attired more sedately in striped tailcoats and cravats. As Sheba served the soup, she noted that none of the guests looked comfortable on the hot August night.

Mrs. Dana was flanked by a man and a woman who had arrived separately. The heavyset man had a salt-and-pepper beard, and Sheba assumed that this was the current beau for the eligible Mrs. Dana. According to Ruby Burton, Mrs. Dana had been pursued by most of the city's bachelors since her husband's death five years before in one of her father's mines in Oregon.

The servants retired to the kitchen after the cold soup was served, then waited to serve the next course until Mrs. Dana signaled by pressing a button on the floor situated under the table near her foot. When the mistress stepped on the button, a bell rang in the kitchen, and Sheba and Hattie went in to clear, while Maud and the woman from the caterer's, whose name was Lorena, brought in the next course.

As she cleared, Sheba stole glances at the guests -- particularly the gentleman sitting next to Mrs. Dana. It was hard to make out his facial features in the flickering candlelight, but Sheba could see he was almost bald and sported a large gold ring on his right hand. His eyes seldom left Mrs. Dana's face and he punctuated his conversation with a booming laugh that made the other diners start.

"Now Susie, I can't imagine what a delightful woman like you could possibly want with those shrieking suffragettes. But the paper reported that you hosted a meeting here for them," the man said, then the door swung shut behind Sheba as she carried in the last of the appetizer dishes.

Sheba mused as the servants waited in the kitchen for the summons to bring dessert and coffee. "I never heard a that, a suffragette. S'pose that's some kinda witch or bad thing."

Maud shook her head. "I don't got no idea. Some craze of the mistress."

Lorena interjected, seeming proud of her knowledge of the world. "A suffragette's someone who's in favor of the vote for women. Mrs. Dana's quite active in that movement. I guess they must be discussing them at dinner." Her face dimpled in a smile and Sheba wished Lorena worked here at the house instead of Maud.

Sheba's voice dropped to a whisper. "That bald man set next to Miz Dana , he courtin' her?"

Lorena patted her hand, putting Sheba in mind of recalled nighttime conversations among the orphans about Miss Eva. "That's Dr. Potter. He's been Mrs. Dana's beau for several months now." Lorena lowered her voice. "But my guess is that she won't be seeing him much longer. He's not her type." She nodded and glanced toward the dining room. Everyone in the kitchen started when the bell sounded, and then they dashed to bring out the trifle and coffee.

As Sheba cleared the main course to make way for dessert, Mrs. Dana directed a question at the woman on her right, who had sat silent for most of the meal. She wore a sheath-like dress and a turban of the sort colored women favored; but this lady was white. When Lorena set the dessert plate in front of her, the woman touched it tentatively. Only then did Sheba realize that the woman was blind.

A wistful smile playing over Mrs. Dana's face. "Celia, I do hope the spirits will favor you tonight. It would be such a pleasure to talk with dear Mama."

Celia leaned over to touch Mrs. Dana's arm. ""Yes, my dear Susan, I do believe we might be able to contact some of our departed souls tonight."

Mrs. Dana caught the woman's hand and held it to her face. "Oh Celia, I do so need the spirits' advice and counsel." She looked down the table, then up at her guests, who gazed at her expectantly. "Now, let's all adjourn to the gallery for a session with the Ouija board. It promises to be positively enthralling." An exclamation of approval from her guests greeted her invitation.

Sheba listened as she served the coffee from the silver pot. At the Pleasant Grove Baptist Church, she had witnessed people praying for their dead relatives, sometimes weeping and throwing up their hands at wakes. But no one ever tried to bring back folks from heaven. This had to be craziness that Mrs. Dana was discussing with this strange blind woman and her guests.

Back in the kitchen, Sheba and Hattie busied themselves with the dishwashing, while Lorena packed up the dishes from the dinner and prepared to leave. Maud listened at the door to the dining room and finally announced, "They've gone into the big room. We can clear the rest of the table."

Sheba wondered what was happening with the guests and Mrs. Dana while the maids cleared. It was late, past ten, when the last dish was finally stacked neatly in the cupboard. Sensing Sheba's exhaustion, Hattie waved her toward the stairs." You go on up to bed. I can do for them if'n they need somethin'."

Too tired to satisfy her curiosity about the Ouija board, Sheba climbed the stairs to her very own bedroom, across from Hattie's. She folded her clothes and put on her long white nightgown, then washed up in the bathroom. She was even brave enough to use the indoor privy that was part of the bathroom the two women shared.

On her way back to her bedroom, Sheba noticed a door next to the bathroom that led out onto a balcony. Despite her weariness, she opened the door, stepped out and walked along the open sleeping porch in her bare feet, enjoying the cool breeze that had started up after the sun went down. The porch ran the length of the house wing and was wide enough for two mattresses end-to-end. Looking out over the dark courtyard, Sheba could see the tall patterned glass windows of an enormous room in the adjoining wing of the house.

The dark room was lit only by candles. In the flickering light, she could make out the forms of Mrs. Dana's guests gathered around a low table. Abruptly Celia rose from her chair, her head thrown back in a scream that pierced the night air.

Sheba covered her ears and, ducking her head, she fled through the door and into her room. She jumped into bed and pulled the sheet over her head. But tired as she was, she lay awake, shivering despite the heat, until she heard Hattie's heavy footsteps around midnight. When the other bedroom door squeaked shut, Sheba relaxed into the feather pillow and closed her eyes.

Kate Howard

The next morning, Elliott waved the *Springfield Record* in front of his father, Harry, a slender, elegant man with a handlebar mustache. At that moment, Harry was seated before a plate of fried eggs and potatoes at Loper's Restaurant, thought by some to be downstate Illinois' finest eatery. "Read that, Dad. Front page news. My story. I told you it wouldn't be long."

As he watched his father survey the front page, Elliott stifled a grin – there was no point in looking foolish in front of the breakfast crowd, who stared at him as Harry perched on a stool at the back bar. That would show them – he knew the opinion of most of the well-heeled patrons, most of whom were eating before departing to oak-paneled offices in businesses or plush rooms at the State Capitol. The Loper boy'd never amount to anything, that's what they thought. Not like Harry, a respectable businessman. He was cheerful, with reason to be so: he was a man of principle and a success in the eyes of the world.

"This here your story, the piece about the colored man on the Interurban?" Harry spread the paper on the bar and pointed to the two-column story in the lower left corner of the page.

"Yessir, that's my article. I was working graveyard shift last night and the alarm sounded, so I took off. Guess it was worth my while." He couldn't keep a smile from splitting his face.

Harry looked up at Elliott and grinned, his eyes crinkling with delight. "Nice reporting, son, but I don't see your byline. So I don't know it's you who wrote this, unless you tell me." He opened the paper and glanced on page two. "Guess it's not continued from the front. The whole thing's on the front page."

Elliott sat down next to his father on the barstool. "Well, only real feature articles get bylines Dad. See, none of the articles on the front page have 'em." He opened the paper to page three and read aloud 'Earthquake Aftermath Wrecks Havoc for San Francisco by Stephen C. Bell, Associated Press' That's a feature piece from the wire service. We run local features too, with bylines."

Harry picked up his fork and began cutting his soft-cooked eggs, then mixing the yolks with the crusty fried potatoes. "Well, that's what you want, a byline. Then you've made a place for yourself, folks get to know you, doors will open." He chewed the eggs and potatoes with relish, then wiped his gray moustache with the linen napkin on the bar.

Elliott's elation evaporated. His father was a kind man, but demanding, especially of his only son. "I know Dad. That's what I'm aiming for. But this is the first step. Getting a real news article on the front page."

Harry put his hand firmly on Elliott's shoulder and the young man felt calmer. "You done good Elliott. I'm proud of you. It's the start of great things." He turned his attention back to his breakfast and a colored waiter stepped behind the bar, then sidled up to where Harry was eating.

"'Scuse me Mr. Loper. Hate interruptin' your breakfast, but, well, we havin' some trouble in the kitchen." Harry pushed his plate back and rose from the barstool.

"No trouble, Walter, I was done anyhow. I'll be back directly." Harry turned to his son, who also rose. "I guess you'll be off to cover some story or other." Elliott knew his father had done as much as he was capable of to show that he was proud of his son.

He grasped his notebook. "Actually, I'm off to do a little investigating about that streetcar holdup. Maybe it'll lead to another piece." As he strode out the door, he imagined that the eyes of the diners followed him. He hadn't far to walk down the broad streets of downtown in the early morning light of late summer. The few trees bordering the old State Capitol lawn cast a deep shade and the grass stretched from the brick sidewalk like a green carpet.

As he advanced purposefully down Fifth Street, Elliott pulled a piece of paper from the breast pocket of his houndstooth jacket. "126 East Jefferson, Howard's Boarding House." The address he had gotten from the police was only a few blocks from his father's restaurant. He was relieved that the boarding house was on the outskirts of the Levee. Even at this hour of the morning, the vice district still crawled with activity. Drunks sleeping off benders from the night before, ladies of the evening hanging out laundry, saloon keepers sweeping their establishments: he had glimpsed this from infrequent forays into the Levee as he traversed the city and he had learned to avoid the area if he could.

As he walked by Thompson's Grocery, Elliott admired the golden apples shining in the cart outside the entrance to the grocery. Somewhere in the cool depths of the store, a man spoke in agitated German.

Howard's Boarding House stood midway down the block, a two-story structure with peeling green paint. A shingle bearing the name of the establishment hung over the front door, which sagged open. Elliott grasped his notebook, then advanced up the front walk to the narrow porch. Two, straight-backed chairs guarded either side of the front door. A slight push from Elliott admitted him to a small anteroom, its wallpaper crowded with large roses. The room opened into a narrow dining room, empty save for a colored servant who was clearing the table. She looked up as Elliott entered.

"Good morning. I was wondering if I might have a word with Mrs. Howard." The woman stopped and stared at the floor. "You see, I'm a reporter

15

for the *Springfield Record* and I'm working on a story." Elliott held out his "Press" card to the woman, who continued to refuse to meet his eyes and ignored the card. She turned and vanished through a swinging door at the back of the room.

Assuming she had gone to fetch her mistress, Elliott turned his attention to the heavy oak bureau in the anteroom. Standing as tall as him, the top of the bureau was carved with leaves and vines and several pegs stuck out from the carving to accommodate hats and umbrellas. An ornate gilt clock, which appeared to have stopped at half-past three, stood on a marble shelf with two drawers underneath. Curious, Elliott pulled the top drawer open revealing an assortment of playing cards and gloves. Handkerchiefs embroidered with roses and lilies filled the bottom drawer, then something shiny caught his eye. He pushed a handkerchief with his finger to get a better look. The shiny object lying beneath a layer of handkerchiefs was the pearl-handled gun, the initials 'KH' scratched above the Colt insignia.

Elliott pushed the drawer shut as a heavy-set woman lumbered into the dining room, followed by the colored servant. When she saw him shutting the drawer, the white woman turned to her servant and struck her sharply on the face. "You good for nothin', you shouldn't a left him," she sneered, and the servant put her hand to her cheek. "And see you get this table cleared right now." She directed her attention to Elliott, who stood motionless in the entry. "Well, what'd you want? I don't guess you need a room."

Elliott stepped forward and offered his hand. The woman wore a white apron stained with coffee and something yellow. Her mouth and eyes turned down in a look of jaded contempt. "I'm Elliott Loper, a reporter for the *Springfield Record* and I wondered if you might have a few moments to talk with me. You see, I reported the story about the incident on the streetcar last night, the incident that involved your weapon."

Police Chief O'Connor had called Elliott late that night, after he had filed the story for the morning edition. "We know the owner of the gun. Names Howard, Kate Howard. Runs a boarding house downtown. Craig says he took the gun from her. She's coming down to get it."

Whether or not there was a story involving the gun's travels from Howard's Boarding House to Joe Craig's shaking hands was what Elliott was hoping to determine by his visit. But, face to face with the arrogant Kate Howard, Elliott felt his resolve failing.

Her voice dripped with derision. "I don't have to talk to you. Why I ain't even heard of you. You sure you're a newsman?" She stared at Elliott, who felt suddenly like a boy of ten.

"Oh yes ma'am. Why I have this card to prove it and my editor, Mr. Anderson, would be glad to vouch for me." By now Elliott was less certain of the value of the 'Press' card, but he continued to offer it to Kate. She pushed it aside.

"Look here sonny, why should I give you the time of day? What's in it for me? Now, get outta' here so's I can get some work done."

16

As she pushed him towards the door, Elliott regrouped and fired what he hoped was a winning salvo. "It would be free publicity for your boarding house, front page, we have thousands of readers." He hoped he was right.

To his relief, Kate stopped and looked at Elliott, as if seeing him for the first time. "Well, you got a point there son." She pulled at her chin and then crossed her arms over her sagging bosom. "So what'd you want to know?"

Elliott pulled his notebook from his jacket pocket along with a stubby yellow pencil. "Well, Mrs. Howard, I have reason to believe that the gun used in the altercation on the streetcar last evening is yours, and was taken from you to commit this crime."

"Yeah, no count nigger lifted it from me. That fella, Craig, he's a real pest. Always here messin' with her," she nodded to indicate the servant in the dining room a few feet away. She leaned toward Elliott. "Them niggers, you want my opinion, they nothin' but trouble. Lazy, thievin' heathens. And breedin' like rabbits, I'll tell you. Like to run us white folks outta' town." Elliott's pencil was poised above the notepad, but he found himself unable to write. Never in his life had he encountered a woman like Kate Howard. She continued, "I wouldn't have 'em in my place, 'cept you can't get white help so cheap." She raised her voice, "After you get that table cleared, you start them dishes."

He cleared his throat. "To get back to the story ma'am, how did this fellow obtain your weapon?"

She rested her watery brown eyes on Elliott and answered without a pause. "Oh I always keep that gun locked up in my safe with the rent and such. That Craig, he threatened me at knifepoint and demanded my revolver." She examined the rose wallpaper, then continued, "And while he was at it, he took my rent money."

Elliott looked carefully at Kate Howard. "I'll check with the police, because they will certainly have a report of this horrendous crime. It's odd, but I don't recall that the *Springfield Record* did a write-up."

She shook her head, loosening even more mousy brown hair from her bun. "Oh them police, they don't help nothin'. They're worse'n useless, you ask me. This guy Jones, big guy that lives here, I'll call him I want somebody caught and beat."

Elliott scratched his head. "I just don't understand the motive for Craig's crime."

Kate smiled, exposing her long yellow teeth and a substantial amount of gum. "Hell, he was just a drunk nigger. There's your story son."

Behind Kate, the colored woman silently reentered the dining room. Elliott offered his hand again, which was ignored. "Thank you for your time, Mrs. Howard."

She stood in the doorway as he went down the steps into the midday sun. "Front page story, remember." She pointed her finger straight in the air, toward the red and black shingle above the door. "Howard's Boarding House. Get it right."

17

Hattie's Tale

Although Hattie was a colored woman like herself, it still took Sheba several days before she found out anything more about the other live-in maid. They seldom shared the same tasks, and when it came time to go to bed, Hattie retired the instant the sun set, her snoring rattling with regularity across the hall in the other bedroom. One morning, about a week after she had begun working at the Lawrence house, Sheba awoke to find a hand with fat fingers shaking her shoulder. For a minute she was disoriented, then a soft voice said "Wake up child." She opened her eyes and looked up at the large, comfortable figure of Hattie, already clothed in her black dress and white apron.

"What?" Sheba sat up and looked at the clock on the bureau. She had overslept, something she was prone to do. Here it was almost six and she hadn't set the alarm. The dinner party of the previous night had ended with bowling in the house's duckpin alley in the basement where Sheba was needed to reset the pins and return the balls to the gentlemen playing the game. She had gone to bed at two o'clock in the morning and would have slept all day if Hattie hadn't roused her.

Hattie shook her head, as if to erase her fears. "Don' worry. I reckon they won' be up for hours after that ballyhoo last night. I jus' thought maybe I better wake you up." She seemed in no great hurry, but was instead bent on exploring Sheba's room. She wandered over to the bureau and started examining Sheba's hairbrush and hat, then threw a glance at her Bible, a gift from Pastor Ball and his wife. Hattie threw her a suspicious glance. "Kin you read?"

Too tired to pull herself out of bed, Sheba nodded from her pillow. "A little. My pastor's wife, Miz Ball, she done teach me. I cain't read all a that tho'," she said, as Hattie riffled the Bible's pages.

"Hummp." The older woman finished her prowling and sat heavily at the foot of the narrow bed, causing the springs to creak loudly. She rested her hands on her knees and turned her large head toward Sheba. "You better be shakin' a leg little better, girl. Seem like you slackin' a'ready."

Sheba winced. So Hattie had noticed that she didn't take care to dust all the way down the living room steps and clean out every corner in the endless panes of stained glass.

Hattie continued, "Don' think you won' get fired if you don' do the work. I done seen five girls turned away in the last month. They all jus' dyin' to work here, gots their heads full 'o stories 'bout this house." She turned away. The breeze blew in from the open window and the weak, early morning sunlight showed the carriage house roof across the courtyard, half obscured by the flickering leaves of the trees. "Course it's true 'nuff too. I don reckon I ever had a place this good before." She spoke reflectively. "Course I been here a good bit of time, even 'fore this house. Why I done worked for Mr. Rheuna after I came up from New Orleans."

This was the most Sheba had ever heard Hattie say, and she was eager to hear more about Hattie's past. "You come from New Orleans? That's down south, ain't it?"

"'Bout as far south as you cin git. New Orleans be home, but it weren't good place after the war," Hattie paused to gaze off in the distance, seeming to remember better days. "After the big war, me and some of t'other free coloreds, we came up here with Mr. Will Donnegan." She nodded and crossed her arms. "Mr. Will, he right fine and he do pretty well for hisself, specially since he's colored. Why after the war, I wager he done brung near a hundred of us up here and found us situations or work in the mines. No tellin' what we would a'done without him." Hattie pointed toward the west, "He done live close by, we kin go see him sometime." Suddenly Sheba heard a bird, a cardinal to be exact, out in the courtyard. "Birdeeee, birdee-birdee," the "cardinal" sang.

Hattie looked out the window into the shady courtyard. "Oh that jus crazy Thomas. When he ready for breakfast, he just comes 'cross the yard from the stable where he sleeps and he whistles so's we let him in." Sheba jumped up and ran to stand next to Hattie at the window. Thomas was standing outside the kitchen door looking straight up at her and smiling. He pointed at the door, gesturing for her to open it.

Sheba turned back to Hattie, whom she was beginning to like more and more. "Kin you let him in? I gotta' git cleaned up." With horror, Sheba realized how much time they had wasted. She would hate to be dismissed from this position. And then of course there was Thomas, who she suddenly did not want to see her look so disheveled.

Hattie seemed unconcerned about the time and moved slowly toward the stairs. "Well, 'member what I said. No slackin'. An' be downstairs by half-past six."

Sponging herself quickly all over with water from the sink, Sheba hummed to herself, thinking of Thomas and wondering about Mr. Donnegan. She had never met a man who brought slaves north for jobs, giving them new lives. Although, as she dressed, Sheba also remembered the colored children turned away by the orphanage for lack of space or food. There seemed to be no place for colored people here in Springfield, the home of the revered Mr. Lincoln. Sheba turned the idea over in her mind as she dressed, determined to visit Mr. Donnegan if she had the chance.

December 1906. A Crackerjack Idea

Mrs. Howard's parting comments notwithstanding, Elliott had been unable to cobble together even the semblance of a follow-up article on the streetcar hold-up by Joe Craig. He had tried though, Elliott rationalized in later discussions with his father regarding his career path or lack thereof. After several failed attempts at contacting Craig, whose paramour left employment at the Howard establishment shortly after his visit, Elliott had submitted a story, based only on conjecture, to Mr. Anderson, who had crumpled it and tossed it in the wastebasket in front of Elliott. "The facts boy, that's what we're about. That's what good reporting is. And this ain't facts."

So he sat, in the half light of a December afternoon, trying to invent a new way to communicate an individual's demise for the day's obituaries. "Mrs. Henry (Maude) Johnson was laid to rest at Oak Ridge Cemetery Tuesday last. The mother of five men, Mrs. Johnson was mourned by all..." He sighed. Surely these people deserved better than this.

His eyes lit on the *Springfield Journal* that lay open on his desk, atop a thick stack of pages that he would take to the typesetter later on. Each morning it was Elliott's job, as junior reporter, to purchase copies of the four competing Springfield newspapers from the newsboys who clustered at the corner of Adams and Fifth Streets. The *Springfield Record* had no reservations about borrowing or stealing ideas from another paper – indeed it was all part of the game.

The *Journal* article that caught his attention sported the dire headline: "Houses of Vice Proliferate on Levee." He pulled the newspaper from his desk, flapped it to make it stand up straight, and then began reading. "Our fair city gained yet another House of Ill Repute yesterday when Mamie's opened its doors at Ninth and Washington in the heart of the district known as the Levee. This brings the total number of such businesses to twelve, by this reporter's count. ..."

Elliott jumped to his feet and dashed for the corner office where his editor, Charles Anderson, gazed at a stack of dog-eared grayish white pages from under his green visor. A single light glowed above his desk, the naked bulb casting harsh shadows on the long columns of typeset copy and giving a shine to the top of his bald head. He looked up as Elliott skidded into the room. "You done with those obits yet, Loper?" He glanced at his silver wristwatch. "We're on a deadline you know. Gotta' have 'em by six."

"Yes sir, Mr. Anderson. No problem meeting that deadline." Elliott paused and adjusted his collar, which seemed to be poking his Adam's apple. He cleared his throat as the older man sat back, his chair creaking, and folded his hands across his paunch.

"So what d'you want, Loper? Cat got your tongue?" He smiled, but there was no kindness in the lined face. Elliott resisted the urge to squirm.

"Sir, I've got an idea for a story that's sure to sell papers. Why if we run this, it's guaranteed we'll outsell the *Journal* and *Register*." The editor continued to stare at the galleys in front of him, then pulled a grease pencil from in back of his ear and began to mark on them. "Mr. Anderson, do you want to hear the idea? I just know it'll fly." Elliott paused, wondering if the editor had suddenly gone deaf.

Anderson put down the grease pencil and looked Elliott straight in the face. "OK, you got two minutes. What's the story – and it better be good, cause I'm tired of listening to no-count reporters who get tired of writing obituaries."

Elliott pushed the front page of the *Journal* on top of his editor's desk, scattering galleys to the left and right. "See here, they've gone and opened another brothel on the Levee. That makes twelve, according to this article."

"Yeah, so what? What's one more brothel in this town? You got no story there kid, at least not one that's new."

Elliott's collar felt like it was choking him. "Well sir, what if somebody, like me for example, went down to the Levee and interviewed some of those women who work in the houses? Found out why they're doing what they are, maybe talked to some of the owners, maybe even some of the customers. See why there's so many of these places opening up all of a sudden. Now, there's a story." He braved a smile at the editor, who had stopped marking galleys and was perusing the article.

Anderson took the paper in both hands and looked up at Elliott. "You know, you might have a story here, Loper. It's an idea." He dropped the paper on the desk and looked about the busy newsroom, where men typed or shouted into telephone mouthpieces. "But why should I have you do it? You're new, got no experience. If I were smart I'd put Lewis on it." Lewis was the top man in the reporting group and routinely covered the Governor and Statehouse beat.

"Well sir, Lewis would do a crackerjack job, but isn't he pretty busy now, what with the special session of the legislature and all?" The state legislature was considering a temperance bill that would effectively put the Levee out of business. A big story there too.

"You've got a point there, Loper." Anderson stood up, his suspenders cutting into the shoulders of his dingy white shirt. "I've got a good mind to let you do this, just to see what you're made of. But it's got to be done by next week, because we've got that special New Year's Day edition with twenty-four pages to fill. And mind you, you better get all the obits written before you even think about this story."

21

Elliott fought the urge to embrace Mr. Anderson, and instead beamed his broadest grin. "I appreciate your confidence in me, Mr. Anderson. You wait, it'll be the best story we've run in months. May even expose some practices that need to be brought into the light of day."

"Yes, yes. Now get back to work." The editor adjusted his visor and dug into the pile of galleys again as Elliott strode triumphantly from the room. He'd get started right away, and the first step was to visit Mamie's Bordello.

The Levee was famous, at least in Springfield, for its plentitude of brothels, taverns, gambling halls, and other establishments catering to the shadowy side of humanity. It had started simply with a saloon or two, back in the days before the Great War. Over the ensuing half century, the area had ballooned like a foundered sheep, fed by the unfettered appetites of the legislators who came to the state capital, the miners who worked the coal mines surrounding the town, and, according to some, the voracious needs of Negroes. Although there were only about three thousand colored people in Springfield, in 1906 the city had a higher percentage of Negroes than any other major city in Illinois.

According to an editorial in the *Register*, a "dissolute and criminally-inclined" class of blacks frequented the Levee's twenty-two saloons, twelve brothels and numerous gambling parlors. As Elliott crossed Washington Street, he wondered if the newspaper's assertion would be proven true. The shadows of the light poles were short in the midday December sun and there were precious few people strolling the sidewalks of the Levee. He paused and looked up and down Washington, past Fishman's Pawn Shop, Dandy Jim's Saloon, and an unmarked building that almost certainly was a brothel, judging from the women who showed themselves unabashedly to male passersby from the tall windows.

A slender white woman with red hair in a bun called from the house's second floor window as he drew near. "Hey pretty boy, what you doin' out this way?" She waved an arm at Elliott and he felt himself flush red – the women he knew weren't so forward.

"I – uh – I'm a newspaper reporter working on a story," he called back.

The woman's eyebrows rose. "What'd you mean? Somebody die?" She turned to an older woman whose face appeared suddenly at the window. "Harriet, don't this beat all? He says he's a reporter." She turned to yell down at Elliott, "Hey, you gonna' do a story on us? We get our pictures in the paper?"

In light of this warm welcome, Elliott abandoned his resolution to press on to Mamie's. Surely one brothel was as good as the next. He paused before turning up the front sidewalk to the house, glancing furtively down Washington Street. He considered it quite unlikely that his father's acquaintances would frequent this part of town, at least in broad daylight. But, aside from a trash wagon being pulled down Seventh Street by a weary spotted horse, there was no living being in sight.

Elliott walked up the sidewalk and stepped onto the front porch, once painted a cheerful blue but now chipped badly. His boots creaked on the old wood and his footsteps seemed unnaturally loud as he took the three steps toward the front door. Appearing out of the gloom was a woman whose lined face was topped by a mountain of orange hair with a feather waving from its peak. "You come for a good time, sonny. You done picked the right place. Can't go wrong at Sal's." The woman pushed the door open with one hand, the other pulling at the lace collar that surrounded the sagging skin of her neck. She stepped aside to admit Elliott

He turned to face the madam, who leaned heavily on a wooden cane as she looked him over. "Well, you see ma'am, I'm here on business, not pleasure."

"Oh right, sonny, strictly business," she leered, showing a mouth missing as many teeth as it boasted.

"No really, I'm a newspaper man, and I'm working on a story." He pulled the "Press" card from the band of his bowler and presented it to the woman. By now a small group of "girls" had gathered in the adjoining drawing room and clustered at the doorway, listening with interest. There were five or six of them, dressed in pantaloons, camisoles, and silken wrappers. Young white women, Elliott saw, and middling attractive. A movement in the corner drew his attention. A slender Negro sat on the piano bench, staring at the sheet music. She wore a beige housedress. A servant perhaps.

The madam thrust his press card back into his hand. "Well, if it's a story you want, we ain't interested. We got work to do." One young woman nodded vigorously, while the rest simply stared at Elliott, who felt acutely self-conscious.

Still, he had to try to get this story. "Why ma'am I certainly do realize you're very busy. That's why I came at what I thought might be a convenient time." The woman turned and opened the door, waving Elliott onto the porch. "But you see, there are those in this fair city who don't know what it's like to work in an establishment of this sort. Why it must be somewhat…thrilling. I'd make you all famous, bring in lots of business…" The woman slammed the door.

He pushed his hat back onto his head, hurried out of the house's dooryard, and made his way down Washington Street, considerably discouraged. He was chagrined that he had been unable to think up convincing arguments for the story. He'd been so interested in winning over his editor, he hadn't thought there might be other obstacles. As he passed in front of Dandy Jim's, he heard a voice at his back. "Mister. Mister. Talk to me. You kin talk to me fer your newspaper."

"What the…" he whirled to see the Negro woman from the house's parlor stopped a few paces behind him, her face contorted in fear, hands dropped to her sides. "I'd be happy to talk with you, but aren't you jeopardizing your job?"

The woman was older than the other girls at the house, nearing forty Elliott guessed. Her face had the fine bones and small features that marked her as a mulatto, with creamy brown skin and rough hair piled on her head. She looked at Elliott, and he saw her features were painted to disguise her age. This was no servant: the woman was a prostitute.

23

"They gettin' ready to get rid a me anyways. I's too old t'be good for business," she protested.

Elliott resisted the urge to argue. He didn't care what motivated the woman. What he needed to establish himself as a bona-fide reporter was an interview, and damn it, here was his chance. He bowed slightly. "Madam, I am very much obliged. You won't be sorry you know."

She nodded and he noticed she was wearing only a sweater over her housedress. She shivered.

"How thoughtless of me. Let us find a place to sit and talk, where perhaps I can purchase you a warm drink."

She nodded at a tavern across the street. "How 'bout there? It's nice in that place and you can buy me a beer."

As the pair crossed the street and walked into the tavern, empty but for a barkeep dozing in front of the whiskey, Elliott's heart raced. He ushered the woman to a booth near the window. "Beg pardon Ma'am. I never did ask your name."

She scooted into the bench facing away from the window and answered, without looking up. "Mae Tully. Now start askin' questions."

Elliott settled onto the bench and gazed at Mae. He beckoned to the barkeep. "Bring her a beer." The woman followed the barkeep's movement as he drew the golden liquid from the tap, then placed the tall glass in front of her on the table. She gulped the drink. "Keep 'em coming," Elliott nodded to the barkeep and opened his notebook. "Now, tell me how you came to work at Sal's."

Story Hour

As the months went by and Sheba fell into the routine of the house, she thanked God for leading her to this position. She spent her days doing the endless cleaning that the house required. For even though it lacked mantles above the fireplaces to collect the knickknacks and framed photographs that rich folks were so fond of, there were still ample wooden ledges and tables to dust and polish, rugs to beat out on the clothesline in the courtyard, and cobwebs to knock down from the corners of the ceilings.

During her first night in the house, Sheba found that train tracks lay a few steps from the courtyard's back wall. Several times each day, a loud, soot-spitting train sputtered by and the small panes of the art glass windows and doors soiled quickly from the coal dust floating through the house. She guessed Mrs. Dana must have had sentimental reasons for wanting her palatial home so close to a dirty old railroad track, and that she had grown used to all the racket over the years. But Sheba herself would have picked a more gracious setting.

The young stablehand Thomas was not much in evidence during the day, but Sheba savored the time during the evening meal when he would tease her about being so prim and proper. Once at the end of a meal, their eyes met and Sheba felt a strange thrill of excitement.

The servants met with the maiden cousin, Flora, daily at nine o'clock in the morning, when she came to the kitchen to give them the menus for the day and any special instructions. She never smiled and wore dark colors exclusively for some reason of mourning they guessed, although they weren't sure for whom. More often than not, Flora gave them special instructions, a dinner party, a reception, a dance for which to prepare the big room or gallery. Sheba assumed that she would like the children's functions that were planned, especially the story hours. The neighborhood children accepted the invitations to these eagerly, probably for the ice cream, a delicacy lately introduced to Springfield, which was served after the story ended.

It was nearing Christmas when Sheba brought the ice cream into the low-ceilinged library at the close of one of Mrs. Dana's story hours. She was greeted with a sight that warmed her heart. Garbed in a pink morning gown, Mrs. Dana was sitting on a low backless stool reading the popular picture book *Little Black Sambo*, surrounded by eight immaculate children, none older than twelve. The girls wore large sashes on their simple dresses and sported oversized hair bows, while the boys were turned out like miniature gentlemen, with matched jackets, ties and knickers. They clustered around Mrs. Dana on the floor transfixed as she read.

> *"And she fried them in the melted butter which the Tigers had made, and they were just as yellow and brown as little Tigers.*
> *And then they all sat down to supper.*
> *And Black Mumbo ate Twenty-seven pancakes, and Black Jumbo ate Fifty-five but Little Black Sambo ate a Hundred and Sixty-nine, because he was so hungry."*

She closed the book and looked at her audience. Sheba backed up a few steps, feeling odd, like she didn't belong in this warm library. One boy, who looked to be about seven, dressed in blue knickers and a matching cap pulled Mrs. Dana's skirt anxiously. "Aunt Susie, Aunt Susie." He stood up and looked at her. She nodded and he continued. "Can tigers really turn into butter?"

"Well Charlie," she said, gathering him into a one-armed hug, "I'm not sure. You see I have never been to Africa."

Still regarding her in disbelief and now joined by several other small boys, Charlie gazed into her smiling face. "I bet you have. Mama says you've been everywhere. Why she said you go to Chicago every weekend and to Gay Paree every summer." Charlie stopped then and stared at the floor, as Mrs. Dana looked around at her other listeners. Sheba wondered if she really did go to Gay Paree, wherever that was, every summer.

Her head swiveling nervously, Mrs. Dana spied Sheba on the stairway with the tray of dishes and saw a diversion as well as a reward. "It's time for ice cream," she cried to the children.

A chorus of delighted cries followed and Sheba placed dishes holding ice cream around the low library table that the children had hurriedly cleared of books that they intended to borrow. Soon silence covered the room, broken only by the only sound of spoons clinking. Mrs. Dana watched them from her low chair, the afternoon light picking out the fine lines on her face and highlighting the silver in her thick ash blonde hair. It crossed Sheba's mind that she resembled a kindly aunt or grandmother to the young children.

Mrs. Dana looked up, catching Sheba dawdling, a habit she had picked up at the orphanage. Her idleness seemed to irritate her mistress. "Sheba, you lazy girl, clean up this mess," Mrs. Dana said as she stood up and stared at the children.

"Yes'm." Sheba hurried to clean up the ice cream dishes, but one child, a pudgy boy, was lingering over his treat. Mrs. Dana was ready to go on to the next event on her busy schedule; but the boy refused to hurry. The other children were getting restless, and the first of the mothers had arrived and was knocking on the door, ready to collect her young one.

"Put the tray down, Sheba, and answer the door." Mrs. Dana looked impatiently at the little boy, then walked determinedly in his direction as Sheba moved toward the door. "Billy, do you know what happens to little boys who don't finish their treat before their mother comes?" She leaned over to tilt the boy's chin up so he was looking at her. He shook his head, his mouth full of ice cream.

"The tigers get them! I believe I heard one creep in and hide in back of the fireplace there while we were reading. One of the tigers that was in the jungle with Little Black Sambo." The little boy gulped down the rest of his ice cream, all the while glancing furtively at the fireplace, as if the tiger would emerge at any second.

Meanwhile, more mothers swept through the door. Ice cream eaten, the children were ready to leave. There was no time to wipe sticky hands, the children were bade adieu, and Mrs. Dana vanished up the stairs. Snuffling, Billy sat on the floor, while Sheba answered the door and dispatched children. Slowly the room emptied. Billy began to suck his thumb. Sheba approached the boy, wanting to comfort him. She leaned over and patted him on the back. "You all right. Ain't no tiger back there."

Billy recoiled from her touch. "Don't you touch me, you dirty nigger." Sheba snatched her hand back as though it had been burnt. A knock on the door signaled the arrival of Billy's mother, a dark-haired lady with an eagle feather in her hat. She ignored Sheba and gathered Billy into the side of her skirt. "Mommy's precious is the last one at story hour. Poor Willums." She patted his fat cheek as they walked through the doorway and onto the porch. Neither the mother nor the son turned as Billy cried into his mother's skirts. Sheba went up the stairs to shut the door behind them, asking God for the strength not to dislike that little boy or his mama, who must have taught him to be so hateful.

January 1907. Fallen Angels

Mae Tully's story and the stories of her friends, many of whom agreed to talk with Elliott, created not just one, but a series of three feature stories for the *Springfield Record* and earned the first byline of Elliott's career. "Lookit this, big brother's gonna be famous." His tow-headed, twelve-year-old sisters, twins Minnie and Stella, waved the newspaper between them as the Loper family sat around the large dining table at their home on South Fourth Street.

"You hush now," his mother, Molly, said and leaned toward Elliott. "Of course, we're ever so proud of you. But really, a story about brothels... I don't think it's quite appropriate for your sisters."

From his chair at the head of the long table, Harry raised his voice. "Girls, settle down. Behave or your brother won't come back for Sunday dinner again." He directed his gaze at Elliott, who was wracking his brain for the correct thing to say to his mother, her doll-like features were crumpled with consternation. "Now, don't you worry my boy, you won't always have to write this... this kind of piece ...this yellow journalism ..."

Elliott could feel a flush that rose to the roots of his hair and he jumped to his feet, startling the twins and knocking over a rose-colored glass of water. "How dare you say my writing's yellow journalism. Why that's the worst kind of reporting...the worst...," he spluttered, unable to complete his thought.

Harry was on his feet in an instant, reaching for Elliott's shoulder. "I never meant any harm, my boy. It's just, well, you have to admit, it's a little sensational." He looked earnestly at Elliott, who pulled his arm away.

"Dad, I don't know what you call 'yellow journalism,' but what I call it is bad, untrue reporting that's done to sell more papers, like Hearst and Pulitzer did in New York. And that's not what this piece is all about, not by a long shot."

Molly Loper was on her feet now, extricating the paper from the girls. "Look at this Elliott, you're writing about women of ill repute for a second-rate paper. I can't even brag about this to my friends." She sank into her chair and burst into tears as the twins rushed around the table to console her.

Harry was still trying to make up for his remark, but Elliott, much as he loved and respected his father, shot him a look that made the older man back off and sit down. "Listen, what I'm doing here is first-rate reporting. Why it wouldn't be published if it wasn't, Mr. Anderson'd see to that."

Harry sat down and gazed at his empty plate for a minute, before directing his gaze back to Elliott. "Well, all I can say is, the *Springfield Record's* way back in circulation from the *Journal* and the *Register* and even the *Examiner*. I know because they're always comin' after me to advertise. It's stiff competition, and I wouldn't put it past them to come up with an attention-grabber like your 'Ladies of the Night' series to grab some circulation away from the others. That's all I'm sayin'."

Elliott relented and sat down. "Of course you're entitled to your opinion, Dad. I'm just glad Governor Deneen doesn't share your feelings about the quality of my reporting." His mother's blue eyes widened and Elliott was pleased he'd managed to withhold this bit of information until the right moment.

"Governor Deneen. Do you mean to say you've heard from him about your story?" His mother gasped as Sukey, the maid, entered the dining room carrying a large tureen and began ladling soup.

Elliott hastened to clarify his assertion. "Not the Governor exactly, but his wife, Mrs. Deneen, did stop by the newspaper office on Friday and she asked to speak with me." Elliott spooned the soup into his mouth and savored the piquant tomato-basil flavor while he watched his parents' reactions to this news.

Harry's eyes sparkled. "You don't say, you don't say… The Governor's wife, Bina Day Deneen. Quite a coupe, I must say my boy. Now what did the fair first lady want from you, or was she just paying you the time of day?"

Molly reached over and look questioningly into Elliott's eyes. "Don't mind him, sweetheart. I'm sure she was coming to compliment you on your fine writing. Why you did raise several issues that I know are close to her heart, like the plight of our city's colored citizens."

He could bear the suspense no longer; it was time to let them know. "Actually, she wanted to locate one of my sources, a woman in particularly dire straits, a Mrs. Mae Tully. She wants to give her a job." There, he'd said it. His mother's face registered shock, his father's pleased surprise. The twins clapped their hands in glee.

"Oh Elliott, you've saved a fallen angel!" Stella's round eyes shone.

Molly shot a stern look at the twins. "How you girls know about fallen angels is a mystery to me. I thought I raised you better than that."

Minnie retorted, "It's in the article Mama, he calls the ladies 'fallen angels.'" She pointed at the newspaper for emphasis.

Elliott interjected. "Mrs. Deneen was so moved by the plight of these women, she wants to give Mae a job in the Governor's Mansion, as a laundress. But I still need to locate her and give her the good news. I'm headed to the house where she works tomorrow. I hope she's still there."

In slightly better graces thanks to his providential news, Elliott departed from his parents' home later that afternoon, his consternation about finding Mae increasing. By the next day he was severely agitated as he walked down

29

Washington Street on his way to Sal's. But surely he had nothing to fear, he thought, glancing up and down the street nervously. After all, Mrs. Deneen's praise of the article in front of all his peers in the newsroom had obviously increased his standing at the paper. At least five reporters and his editor, the impeccable Mr. Anderson, had witnessed Mrs. Deneen's entrance, swathed in a feathered wrap and sporting an elaborate hat festooned with some kind of artificial fruit.

She had been soft-spoken, but her dark eyes seemed sincere as she leaned across the counter toward Elliott. "Your series on 'Ladies of the Night', why it's extraordinary, so well written and reported." She paused and watched as the remainder of the reporters in the newsroom inched closer to the front then she raised her voice a bit. "I've come to you because the plight of one colored woman, Mae Tully, touched me deeply…." She looked up at Elliott, who felt as though he might melt. "Touched myself and Governor Deneen as well. We want to help her and I hope that you can assist me with locating her."

Silence blanketed the newsroom and even the reporters on deadline stopped typing. Elliott smiled. "Of course Mrs. Deneen. It would be an honor to be of service to you and the Governor."

So that was why, on this bitterly cold and icy January day, Elliott came to be visiting a brothel for the second time. He turned up the walk toward the now-familiar looking establishment, but the door was uncharacteristically closed and the madam could not be roused, despite his pounding on the wooden door.

Shoulders hunched, he crept away from the house. He could not disappoint Mrs. Deneen. There was too much riding on this connection including, he dared to hope, a possible interview or future story with the Deneens. He briefly entertained the pleasant thought that perhaps in future they might become friends. Perhaps they had a daughter of marriageable age, although he vaguely remembered a report of somewhat younger children. Anything was possible, if only he could locate Mae Tully.

A wagon pulled by a bulky brown horse made its way down Washington, entered the alley behind Sal's and stopped. "Springfield Ice Company" was emblazoned in gold paint across the side of the enclosed wagon, and Elliott watched as a teenaged boy jumped from the seat next to the driver, went to the back of the wagon, and pulled a block of ice from the interior with oversized tongs. Flinging the tongs over his shoulder, the boy hauled the ice to a small door in the back of the house and loaded it in, then bounded back to the wagon. Elliott beat him to the seat.

"I need to speak with Mae, the colored woman who works here." The boy had a pinched face and his nose was blue with the cold. Elliott pulled a nickel from his pocket and handed it to the boy, who squinted at him in surprise.

The boy pocketed the coin and responded. "She's gone mister. Girls said she got fired, on account of she's too old. I heard she went to the Leland Hotel, workin' in the laundry."

Elliott couldn't believe his luck. "Much obliged I'm sure," and he held out his hand for the boy to shake in confusion before the driver clucked at the horses and headed down the street.

Minutes later as Elliott entered the sumptuous lobby of the Leland Hotel, replete with plants, velvet settees and heavy gold-framed mirrors, he noted that the only colored faces belonged to the red-jacketed bellman and the smiling elevator operator. A few businessmen smoked cigars in the corner of the room, empty otherwise of life.

"How may I be of service, sir?" A thin, bespectacled man behind the desk looked at him quizzically.

Elliott remembered coming to this lobby as a child to dine on roast squab at the hotel restaurant after attending church at the Cathedral down the way. Despite several years' passage, the place always put him in mind of tight black shoes and endless adult dinner table conversations. "I need to speak to someone on your laundry staff."

The man behind the desk looked Elliott up and down, as if reassessing him. "Indeed. Well, you'll need to discuss that with our housekeeping manager, Mr. Davis. Just go down those stairs and you'll see his desk." He pointed to a door in the hallway next to the elevator.

As the door closed behind Elliott, blocking out the shining lobby, he descended the narrow, dark stairwell into a small hallway almost entirely taken up by a metal desk, behind which sat a bulky man in a wrinkled suit, snoring loudly. Elliott rapped on the desk with his knuckles and the man woke with a snort. "Yessir?"

"I'm trying to locate Mae Tully on a matter of utmost importance. I'm told she works here."

"She does, but she works night shift. Don't come on till five. You can leave her a note here if you want." The man leaned back and put his feet up on the desk.

On a piece of paper from his reporter's notebook, he wrote "Mae. Must see you on extremely important matter. Meet me at Dandy Jim's at three o'clock tomorrow. Elliott Loper."

He eyed the man, who struck him as extremely unreliable. "All right. Please see she gets this." He wondered how she would read it, but decided the note was his only alternative. He pushed the folded note across the desk at the man, who was already snoring.

A Trip Downtown

Sheba was still musing about the story hour as she walked down Fourth Street toward town on her Tuesday off. She surmised that children could be as cruel as their parents, or as kind, depending on who raised them. It just seemed to her that most white folks thought colored people were about the level of dogs. She hadn't experienced this before coming to the west side of Springfield and it troubled her. She made a mental note to ask Pastor Ball what Jesus would do if confronted with a child like Billy.

She was enjoying her walk, savoring the freedom from dusting and mopping and sewing that the day promised. Last week, Mrs. Dana had started her on a sewing project, a relatively simple daytime gown in pale lavender muslin, and Sheba thought she was capable of the challenge. But Mrs. Dana wanted the dress done by next week so she could wear it to an "at home," a ladies card party where a half-dozen women from the neighborhood gathered to play at whist and exchange gossip.

Sheba gazed at the churches with their tall steeples to the left and right of the street as she neared downtown. Even more impressive was the Governor's Mansion on her right. Surrounded by an iron fence and strictly off limits to colored servants like herself, the mansion's large yard beckoned, even now, covered with snow. The house itself was hidden in the trees.

Sheba started as a soft voice behind her said "You know who that house b'longs to? Governor and Mrs. Deneen, that's who, some pretty high-falutin' friends of the missus." She turned to see Thomas, hunkered down behind the reins of the Lawrence House carriage, regarding her with subdued glee. .

"What you doin' here? Ain't Saturday your day off?"

"Oh, I just be runnin' some errands for Miz Dana, when I see'd you standin' here." Thomas smiled at Sheba, and she remembered that his was the only friendly face on that first evening at the house. "So where you goin'?"

Sheba gazed toward downtown. "I be goin' Downtown t'see what's there, could be some nice stores and such. I got some money," she swung her handbag. "Ten cents. I reckon I kin get a nice hanky or hair pin."

Thomas frowned. "I wager you ain't never been Downtown."

Sheba was reluctant to admit her inexperience to Thomas. "Well, I cain't say I have 'xactly, but when I was at Burtons' we went shoppin' on 'leventh."

His eyebrows were raised in incredulity and she hastened to explain. "See I gotta see Downtown – why I hear they's great big stores and all kinda wonderful things."

He shook his head. "Oh they's some grand places all right. Myers Brothers. Lubin's. Thing is though, they don't take kindly to colored folks just walkin' in. They's some places just for coloreds and some places, well, you leave them to the white folks."

She had thought this might be the case. There were many places in Springfield forbidden to Negroes, and obviously the grand stores downtown were as well. Sheba sighed as Thomas clucked at the horses, then drove the buggy south towards the Lawrence House. He waved as the Morgans trotted down the street.

She had spent many evenings in the kitchen raptly listening to Lorena's tales of the gleaming gold showcases holding hatpins and scarves, gloves and cravats at Myers Brothers. Canes with shining silver heads, bolts of rich and brightly colored fabric, watches and rings, all guarded by well-cared-for and attentive shopladies. She had also treasured hopes of drinking teas and eating cakes at the nicer restaurants. But never mind. She'd figure out where she could go and spend her dime there. With great determination, she set off up the hill towards the mecca of downtown Springfield

By the time she reached Adams Street and the staid brick Court House, Sheba was tired and had slowed her pace. As she gazed through the plate-glass windows, she saw women in enormous hats, gentlemen sporting waistcoats and bowlers, children dragging at their mothers' hands, but no colored men or women. Not even behind the counters, although her eyes strained to see into the depths of the stores, past the shelves and stacks of goods. Sheba stared at the icy bricks in the sidewalk as she walked back past the Court House.

Looking up as she crossed the street, she noticed another colored woman, a middle-aged heavy-set mother with one noisy child, who walked by her and in the door of what appeared to be a dry goods store. The door swung shut, narrowly missing the little boy's heels. Sheba stepped back and saw that the whole row of businesses along this street appeared to be operated for and patronized by colored people. Colored shopkeepers peered from windows and she saw a dark-skinned couple eating lunch at the table near the window of the café next door. Around her the people on the sidewalk were equally colored and white, but the businesses seemed open to all.

"Now what this be 'bout?" she mused aloud, staring up and down the row in amazement.

"What would what be about?" said a voice near her ear. She swung round and stood looking into the pale blue eyes of a fair-haired, bearded young man. He was dressed in a hounds tooth suit and derby hat and seemed to be on his way somewhere. "Well, you must be fresh from the farm never to have been Downtown before." His mouth curled up in a grin, showing even white teeth. Without thinking, Sheba smiled back at him, and a bubble of pleasure formed in her.

33

"This man botherin' you?" A large, very black man came to her rescue from a bench near the Court House steps, but Sheba waved him away.

"Oh no, don't worry 'bout me," she said as she turned to face the young man. "It just so happens that I ain't never been Downtown 'for." She stopped talking, realizing that this person was not only white but also a man. She felt oddly comfortable with him, although he was a stranger, but she was wary. She had heard whispers of colored women who had been treated cruelly, even raped, by white men.

The man stood, smiling at her in the chill January air with people brushing past him. And though she was ready to dodge away at the first hint of impropriety, she was curious about why he had spoken to her. "I do'no why you talkin' to me mister. What you want with a colored girl?"

The man seemed extremely offended, though Sheba could not imagine why. "Well, you seemed confused and I thought I could help. Just being friendly y'know." He extended his hand to her, but she only stared at it, so he put his hand back in his pocket and continued. "I'm Elliott Loper, a newspaper reporter for the *Springfield Record*, and I'm interested in everyone and everything. I was raised to believe we are all equal. As for you being a Negro, well, as I recall a man from our town, Mr. Lincoln, freed the slaves."

Sheba stared at him. "I guess we all free but it 'pears to me that they's some shops I kin go into and some I cain't." She glanced up at Elliott, who was considering her thoughtfully, then nodded toward the shop in front of her. "Is this here the colored section of downtown?"

The sun glinted from the golden stubble of Elliott's beard. "Well, I'd say it's more mixed than anything." He turned and pointed kitty-cornered across the street. "My father, Harry, owns that restaurant," he indicated an elegant establishment where waiters, both colored and white, shook out tablecloths in the spacious dining room.

"Maybe that the Levee." Sheba remembered the unsavory things Ruby Burton had told her about the Levee, where Sheba's mother had disappeared to "work." According to Ruby, the Levee was full of taverns and houses of ill repute. Sheba gazed down the block, wondering what exactly a house of ill repute might look like.

"Why yes indeed, it's down across Seventh Street there." He pointed a block to the east. Sheba could vaguely make out what looked like cafes or shops across that street, but nothing that looked much worse than what was in front of her. She shot Elliott a questioning frown. "I don't recommend you go down there though. You see, there are some rather rough businesses in those blocks and not very nice characters either. So just stay this side of Seventh Street and you'll be fine, Miss...? He stopped since she had not given her name.

"Thank you kindly. I best be goin' now," Sheba said, turning her back. He did seem nice enough, but it wouldn't be proper to tell him her name. She couldn't imagine that they would ever meet again. She walked the few steps from the front sidewalk into the millinery shop, where a woman was trying on a fine hat complete with a stuffed bird in the crown. When Sheba looked out the window after a few minutes, she could see no sign of Elliott Loper.

While she shopped in the milliners, the dry goods store, and the flower shop, a thought began to take shape. With her dressmaking skills, she could have a shop like this, with customers coming in and out the door with a jingling bell. One thing she had learned from Scott Burton was that anyone with the right skills and determination could have a successful business. Whether they were colored or white didn't make a difference, and Scott was living proof of that.

Before she knew it, she was at the end of the block, gazing across the street at the forbidden, tempting row of businesses. Seventh Street was just a brick street like all the others in this part of town. Sheba stood on the edge of this brick, the toes of her only pair of brown boots demurely showing under her black maid's dress. She had considered wearing something else, perhaps the skirt and blouse she'd had on when she came to the Lawrence House, but the clothes from the orphanage now seemed shabby and old.

She developed a plan. With her first week's wages, Sheba bought three yards of brown satin fabric. She would make a fancy Sunday dress for herself and ask Mrs. Dana if she might use the sewing machine. Surely when her mistress was traveling, as she frequently was, she would not mind. Why right now she was packing to go to New Orleans. Sheba wished mightily that someday she too could travel the world like Mrs. Dana. But for now she had to decide whether or not she would cross Seventh Street.

As she gazed across the bricks with brown grass poking up between them, a buggy came through, effectively blocking her view of the large establishment on the other side. Her eyes met those of the rig's driver, which turned out to be none other than the laughing eyes of Thomas. "Afternoon miss," he waved as he drove by. Behind him, the figures of Mrs. Dana and her emaciated cousin were bent together, exchanging some kind of secret to which the lowly passersby could not be privy.

After they had passed, Sheba was emboldened. She had every right to see the more colorful part of the Levee and its forbidden nature pulled her forward, into the street, across the bricks and up onto the wooden sidewalk. She stared down the row of stores, taverns, and other establishments, half expecting Satan himself to emerge from one. The stores all had windows above them, apartments perhaps, Sheba guessed. But instead of being lined with curtains, as with the Burtons' living quarters above the barber shop, these windows were bare. A hairy, pot-bellied man with no shirt sat behind one window, gazing down the street as if looking for someone.

She walked past Dandy Jim's Tavern, late afternoon sun shining in the bar's window, she saw a colored woman who sat in the front corner booth nursing a pale yellow glass of beer. The woman was deep in conversation with a blonde white man. Sheba could hardly avoid looking at them as she walked by the window. As she passed, the man looked up from his conversation and the woman turned around to see what had attracted his attention. Sheba gazed through the glass into the startled blue eyes of Elliott Loper.

Elliott waved his hand in salutation, but Sheba, embarrassed to be seen on this stretch of street, which he had expressly warned her against, walked past with head raised. As she rounded the corner and started down Eighth Street, she heard running boot steps behind her. Sheba whirled and found herself face to face with the young reporter.

"Miss…I'm sorry." He was panting and stopped to catch his breath. Sheba didn't know what to think. She hadn't stolen anything and Mr. Loper had seemed to be deep in conversation with the woman in the tavern when she passed.

"Don't you chase me. I kin walk down this street same's you." She was ready to leave. Her fear of white men returned now, as darkness began to fall.

"I'm so sorry to be chasing you and I do sincerely apologize. But that woman back there, the one in the tavern, she said she knew you." Elliott paused and looked into Sheba's eyes. "I hope you might consider coming back for just a few minutes."

Sheba had no idea who might be sitting in a tavern on the Levee at five o'clock on a Tuesday afternoon and why they might be talking to this young white man. The woman looked nothing like Miss Eva or her sisters—she wasn't near black enough. So that ruled out someone raising money for the Lincoln Colored Home. More curious than afraid, Sheba nodded. "Well, all right, but I ain't goin' in that tavern. I'm a church-goin' woman." She'd never been in a tavern before and besides, she had to be getting back. As she bent her head and started to follow the young reporter, she hoped someone at the Lawrence House might notice if she failed to appear this evening for supper.

Elliott walked next to Sheba along the sidewalk. He held the wooden door as a woman hurried from the tavern into the now-dusky street. Stooping her narrow shoulders and looking periodically at the ground, she walked toward Sheba. Then she smiled and Sheba felt something familiar in that wide grin. "Sheba, don't you 'member me? It ain't been that long." She grasped Sheba's shoulders and hugged her. The scent of lavender water which clung faintly to the woman's clothes jolted something loose in Sheba's memory.

At first she couldn't speak as tears welled in her eyes. This woman was her mother, who she hadn't laid eyes on in six years. Though the Burtons had alluded to her occasionally, it was as though she was dead, not alive and well and living on the Levee. Sheba knew that she had abandoned her, of course, but Scott and Ruby had taken great pains to shield her from this truth.

She stared at her now. Though she guessed her mother was about forty, she looked older and her hair was dyed to stay dark. Her eyes communicated suffering beneath the fleeting joy of seeing her daughter again. Her mother stepped back and sank down on the bench near the sidewalk, looking Sheba up and down, taking in everything about her. Sheba bowed her head self-consciously, and then glanced up at Elliott.

"Aren't you surprised?" He beamed and opened his notebook, which he always carried under his arm. It occurred to Sheba that he must be working on a story for the newspaper. He continued, "I know I was. I was just talking with Mae here about a job opportunity for her, when I glanced up and saw you going by. Mae turned around and said 'There goes Sheba, my little chil'. Go get her quick.' So of course, I ran to fetch you." He paused to make a note in his book, muttering, "I'm sure there's a story here somewhere."

Sheba decided to sit down on the bench near the woman who she now recognized as her mother, still wondering what this woman thought of her. Elliott stood in front of them. "Well ladies, aren't you going to say anything?"

Afraid of the answer she might get if she asked the obvious question, Sheba began to tell the woman, her mother, what had happened to her in the years since they'd seen each other, how she had lived with the Burtons and at the orphanage with Miss Eva, and finally how she had found this wonderful new position at the Lawrence House. As she talked, she felt the old warmth return, and she realized that this woman, who sat regarding her with such solemnity, was her nearest, dearest mother and her only living blood kin.

Suddenly cold, Sheba wondered if her mother might be physically hungry. "You want we get somethin' to eat?"

Mae stood up, straightening her brown dress and shawl. "Oh no, I gotta go -- I got laundry work to do at the Leland. But that other job, Mr. Loper, the one at the G'nor's, it sound real good. You want I should talk to somebody there?"

Elliott nodded. "Yes, yes. Mrs. Deneen will know you're coming. Just make sure to let them know I sent you."

Mae looked at Sheba with pride glowing in her eyes. "Sheba, you have growed up good, my lil sweet girl."

Sheba was speechless. How could Mae leave, after she had just seen her only child? Yet the woman was collecting her bag from the bench, so Sheba caught her hand. "Mama, I got to see you 'gin. I been missin' you somethin' fierce." The woman looked at her with eyes welling with tears, and this time it was Sheba who pulled Mae to her in a hug.

Mae sobbed. "Oh chil', it so sweet seein' you. You doin' good, workin' in that fancy house. Maybe if I get me this new job..." Sheba felt her mother's bones through the satiny material of her dress.

"Mama don't be a stranger. You know where I work." Sheba watched, her stomach churning with sadness, as Mae she moved away down the street.

As she reached for her hanky, she realized it was completely dark. She shivered. "Oh land, it is late. Do you s'pose a streetcar c'ld take me home?"

."It's only six o'clock, it just seems later since it's wintertime. I'm sure the streetcar would take you close to where you live, but I would be honored to escort you back to the Lawrence House. It's not far," Elliott offered.

Sheba was silent for a minute. She did not want this young man to walk her home – she was afraid of what he might he do, what people might think. But the idea of walking home or taking the streetcar alone was too daunting for her to consider. The rough establishments of the Levee were all around and she

37

already imagined she could see men staggering from taverns. As Sheba and Elliott began to walk down Fourth Street she spied a familiar vehicle, the Lawrence House buggy, heading downtown. "Thomas, Thomas." She waved to the buggy and its driver. Thomas turned to stare at her and her escort.

"Why Sheba Tully, what you doin' out so late?" Then his eyes came to rest on Elliott Loper and he dropped the reins to his knees.

Elliott stepped forward. "I'm Elliott Loper. I bumped into…" Sheba could tell he was making a mental note of her name, "Miss Tully this afternoon and, as she was delayed, I offered to escort her home." He glanced at Sheba, who climbed into the buggy seat next to Thomas.

"Loper. You any relation to the Loper what owns that nice restaurant downtown?" Thomas seemed interested.

"Yes indeed," Elliott paused. "That's my father's eating establishment."

"He be a good man, your pa. My cousin works there, says your pa's fair, an' not just to white folks."

Elliott nodded. "Yes, my father is fair and a good businessman. I'm pleased to have met you uh?" Thomas hadn't introduced himself.

"Thomas Cartwright. Good t'meet ya. C'mon we gotta' go." He chucked the reins to start the horses, and then turned the corner for home. Sheba couldn't remember ever being as relieved to see someone as she had been to see Thomas and she settled back on the buggy seat. She watched as the horses clopped their way back to the Lawrence House and wondered why Thomas, who usually didn't stop talking, was so quiet.

A Way to Mrs. Dana

Sheba's image – her oval face framed in frizzy hair and her slender, reed-like figure -- were stamped on Elliott's mind. Her large smile haunted him too. But, more than anything, what intrigued him about the young woman was her dauntless quiet spirit, her unwillingness to accept the limitations society placed on her. She was like a butterfly that he had caught between his cupped hands, wings fluttering against his palms.

He did not share his fascination with the young woman with anyone – that would hardly be seemly – but he couldn't resist recounting the incident on the Levee to his father as they walked from the newspaper office toward the Loper home, where Elliott was dining that night. His sleeping room near the office had little more than a hotplate to cook on, so he often accepted an invitation to dine at the parental home.

Harry walked, calm and patrician. He said very little in response to Elliott's story about the encounter on the Levee, but waxed eloquent about his latest passion – the motor car. "They're the future, my boy. You mark my words, a decade from now, you won't see a horse on this street," his wave took in a wide swath of Fourth Street, damp pavement illuminated by puddles of light from the streetlamps. Several horses clopped down the street, and as one large black carriage with lamps on each corner of its body creaked by, Harry stopped talking. "Look at that monstrosity." He turned to face Elliott, who was staring as the carriage turned onto Adams Street. "That's Susan Dana's carriage, an ostentatious thing if ever I saw one. Good thing people like her so much, otherwise no one'd take to her flaunting her money so."

Elliott stopped short of telling Harry that Sheba was Mrs. Dana's colored maid, even though he thought his father would be sympathetic. "Really bad taste, I must say," he agreed. "I can't help but wonder why people like her."

Both men resumed walking, fighting the January chill, as Harry attempted to explain. "Seems folks respected her father, old Rheuny Lawrence – and maybe they feel a little sorry for her. Her husband, Ed, he never amounted to much – in fact I figure it was kind of a blessing he died in that mining accident. But then of course her parents died so soon after. So now she doesn't have anyone but an old maid cousin."

Harry pulled his scarf closer around his neck and Elliott shoved his hands in his overcoat. "Sure, that's too bad Dad, but she's got scads of money and suitors, or so I hear. And that great big house. I still don't feel sorry for her and I don't see why anyone else should either." He remembered the photo of Mrs. Dana published in the *Record* after one of her society parties. She was far from pitiful, with the glossy sheen of wealth spread across her features.

Harry stopped and so Elliott stopped too. They'd reached the Loper home and lamplight spilled a welcome from the curtained front windows. "I don't suppose you've ever met her." Elliott shook his head and Harry pulled a gloved hand over his moustache. "Because, if you do, you'll see why folks like her. She has a certain charm, maybe it's because she's handsome and blonde and nice to folks. I don't know, she's just … jolly I guess you'd say. The sort of person you want to be around."

His father's description of Mrs. Dana intrigued Elliott. He had to meet this person whom Harry thought so well of, Lord knew he usually agreed with his dad, though he seldom admitted it. So next day at the newspaper, Elliott worked up his nerve to approach Mr. Anderson. Based on what his father had said, he thought the reading public would eat up a story about Mrs. Dana, who was as close to a celebrity as Springfield boasted. And as a side benefit, he might see Sheba Tully again. As Mr. Anderson bent over his desk, green visor obscuring his eyes, Elliott took a risk. "Mr. Anderson, sir, I have an idea for a story that I believe would earn us readers and advertisers too."

Mr. Anderson raised his eyes and squinted at Elliott. "Well, spit it out." Elliott had expected a little more resistance. Although the story on the brothels had been quite well received, the newspaper was still a miserable third behind the *Journal* and the *Register.*

"Sir, I believe I might be able to gain an interview with Susan Dana. If I could, do you believe there's a story."

The editor looked back at his desk. "You'd need an angle, a new angle I mean. Something fresh. We've already run miles of newsprint about that house, and stories about her involvement with the suffragette movement." He stopped and tapped his pencil on his fingers. "Well, let's hear it, your idea."

Elliott was ready, "I was thinking that a story about how she's spending her inheritance might be of interest. The worthy causes she supports, the investments."

Mr. Anderson wrinkled his nose. "Never fly. If she's smart she'll never tell how much she has." He raised his eyebrows quizzically, and Elliott shot another idea forward.

"What about a story about the Lincoln Colored Home? I hear her mother, Mrs. Lawrence, practically built the new place and funded it too."

Mr. Anderson was ready with a response. "No way. That Eva Monroe's been bending my ear since July tryin' to get a piece on the Mary E. Lawrence Reading Room at the home. I got Jensen assigned to that, but Mrs. Dana's no where near the supporter that her ma was."

Elliott ran his hands through his curly hair hoping he could pull ideas out of it. "I don't know then sir, I guess those were my best ideas."

The editor shrugged. "Well, they're not good enough, Loper. So go back and write those obituaries and don't bother me."

As he made his way back through the busy newsroom, Elliott sighed. He didn't have a chance for a story here, now, but if he could only talk with Mrs. Dana, he was sure an angle would present itself. Why his mother and her friends gossiped about Mrs. Dana over whist, she was that famous. Surely there was some aspect of her fascinating existence that would make for good copy. As he pounded away at the typewriter, Elliott imagined scenarios in which he was interviewing Mrs. Dana, discovering secrets that she had never divulged to anyone, until now, until the interview with Elliott.

Shortly before five that day, Elliott picked his way through the crowded streets of downtown Springfield. As he approached the corner of Sixth and Capitol, he could see the sign over the covered entryway to the grand building that was his destination: "Leland Hotel." But instead of entering through the elegant lobby, Elliott ducked down the alley. Two cats stalked mice through the ashes of a burn pile as a woman dressed in black trudged through the mud toward the door in the back wall.

"Mae," Elliott called, hoping it was her. The woman turned. Even in the dim alley, there was something about the grace with which she moved that set her apart. It was Mae.

"Mr. Loper?" He took a step closer and saw tears in her eyes. "I's so glad to see you. I jus' came from talkin' to that Miz Deneen. She say I kin start doin' laundry there at that fine house come next week."

Elliott grinned. He had to admit that he was proud of his role in Mae's redemption. Perhaps it would endear him to her daughter, whose approval suddenly seemed critical. "Why that's grand, just grand. You know Mrs. Deneen wants to give you a chance, a new start on your life."

Mae pulled at her shapeless black hat and lifted the short veil. "God give me this job. He took a poor sinner, and He give me 'nother chance. You be an instrument of God, Mr. Loper." Her hands shook with emotion as she grasped his arm.

He patted her yellow gloves. "There, there. I was only working on a news story. It may be that God put it into Mrs. Deneen's head to have me contact you – I don't know. I daresay I'm not a spiritual man."

Mae's face glowed, as if lit from within. "You kin b'lieve what you want, but I knowed God's usin' you. I been prayin', even while I was doin' that bad work on the Levee, prayin' for mercy, just like Pastor Ball say. And I got mercy, yes I did."

Elliott was getting cold and looked at his pocket watch. It was almost five. "Well, Mrs. Tully, I don't want to make you late, but I do have a favor that perhaps you could help me with."

She nodded vigorously. "You jus' say what you need."

He took a deep breath, aware of her central role in his future success. "I'm interested in talking further with your daughter, Sheba, about her employer Mrs. Dana and I was wondering if you might arrange a meeting. If it wouldn't be inconvenient of course."

Mae stared at the dirt alleyway and a tiger-striped cat brushed between them, staring up at Elliott's face, before pouncing on something moving in a pile of ashes. She hesitated. "Oh, I dunno. Might take some doin' but I kin give it a try. Tell you what, meet me down at Dandy Jim's in two weeks and I'll see what I kin do."

Elated, he kicked at the ashes, sending the cat scurrying. "You're an angel Mrs. Tully, an angel," he shouted after the woman, who disappeared into the bowels of the hotel.

February 1907. The Old Man

Sheba smoothed the newspaper on the kitchen table, while Hattie ironed by the stove. She didn't pause her even swipes across the blue skirt as she addressed Sheba. "You gettin' t'be such a good reader, Sheba. Looks like high time to start book-learnin' good Mr. Donnegan."

Sheba looked up from the headlines, startled. Ordinarily she would have jumped at an excuse to meet Will Donnegan, whom Hattie held in such high esteem. This was the man who had made it possible for a young colored woman to come north, to the land of opportunity that was Springfield. But now she felt inadequate, with her incomplete grasp of the written word. Often as she read aloud to Hattie, she encountered words she could not make out, so she either skipped them entirely or guessed at what they might be. Obviously, she'd done a good job – Hattie thought she was able to teach a respected and wealthy old man how to read. But Sheba wasn't so sure. "Hattie, Mr. Donnegan, why he so old, I don't 'spect he be wantin' to learn readin' now."

Hattie put down the iron on the metal plate and turned to face Sheba. "Chil', he so happy t'be learnin' readin' and writin' 'for he passes on. See his chillin', they respect him more like if he do."

Faced with Hattie's resolve, Sheba relented. After all, she couldn't imagine he'd be too particular. So it was arranged that their next free day, Sheba and Hattie would take a short walk to Will Donnegan's large and pleasant house, well situated near the affluent Aristocracy Hill. Sheba was finding that Springfield was full of contrasts like this. In some neighborhoods on the west side, white and colored folks lived next door to each other, but had no dealings together. Aside from Mrs. Dana and young Mr. Loper, white folks had nothing to do with her. She might as well not have existed.

Hattie pointed to a brick two-story building with paper cutouts of flowers decorating the windows. "We 'most there. This here's Edwards School." It was early afternoon and Sheba could see the tops of children's heads at desks through the windows. As they passed the deserted playground, the wooden swings swaying idly in the cold February wind.

The women crossed Edwards Street, and then turned up the sidewalk toward a well-kept house with gingerbread trim. An elderly white lady sat near the front window, doing some handiwork. As the women approached, she looked up, and then dropped her needlework and, with amazing quickness for such a very old lady, she came out the door and down the steps. "Hattie Patois, how good to see you."

Hattie stopped herself halfway into a servile bow and straightened to smile into the woman's face. "Right good seein' you, Miss Sarah."

Confused, Sheba wasn't sure who this woman could be, since Hattie had clearly said they were visiting Mr. Donnegan, a colored man. The lady seemed to realize Sheba's question and answered it before she could put the words together. "You're Sheba. Hattie said you were comin' to help Will learn readin'. I'm Mrs. Donnegan." The woman had a trace of an accent, maybe German. Her small face was a mass of wrinkles and Sheba wondered what kind of story she and Will had of their time together in a community like Springfield. The small woman opened the front door for the guests and seated them in overstuffed chairs of the parlor, then asked if they might like some tea.

"Lord yes. And let's commence the learning." Hattie was beside herself, proud of having brought Sheba for the benefit of Mr. Donnegan.

Mrs. Donnegan rose and called up the curving stairs. "Will, the young lady who says she's gonna teach you reading's here. Come on down." Then she sat down as if tired by the exertion. She looked at them and, when she had recaptured her breath, said "He likes to lie down after lunch, so he might be a little bit gettin' down here."

They heard a creak at the top of the stairs and saw an elderly colored man dressed in a white shirt and brown trousers, not stooped over like his wife, but moving slowly nonetheless, stepping carefully down the stairs, holding tight to the banister. When he reached the landing, he paused and looked down at the group in the parlor. "Hattie Patois, it's mighty good seein' you. And this fetchin' young woman, I b'lieve you better introduce me."

As he attained the bottom of the stairs, Sheba examined him. His face was long and thin, like the rest of him. White, very short hair covered part of this head, while the top was a shiny brown. Soon, Sheba and Mr. Donnegan sat in the parlor writing simple words on a slate. Close enough to hear, but far enough away not to interrupt, Hattie and Sarah sat in the living room trading gossip about people Sheba did not know. Most of the conversation concerned various servants and the houses where they were employed, along with choice bits about the employers.

As Mr. Donnegan attempted to form the letters for "DOG" on a small slate, Sheba wondered how he had managed to bring all those folks up north to work in Springfield and begin new lives. But she hesitated to ask him, since she didn't know him well and she thought he might take it as prying. Instead, she patiently instructed him on the alphabet and listened to Mrs. Donnegan and Hattie, who now were off on a more interesting tangent.

"Let's hear the latest about Miss Susan and her dried up old cousin." Sarah asked and waited, obviously dying for a bit of gossip about the most interesting woman in town. Hattie let Sarah wait a minute as she sipped her tea. Placing the delicate cup neatly on the thin saucer, she put both hands on her knees and

44

leaned conspiratorially toward Mrs. Donnegan. Sheba leaned their way too, worried she might miss something. But Hattie's stage whisper was loud enough for even poor deaf Mr. Donnegan to hear.

"'Course I hate sayin' anythin' 'gainst the missus, and land, she been good to me, but you oughta see some o' those 'spirit' types done come for meetin's with the dead folks." Hattie paused to let out a loud guffaw and ceased even the pretense of a whisper. "Land, this lady Miss Celia – she be blind so's she conjures better. She does put on! You oughta hear the hootin' and hollerin' goes on at those séances." Hattie was laughing so hard she began to perspire and pulled out a handkerchief to wipe her brow.

Sarah protested. "I just don't believe it. I reckoned she just did those Weeje boards or whatever they're called. Talking to the dead – I s'pose next she be talkin' to Mr. Ed." Sarah had apparently known the late Mr. Dana.

Hattie regained her composure and considered her next response. "Not so's you'd think. It's mainly her pa she hankers for, she did favor him. He used't call her 'Tag' when she was just a mite. Short for 'Tag-A-Long,' ain't that queer?"

Sarah gazed toward Sheba and Mr. Donnegan. "I should say so. They say they called her 'Little Rheuna.' I think it's plum funny how she does resemble her pa so much."

Hattie nodded. "Oh, I seed it before, but she's real funny 'bout him. 'Course she be spendin' his money like no tomorry on fancy parties and trips and that there house," Hattie paused. "But then it seem like she feel bad and jus' want him to say it all right." Sheba started as the volume on Hattie's voice raised abruptly. She slapped her knees and laughed. "But he dead! Been dead these five year. And that Miss Celia, she be fillin' Miss Susan full of lies and such like, tellin' her her pa's talkin' to her and all. She be so sad and lonely and worryin' all the time…"

Sarah patted Hattie's shoulder. "Why, you been working for them Lawrences for well nigh twenty years. You seen Miss Susan grow up and marry and go off with her husband, then come back here and see everybody die off on her."

Hattie recovered enough to eat another cookie and add, "Well, she so flighty al'ys, never had no head for figures at all. And Mr. Rheuna's money he worked so hard for, it's jus' gonna slip through her fingers, you mind my words." Meanwhile, Mr. Donnegan had mastered "dog" and "cat" and "mat" and Sheba thought that would be enough for today. Besides, she wanted some tea and cookies.

As they pulled their chairs up to the tea table, a bell outside the schoolhouse across the street rang and a stream of children shot out of the building. Boys in knickers and girls in jumpers and white blouses with big hair bows ran across the school yard and scattered as they reached the street. "Race you home," yelled one boy, heading straight across the street.

Another boy just behind him responded, "I can beat you easy. But hey, no fair cutting across Nigger Donnegan's yard. He'll catch you and boil you in a pot for dinner." Sheba looked at Will Donnegan to see his reaction, but he was quietly drinking his tea and conversing with his wife. Perhaps he hadn't heard the boy, deaf as he was. She turned to look at Hattie, who shook her head. "Don' fuss over them boys' filthy mouths. They most all talk like that."

Sheba watched as the boys ran down the street. Soon the schoolyard was empty. Will looked up. "We love t' watch those chillen at that school. Some of those chillen, they real nice."

Hattie stood up. "We gotta be back by dinner time. Sure was a right pleasure to see you'all. Mr. Will, you take care and Sheba'll come back t'give you 'nother lesson."

As they walked home in the late afternoon sun, Sheba wondered aloud. "You somethin' Hattie, bringin' me to see Mr. Donnegan. He a right 'spectable ol' man, brung a bunch 'o slaves up here for honest work. I 'magine even white folks do respect him." She was silent, watching the bricks in the sidewalk and thinking how many people had better lives because of Will Donnegan.

Hattie stopped in her tracks. "I swan Miss Sheba you slow as molasses sometimes. Mr. Donnegan be a colored man married to a white woman. They ain't nothin' white folks hate so much, 'less it's seein' a colored man get rich."

They turned into the courtyard of the Lawrence House, its silhouette blocking the darkening Springfield skyline. Hattie shook her head and went up the steps and in the back door, while Sheba turned west to watch the sun begin to set, making the sky blaze. Almost like fire set by a mob running wild in the night. She shivered, cold, and went in.

Dandy Jim's

Two weeks later, Elliott sat in the same booth at Dandy Jim's Saloon that he and Mae had occupied that fateful day when Sheba had passed by. He pondered his cup of coffee, amazed at his good fortune. The odds were against such a choice coincidence, yet there it was: Mae's daughter was employed at the home of the illustrious Mrs. Dana. And she was pretty too. He looked up as Mae, swathed in a brown wrap, entered the saloon through the swinging front door, letting in a gust of icy February air. Her wrap had a hood, which she kept up, obscuring her features. Elliott thought this curious, but was overcome with a desire to know if the woman had secured him an interview with her daughter.

As she seated herself in the narrow wooden booth, Mae let her hood drop to show her face now devoid of paint and unremarkable. She had apparently stopped coloring her hair as well, and now it was beginning to turn silver at the part and above her ears. She looked straight at Elliott as the barkeep placed a glass of beer in front of her. He suppressed a shiver as her watery eyes met his and smiled in what he hoped was a cheerful fashion. "Well, Mrs. Tully, I'm eager to hear how the new job is going." He could barely restrain himself, so eager was he to get to his request.

Mae regarded him soberly. "Oh yessir, it's a fine job. Lots better than the hotel." She looked down at the table as if her glass might have disappeared, then took a gulp of beer. "And, a course, lots better than Sal's." She grimaced, then smiled, the gaps for missing teeth reminding Elliott why Mae avoided the expression. "That Miz Deneen, she jus' a peach, and the G'vnor, well somebody tol' me his folks be Abolitionists so's he's specially kind to us coloreds."

Elliott leaned across the table. "Yes, yes, it does sound like a capital job. But have you had the opportunity to talk with your daughter about meeting with me? Regarding an interview with her employer, of course."

Instead of answering him, Mae looked up from her empty glass, then hailed the bartender. "Bring 'nother, please sir." Her eyes slid back to Elliott, who pretended to concentrate on stirring his coffee. After a minute she sighed. "Well, I ain't 'xactly talked t' her. But a fella, friend 'o mine he works there, maybe he kin get you that interview."

Elliott felt his hopes draining with the beer Mae was emptying from the glass. Still, if this was the only way…. "So tell me what I need to do." He pulled his notebook out, ready to write instructions.

Before Mae could answer, Harry Loper rushed in from the cold afternoon, frost on his breath, striped muffler securely fastened above his immaculate black coat. "Elliott, my boy, what a surprise to find you here," Harry boomed, clapping his son on the shoulder while surveying Mae carefully.

Elliott jumped to his feet, while Mae sank back in the booth as if trying to vanish. "Why Dad, what are you doing on the Levee at this time of day – or any time, for that matter?" Elliott knew his father had a sterling reputation to protect. It simply wouldn't do for a prominent Springfield businessman to be seen in this part of town.

The smile left Harry's face. "It's not a pretty story that brings me here son. You see, I employ a cook who lives above a pool hall down here and he didn't show up today. I got to worrin' about him, whether he was in trouble or just lazy, and figured the quickest way to find out was to just pay him a call." He gestured for Elliott to sit down and slid onto the bench next to him, pulling off his gloves. "Turns out he had been out late last night and was…ahem…" He looked pointedly at Mae, who avoided his glance. "But I can't imagine what would bring you to Dandy Jim's this time of day."

Elliott resisted the urge to squirm. He was his own man, twenty-five years old with his own job and place. He wasn't accountable to his father regarding his whereabouts. Harry waved at the man tending bar, who appeared to be falling asleep. "Barkeep, let me have a sarsaparilla." He turned to his son, fixing him with his gray stare, unnerving Elliott so thoroughly that he blurted a response to his father's inquiry, despite his best intentions.

"It just so happens that I'm meeting with Mrs. Tully here on business, she's providing me with a lead to a possible story." Surely that was a defensible explanation for his appearance in the Levee tavern.

Harry poured the dark brown sarsaparilla from the bottle into a frosted mug and took a swig with relish. "A story now. What kind of story?"

Elliott stiffened his resolve not to tell all to his father. "Well, I'm not really at liberty to say… you know someone might steal the story."

Harry shot his son a sharp glance. "Come, come, Elliott. I'm not goin' to tell anyone. I'm your dad for Pete's sake." He looked out the window into the darkening street. "You know, you sittin' here with this lady, that might strike folks a little odd. But you sittin' here with your dad, well, that's not so queer."

Trapped in the corner of the booth, Elliott sighed. Of course, his father was right. He was always right. "Well, then sir I'll tell you. Mae's one of the ladies I wrote about for my news story awhile back, the story that helped her get a swell job at the Governor's Mansion. Bein' as she's got that job through my story, she's goin' to get her daughter who's a maid in the Lawrence House, to set me up with an interview with Mrs. Dana. Course I do know her daughter, we met downtown." Elliott hoped this last piece of information would put a better light on what appeared suddenly to be a case of white man taking advantage of a colored woman.

It was no good. Instead of congratulating Elliott on his ingenuity, Harry's face went red with anger. Elliott had seen enough of his father's rare temper growing up to know the older man was genuinely riled. "Well Elliott, I sincerely hope you're good friends with this daughter, because I don't doubt she'll lose her job over this." He slammed his fist on the table, shaking Elliott's coffee cup. "You ain't got any idea what you're doin', do you boy? That girl's job's nothin' to you, you swell newsman. But you'd let her get fired from probably the best job she ever had -- just for your damned pride. For Elliott Loper's career." Harry pushed away from Elliott and stood up, then addressed Mae for the first time. "Ma'am, I don't know your daughter, but if she values her job, she won't do this and you won't ask her to." He swung to face Elliott. "And you won't put this woman in the untenable position of having to appear ungrateful if she refuses." Harry pulled his muffler tight around his throat and strode into the night of the Levee.

Shaking, Mae pulled her cape over her head, then leaned forward, staring into Elliott's face. "Oh, Mr. Loper, I don't want Sheba to lose that job. Why God done sent her there to that house and softened that lady's heart." Tears crept down her smooth brown cheeks.

Elliott pulled a handkerchief from his breast pocket and offered it to Mae, who ignored it and dabbed at her face with her fingertips. Elliott felt confused. Surely his father was being an alarmist, as usual. Sheba had nothing to fear, he was certain. Still, Mae was in a state and he felt he would be pressing his advantage if he insisted on the interview now. Regardless of the truth of the situation, regardless of what he stood to lose, he must withdraw. It was a point of honor. "Of course she won't lose the job but I wouldn't dream of asking her to risk it. Please leave now and forget I ever said anything. And don't worry, there's nothing you need do to pay me back for the favor. You earned that job yourself, fair and square."

Between sobs Mae choked out, "I – I'm beholdin' to you Mr. Loper – don' think I ain't." She gathered her wrap around her and rushed out the tavern door, into the night, taking with her his last hope of success, or so Elliott felt. He had counted on the interview to open doors for him, to create a path he could follow higher up the mountain of personal fame, into the realm of the great journalists.

He sighed. He knew only one thing for certain and that was that he couldn't stand another day of writing obituaries at the *Record*. He needed to start fresh in something other than news writing. Sure it was his love, writing, but he loved many things. He gazed aimlessly at the balled-up handkerchief on the table. As he moved to stuff it back in his breast pocket, his fingers brushed against the smooth metal case of his pocket watch. He pulled it out and popped the case: it had been a gift from his parents for his twenty-first birthday.

Elliott stared absently at the face of the watch, soothed by the cool feel of the case. It was a real peach, he had to admit, and he'd hinted that he wanted it for years. The slender hands swept along the clean white face, transporting the distance between the curly Arabic hour numerals. Smaller numerals representing individual minutes edged the outer rim of the face, while on a small dial at the bottom a single hand spun, counting off the seconds. At the center of the two-inch watch, a single word, "Illinois" proclaimed, in an assured and stately fashion, the manufacturer of this piece of precision mastery.

The Illinois Watch daily assured that the many trains across the nation did not collide. Elliott sat up and snapped the watch case shut. This beautiful piece of worksmanship was made right here in Springfield, at the Illinois Watch Factory, rumored to be the best place in town to work. And by Jove, that's where he'd go. The Illinois Watch Factory. Tomorrow. Elliott put his watch back in his breast pocket and walked out into the night of the Levee, heart suddenly light.

Mr. Wright

Sitting in the warm kitchen of the Lawrence House and reading aloud from the *Springfield Journal*, Sheba listened as the large clock on the wall ticked off the seconds. Close by, mending a torn nightgown, Hattie hung on every word while Thomas leaned against the counter, looking bored. "A reception was given by Mrs. Susan Dana at her home Friday last highlighted by an account of the hostess' travels to St. James Court where she met England's King Edward VII. Red and white cut flowers, ferns and palms were arranged in tasteful display in the reception area and anterooms," Sheba paused and made a face. "Where you s'pose them 'anty rooms' is?" she laughed while Hattie urged her to read on.

"Guests in attendance included the Honorable Governor Charles and Mrs. Deneen, George Dallman, the Misses Alice and Tillie Treadway." Sheba looked up as Miss Flora appeared in the kitchen doorway, her small eyes squinty with worry. Both servants rose when she stopped. Mrs. Dana might sit and talk with them, but not Miss Flora. "Girls, I wanted to let you know that we will be honored," she paused and sighed, "honored tomorrow by a very important visitor who will require the house to be spotless."

Sheba and Hattie looked at each other in concern as Miss Flora continued, tapping the table with a pencil to accentuate her words. "Mr. Frank Lloyd Wright, the architect and designer of this wonderful house, will be visiting at Mrs. Dana's request to make some adjustments to our house regarding lighting and cooling. So, we must be sure the house is at its very best."

Since Mr. Wright was to be the lone male guest of two unmarried women, Sheba assumed that he would stay at the Leland Hotel a few blocks away. But as Miss Flora turned to leave she added, "Mrs. Dana has requested that Mr. Wright sleep here – as the house's architect it is only fitting."

Sheba's mind was filled with questions, the most practical having to do with logistics, since the house was not designed for overnight guests. Miss Flora usually used the only guest bedroom as a dressing room. She couldn't resist asking, "But where'll he sleep?"

Miss Flora turned with evident pain at having to answer such a question. "Why in Mrs. Lawrence's old room of course. It's empty and would be the perfect room for a gentleman. See that it's ready for him tomorrow." And she stalked out through the butler's pantry.

Hattie lowered her voice and looked steadily at the door, in case Miss Flora came back. "Miz Dana won't 'lo it, no how, no ways. Why it like some kinda shrine to her mama in there." She was whispering now. "I do b'live it's hainted. I seen Miz Dana doin' spirit writin' and like that in there sometimes. Maybe the old lady's ghost's there."

Sheba sat down and looked at Hattie incredulously. "Folks' spirits cain't come back after they's gone. God takes they souls to heaven." Sheba couldn't imagine that Hattie seriously believed such nonsense. It was one thing for a flighty woman like Mrs. Dana to have such fancies, but quite another for a hard-working plain woman like Hattie.

Hattie pondered this pronouncement, wringing her dishcloth with care and furrowing her brow. "Well, even if it ain't hainted, it ain't fittin' that man be stayin' in Miz Lawrence's room anyhows."

Sheba stared at the table, pondering the famous man, thoughts of spirits far from her mind. Frank Lloyd Wright – she'd finally get to meet this man she'd heard so much about. He might be a devil from what Hattie told her, or he might be a prince, from the way Mrs. Dana carried on about him. Either way, it would be thrilling. Now she could see if it was true, if he was really the genius people said he was.

The next day was spent in a flurry of cleaning and Sheba even took the special step of swabbing the individual panes of art glass behind the fountain in the sitting room while Hattie busily dusted the empty bedroom that opened off the corner.

Coming down the steps from the second floor Mrs. Dana spoke, startling Sheba. "What are you doing?" She sounded perturbed and Sheba dropped her rag, while Hattie moved out of the bedroom, twisting her dustcloth in obvious agony.

"Ma'am, Miss Flora said get this room ready for Mr. Wright to sleep here tonight. That's what she said." Hattie stopped and bowed her head.

A scowl spread over Mrs. Dana's porcelain features. "That's just ridiculous. Mr. Wright can sleep in the guest room next to Flora's room. It's perfect for him." She swept toward her mother's bedroom. "Besides, this room mustn't be disturbed. No one will ever sleep here again. It's Mama's room." She gently closed the door, the two maids watching in silence. Sheba looked at Hattie, who avoided her eyes. They spent the rest of the afternoon readying the guest room for the architect's arrival, with Miss Flora barricaded in her bedroom, just off the same upstairs hallway.

As the sun was beginning to set and the evening train was rattling south towards St. Louis, the front doorbell rang. Opening the door, Sheba saw a man in his mid-thirties with arresting blue eyes and long brown hair that flowed over his collar. He was dressed in an old-fashioned manner with a wide tie and cravat. Sheba glanced down and noticed that he was wearing riding breeches and held a small valise in one hand. He smiled. "Greetings. Mrs. Dana is expecting me. I'm Frank Lloyd Wright."

Although she'd known he was coming, Sheba was too stunned to speak. He was not handsome in the traditional sense, but something about Wright compelled the attention. Sheba pulled the door wide, noting that he was at least two inches shorter than she. "Come in, sir. I'll go fetch the missus." As she mounted the stairs to the upper story, she noticed Wright was studying the furniture and art glass, stooping to see the underside of the umbrella stand shelf and muttering to himself.

When she heard he had arrived, Mrs. Dana flushed and moved quickly to the entry hall, where Wright was making a close study of the statue. "Mr. Wright, what a pleasure to see you. We are so glad you could come."

He took one of her plump hands and kissed it, looking up as she smiled. "My dear Susan, the pleasure is entirely mine." Sheba stood in the next room, enjoying the sight of her mistress melting in the glow of the architect's attention. She was already beginning to see why Mrs. Dana had given this man such a free hand with the design of her house.

"You are a picture. I have never seen you look finer, Susan. And the house, it is impeccable." Wright and Mrs. Dana sat side-by-side on a settee to one side of the arched fireplace. Sheba recalled that this man had designed not only this house, but the glass in the windows and lamps, the odd angular furniture, the lovely and mysterious flow of the great house's rooms and hallways. He sat amid his creation, gazing serenely at Mrs. Dana's animated features, his eyes never leaving her face.

Sheba was aware she was eavesdropping and could feel the pull of work she was needed for in the kitchen, but she stood motionless and unseen in the living room, fascinated by the pair. Wright was married and had six children, according to Hattie, but at this moment he seemed to exist only to listen to Mrs. Dana as she outlined her plans for dinner. "I have had the Governor and his wife here on many occasions, and they are both very complimentary of my lovely residence. Of course, you will meet them tonight at dinner."

Sheba heard a sigh and craned her neck for a better view of the couple, who were seated with their backs to her. She saw Mrs. Dana lean forward and Wright appeared to be holding her hands between his. "I do so wish Mama were here too. She did so love this house."

The architect spoke, "Ah yes, Mother Lawrence, God rest her soul." Then he looked away, across the darkened sitting room where the fountain gurgled quietly, toward the closed door of Mrs. Dana's mother's bedroom. "I am rather taken with that bedroom on the main floor that I designed especially for her. What an excellent idea." To confirm the truth of this pronouncement, Wright rose and strode over to the vacant bedroom, opened the door and went in.

Sheba was amazed by how quickly Mrs. Dana reached her mother's bedroom from the settee. She was visibly flustered, and patted her breast with a handkerchief. As she advanced into the bedroom, she called, "Mr. Wright, what are you doing?"

They had moved out of Sheba's view, but this conversation was too good to miss. Sheba had to go into the room recently vacated by the pair to hear what they were saying. She made a pretense of poking at the fire, but was careful not to make too much noise.

The architect's boots clomped on the wooden floor as he toured the bedroom. "You should be using this bedroom, Susan. Why do you keep it shut up?"

There was a pause. "This is Mama's room and it will stay Mama's room, in her memory." Another pause. Sheba strained to hear the pair, then Mrs. Dana's quiet voice cut through the silence. "Sometimes I come in here and feel her tender hands on my shoulders, comforting me."

Wright seemed not to hear this remark and his voice was somewhat muffled, as though he were facing away from the door, perhaps toward a wall. His next remark indicated he was facing the inside wall, where Mrs. Dana had hung several travel photos. "Hanging of pictures on walls disturbs the organic flow of the house. Yet, despite what I've told you Susan, you insist on hanging these photographs of God knows what. I'd at least have expected some of your fine Japanese prints if you are planning to desecrate these walls."

Cautiously, Sheba moved into the sitting room. Now she could see Mrs. Dana in profile as she stared at a framed photograph on the bedroom wall. "Mama loved those pictures. See, here are Edwin and I on camels in front of the Great Pyramid." But Wright was not looking at the photograph: behind Mrs. Dana, he stared out the art glass windows at the fading light coming over Lawrence Avenue as a lone carriage made its way westward down the street.

Mrs. Dana turned toward Wright and reached out, seeming to want to grasp someone in the room, though it was empty save for the architect and herself. "Mama is here, I can feel it. I've asked her to contact me here in spirit letters that Celia writes for me. She's my medium you know and she assures me that Mama is here, in this room, watching me." She looked at Wright, who stopped on his way out of the room and gazed into Mrs. Dana's eyes.

"Susan, there's no one here. This is a superbly designed bedroom, that's all. And it's being wasted." He put his hand on her shoulder, then continued out of the room. Narrowly missing being discovered, Sheba ducked into a corner of the dining room. She could hear him ascending the stairs to the guest room, calling back, "I'm going to settle in, but I'll be ready for dinner at eight."

From the dining room, Sheba peered into the gathering darkness of Mrs. Lawrence's bedroom. She saw the white figure of Mrs. Dana seated motionless on the bed. Quietly Sheba slipped through the swinging door into the bright bustle of the kitchen.

54

The Watch Factory

Even on this cold February morning, Elliott thought the three-story, red brick structure looked somehow inviting. As he trudged nearer the imposing building, he glimpsed movement behind the deep windows, tall as a man, that honey-combed the two wings and the center building. The rows of bare-limbed trees that lined the sidewalks angling out from the large center door looked oddly welcoming. Above the door, white block letters spelled out the words "Illinois Watch Factory."

He drew a deep breath as he swung open the heavy front door, realizing for the first time that he was slightly nervous about his interview at the factory. He'd submitted his letter of resignation to Mr. Anderson at the *Record* the week before, following the unfortunate incident at Dandy Jim's. Still chagrined at being made a fool of, Elliott hadn't spoken to his father since, though it was rather hard to avoid a man of Harry's prominence in Springfield.

His boots made a ringing sound as he crossed the shiny lobby floor and entered a room marked "Reception." Inside a dark-haired woman with a broad nose and shiny forehead typed assiduously at a desk but stopped as he entered.

"How can I help you, sir?" She didn't move her gaze from the paper in the typewriter.

Elliott was a little taken aback: he wasn't used to being ignored by mere day laborers. "Good day, ma'am. I have an appointment with Mr. Maisenbacher regarding employment. My name is Loper, Elliott Loper." He stopped not wanting to volunteer any more information.

The woman picked up a speaking tube mouthpiece, removed the cap, blew into it, then spoke. "Mr. Maisenbacher. Elliott Loper is here to see you." She put the cap back on the tube, finally glancing in Elliott's general direction. "Please have a seat right there and he'll be with you shortly."

Elliott sat down in one of the straight-backed chairs that lined the walls of the small room. He was directly opposite a door with a frosted glass window over which was emblazoned in gold letters "Corporate Offices." Occasionally a dark form moved in back of the doorway, and Elliott wondered if the heads of the company, the father and son both named Jacob Bunn, were in the offices that day. Of course, his father knew these men and doubtless could have

55

greased the wheels by providing an entrée for Elliott, had he been on speaking terms with the older man.

The doorway to the lobby swung open to admit a florid man with grizzled hair and a handlebar mustache. Elliott rose to his feet as the man approached. "Mr. Maisenbacher?" He stretched his hand and looked into man's face. "Elliott Loper, sir. Pleased to make your acquaintance."

The man gripped his hand and greeted Elliott in a deep voice overlaid with a thick German accent. "Yah, pleased t' meet you too. You come dis way and I talk wid you." He strode back through the doorway with Elliott following in his wake. They passed through a long room off the lobby containing rows of tables next to the tall windows, through which diffused light spilled. Men and an occasional woman sat at these tables perusing stacks of paper. A two-headed lamp stood in the center of each table, with a light for each side.

"Hullo, Mr. Maisenbacher. Mornin' sir." Almost every employee looked up to greet them as they passed, some offering smiles. A friendly place, or so it seemed, Elliott surmised. By the time they were seated in Maisenbacher's narrow office at the back of the room, he was even more determined to land a job at this place.

"Sit down, Mr. Loper, and den tell me why you tink you make a good employee here." The manager settled in the wooden chair behind the desk, then leaned back, the chair emitting a loud squeak.

Elliott had come prepared. He didn't have any manufacturing experience, but he hoped to show he was a good worker. "I think you want someone like me. I hold out for the best. And I'm reliable and can write a good hand and have lots of experience, why I've been working since I was fifteen." He stopped and Maisenbacher remained silent, making Elliott nervous.

The man steepled his fingers and seemed to study his fingertips. "You ain't had no factory experience. So maybe you don't know but what we make gotta be perfect. Cause if it ain't, people die, they die in train wrecks if our Illinois watches ain't accurate,." He stared at Elliott, then smiled, displaying uneven gray teeth. "Some of our parts is so small you gotta use a glass just to see them good. You think you could work with them?"

Elliott saw his chance. "Oh yes, sir. Why ever since I was little boy I've been making sailing ships and putting them in bottles. You ought to see those tiny riggings and masts. I had to use tweezers to handle them."

Maisenbacher looked at Elliott. "That's interesting, son. Maybe you would fit in. Let's just take a walk around the factory so's you can look at how we operate." And with that, he rose from his chair and strode out the door.

Unlike other factories that Elliott had seen in the course of his reporting career, the watch plant was amazingly clean. The pair walked along the hallway's shining wooden floor, its white walls interrupted at regular intervals by doors. The German stopped, then turned to Elliott. "You know why this factory's so clean? Well, I tell you. See, you can't make fine watches in de dirty plant. The grime, why it get in the works. Even a speck of dust makes a timepiece so it ain't precise. We gotta keep the place clean." Maisenbacher opened a door, then stepped back and gestured Elliott inside.

As the manager entered the rectangular room, several of the workers looked up at him and two men nodded before returning to their tasks. The room was lined with tall, arched windows through which the bright February sunshine spilled. Around the circumference of the room were narrow tables and in front of each table, at equal intervals, sat an employee, either a man in white shirt sleeves or a woman in a white blouse. Above each worker, a light dangled from the high ceiling, lighting the tiny pieces they were assembling on trays directly in front of them.

"This here's our Escape Room. You know what an escapement is?" Maisenbacher asked. Elliott shrugged: it seemed clear that his lack of knowledge about watch-making wasn't a black mark against him. Maisenbacher sidled over to the nearest worker, a man with brilliantined brown hair, nattily clad in a herringboned waistcoat and black bow tie. "Hey, Joe. Wanna show this fellow what you're up to?"

The man removed what appeared to be some sort of binoculars and looked up from his work. "Sure thing, Mr. Maisenbacher." He picked up what looked like a tiny wheel and held it at arm's length. Elliott inched closer, marveling at the minute detail and the microscopic teeth encircling it. He made a move to take the piece from the man so he could examine it more closely, but the worker pulled it away. "Don't touch it. You might drop it." He put the wheel down carefully on the felted work surface and turned back to Elliott.

"That's an escape wheel. Sounds funny but it makes sense. See the escapement was named because it allows the movement given to the train of the watch by the mainspring to escape or to run down at the right rate. Of course, our escape wheels are perfect, so our watches are guaranteed to keep accurate time." The man looked at Maisenbacher for approval and when the boss nodded, he turned back to his work, smiling broadly.

Maisenbacher turned to Elliott, rubbing his hands together as they walked from the room. "That's the kind of work we got here. It's close and it gotta be done right, but the workers, they're proud of what they do. Joe there, he makes the best damn escapements in the nation, maybe the world."

Down the hall, they turned and entered a room that seemed, at first glance, to be very similar to the first. Large and lined with windows, it was also filled with tables, but these were occupied only by women and several girls. Mostly young, none over thirty and several who looked to be less than fifteen, the workers were dressed neatly in dark skirts and long-sleeved, high-necked white blouses. As they neared a table, a fetching woman looked up from winding a pocket watch. Her greenish-gray eyes met Elliott's and she brushed a curly brown tendril from her forehead. "Morning, Mr. Maisenbacher."

"Morning, Hazel. How's the timing business dese days? Keepin' those watches goin'?"

The young woman blushed and Elliott realized that he had been staring at her fine-boned face and porcelain complexion. This was not the type of woman he had expected to find working manual labor at the watch factory. She seemed better suited to a tea table or promenading round the square on Sunday afternoon. He looked at the woman seated next to her, a chubby fair-haired girl who smiled, showing large teeth. Several of the women seemed to be regarding him now, and he realized that a single gentleman might present interesting possibilities to this roomful of women.

Hazel found her tongue finally. "Oh sir, we do keep these pieces going, and turn them just so, for when they're tested." Her words had a lilt to them, an accent he couldn't quite place. Hazel refused to meet Elliott's glance again, but he wasn't ready to give up. He felt something, a faint but insistent attraction.

"Well Miss, I'd like to work here at the watch factory. What do you say about working here?" Elliott wondered what kind of a response he would get from this shy flower. All the women in the room, about twenty of them, were now watching the threesome.

Hazel looked up, her pointed face rosy. "Why sir, the Illinois Watch Factory's the best place to work in Springfield, maybe in Illinois. The girls here are friendly, just like family." It was an Irish accent, Elliott decided, and quite beguiling at that. Hazel paused and the blonde girl next to her grasped her hand. She shook her off and continued. "There isn't any swearing and it's neat and sunny. And on warm days in the summer, we all go over to Reservoir Park on our lunch hour." She looked at Maisenbacher, who nodded. "But maybe the best part is the band. You might have heard of our band, it's led by Professor Louis Lehmann, and he came all the way from back East."

Elliott had indeed heard of the Illinois Watch Company band, in fact he remembered a newspaper photo of the group, its members clustered around a large bass drum bearing the band's name. The men were smartly outfitted in nautical blue uniforms with shiny brass buttons and they sported caps with tiny watch emblems. Besides entertaining at employee functions which the paper had often reported on, the band was a community fixture, performing at gala dinners and marching in parades. This company must be something special if its employees found time to play in a band several times a week after work.

"Thanks girl. Now you and these others best be getting' back to work," Maisenbacher said. Elliott threw what he hoped was an engaging smile to Hazel, then followed the manager from the room.

As they walked back toward Maisenbacher's office, the older man peppered Elliott with questions about his past employment, his references, and his family. Seemingly satisfied with Elliott's responses as they reentered his office, Maisenbacher seated himself behind the desk again.

"OK, now I wanna tell you somethin' about workin' here. Because I want you to come here if you think you'd be a good worker for us." He raised his salt-and-pepper eyebrows and fell silent.

Elliott realized that this was his opening. "You can be assured that I desire to work here and that I will do my very best to be an excellent employee. Thank you, sir." He extended his hand, only then realizing that he had no idea where in the factory he was to work.

But Maisenbacher seemed unconcerned with the exact position Elliott would fill. Instead he stared at Elliott. "Now listen son, I'm gonna give you some advice right now, 'for you start. Because all our workers been told how to work and they do it. That's why we make the best timepieces in the world. See you work like you dance. You gotta make every move count and don't make a single move you don't have to make. Don't waste a single second – seconds are slippery little things that slide away before you know it and they never come back. And you know what, they take part of your pay envelope away with them. So you gotta time your own work yourself and figure out how many you can do per minute. Then keep to that pace."

"Excuse me sir, but how many of what? Where exactly did you have in mind for me to work?"

The man was examining a long, ledger page with names written on it in a large, even hand. Showing faintly behind some of the names was writing that had been erased, although not completely. Probably names of employees who had departed, Elliott surmised.

Maisenbacher turned the page and ran his finger down the edge, then stopped. "We'll put you in jewelling, we gotta a couple vacant spots there. Work hours is Monday through Friday from seven to five o'clock. You get off at noon on Saturday. Twenty-five cents an hour. Best place to work in Springfield, you heard what that girl said. What do you say?"

"You bet! When can I start?" Elliott jumped to his feet. His new beginning, at this sparkling factory full of friendly people and pretty girls. It was too good to be true, and maybe here he'd be able to shrug off his dreams of becoming a famous newsman. Maybe if he gazed into the lovely Hazel's green eyes long enough he'd even forget Sheba.

A Discussion of Spirits

At the Lawrence House, the hours before the dinner with Wright held many preparations for the elaborate meal, though there were to be only five diners in all. Sheba placed the final pieces of silver on the table, then looked up, pausing to admire the shadows cast by the chandeliers in each corner of the room. The silhouettes of triangular butterflies fluttered on the mural that encircled the wall above the table.

She hadn't time to enjoy the beauty of the butterflies: she had to help Mrs. Dana dress for dinner, a task that was alternately a chore and a pleasure. Mrs. Dana required considerable attention and often changed her hair and garb more than once; however, now that she was more familiar with the girl, she sometimes confided in Sheba. To have a wealthy white woman like Mrs. Dana trust her was an honor Sheba never dreamed could happen.

Sheba hastened through the upstairs back hallway and across the musicians' balcony above the dining room while snatches of "The Cascades Rag" ran through her head. The tune had been played on the Victrola at a previous evening's party and its syncopated beat had caught Sheba's fancy. It appealed to something deep inside her, tugged at her emotions the way a hymn might, sung full force by the assembled congregation at the Pleasant Grove Baptist Church.

"That song is just a sensation," one of the guests had remarked. "A colored man, Scott Joplin, wrote it for the 1904 World's Fair. It's amazing."

Governor Deneen had nodded in time to the music. "Indeed. A sensation. The coloreds have a real feel for this kind of music." The Governor had turned to his wife, Bina. "This is a toe-tapper," he had exclaimed, pulling her from the settee, then two-stepping around the room. The Governor and his wife had cut a fine figure stepping neatly across the large Oriental carpet. Sheba had watched from the corner, giving herself up to the hypnotic pull of the rag.

Arriving at her mistress's bedroom, Sheba knocked at the door, then opened it and climbed three steps into the room. Mrs. Dana had already begun her toilet and was seated before the oak dressing table, gazing at her own face and shoulders in the mirror. "Sheba, I particularly need your attentions tonight – you see, for Mr. Wright I must look especially well."

Mrs. Dana seemed withdrawn, which Sheba attributed to the conversation with Wright that she had overheard in the vacant bedroom earlier that evening.

His disparagement of the existence of spirits had obviously dismayed Mrs. Dana, so Sheba tried to put her mistress in a better mood. She felt maternal toward the older woman, who sat in front of her, patting on powder while Sheba worked to pull her thick, ash-blond hair into a loose knot atop her head. In spite of the fact that Mrs. Dana could be haughty and remote, Sheba had grown fond of her, due in a large part to the dressing room confidences. Over the months she had heard accounts of the young Susie Lawrence's courtship by Edwin Dana; the pitiful deaths of her two infant sons in Minneapolis, where the young couple had lived; and finally, the barely disguised yearnings for Wright. Mrs. Dana was never clear the extent to which she carried her admiration for the married architect, and Sheba didn't want to know, because then she'd be bound to tell Pastor Ball and she couldn't imagine what he would do.

Tonight, the electric lights in the butter-colored sconces on the bedroom walls cast a dim-but-appealing light over the dressing table. Across the room stood a matching dresser and next to it, a single bed, just like the one her mistress slept in. These were doubtless intended for some future husband, an optimistic gesture on Mrs. Dana's part, Sheba had decided.

"This looks right nice," Sheba commented, pinning a large sapphire brooch on Mrs. Dana's dress, just at her shoulder. It glittered on the pale blue evening dress, drawing attention to the middle-aged woman's still-lustrous skin. She looked over Mrs. Dana's head and into the dressing table mirror, glimpsing her own face. Above the elegant matron she saw a slender young woman with almond eyes and smooth complexion, her face expressionless, like a mask.

"Sheba, please catch up that curl, the one just behind my neck." Sheba's attention was drawn back to the woman seated before her, her features tonight eroded by the signs of age, graying hair, and a softening jaw line. Sheba fixed the loose curl and Mrs. Dana turned to her, standing up and straightening her evening dress. "We are so honored by Mr. Wright's visit. I assume he found everything to his liking."

Sheba wasn't sure what this meant, but Mrs. Dana was staring at her with piercing blue eyes that demanded a response. "Well, he did move some thin's in the big room just 'for I came up." Sheba could not lie. She looked down, embarrassed, hoping Mrs. Dana would change the line of questioning.

Her mistress gave a low laugh. "I'm sure he can do as he pleases, but doubtless he didn't move much."

She paused, so Sheba felt she should say something. After all, Mrs. Dana did have a right to know. "Well, ma'am, he took down those nice p'ctures 'bove the fireplace, an' he moved that music stand an'…" She stopped as her mistress collapsed onto the bench. She wondered what she had said to cause such an abrupt change in Mrs. Dana's mood.

The older woman sat, face in her hands, gazing into the mirror. "Oh Sheba, it's just as I expected, as I feared. I can never please him, it's never right here for him." Her voice was almost a whisper and Sheba was worried she would begin to cry, which would make her face all splotchy for dinner, surely not what she would want for Wright.

Before she could say anything, Mrs. Dana raised her head, gazing at Sheba's reflection in the mirror. "He's a genius, just a genius, you see, and this house is a wonderful display of that prodigious talent." Her eyes filled with tears and she closed them. "But Sheba, I have to live here. This is my house. Their spirits are here -- Mama and Papa, Edwin, even my dear little baby boys." After a moment, she sighed, dabbed at her eyes, then took out her gloves from a drawer and began putting them on. Relieved, for she didn't know how to comfort Mrs. Dana, Sheba put away the toiletries and dusted the dressing table of any lingering powder.

Mrs. Dana straightened the folds of her satin gown and glanced at the clock on the dressing table. "My goodness, look at the time. Well, I'm ready for dinner. I do so enjoy Governor Deneen and his sweet wife. And now they'll be meeting Mr. Wright." Restored, at least temporarily, by the anticipation of a dinner with the architect, Mrs. Dana swept from the room, the scent of floral perfume lingering after her.

When Sheba was finished laying the fire and getting out nightclothes, she went down the steps into the kitchen to help Maud and the others. Soon the other guests arrived and Sheba began to serve the five diners: cousin Flora, dressed as usual in severe black; the Governor and his wife—he in black tie and tails, she in an elegant white sheath and a headdress of white plumes; Wright, in a bow tie and cummerbund; and Mrs. Dana, who seemed to glow in the pale blue gown.

As Sheba served the squab and asparagus, Wright waved his hands, animatedly describing his latest projects near Chicago. He had captured the attention of the Governor and his wife who paid scant attention to their food. Sheba quietly removed the plates, listening surreptitiously. Now the Governor was telling about the Levee and its many dens of iniquity. Sheba had heard the taverns and gambling dens decried often by the aged men in her church and even by Pastor Ball from the pulpit.

"They tell me most of these businesses are run by the colored, that they're to blame for all this drunkenness and vice. But I don't know—seems to me plenty of white folks patronize those places. Why I believe some white men come to town just to visit." He stopped himself and looked up at his wife. "Well anyway, it's just hard to believe that the Negro is behind all this." The Governor looked askance at Wright, who appeared somewhat bored and attempted to change the subject to his own philosophy of life.

"Well sir, all races can appreciate fine architecture – it's is the great leveler of mankind," Wright proclaimed, waving his hand to indicate the spacious room, its barrel-vaulted ceiling rising into the second story. He looked directly at Sheba, who had never been recognized in a gathering of white people before and addressed her. "Why young woman, don't you feel the nature of God in this house?"

Shocked, Sheba balanced the dirty plate, looking from Mrs. Dana, to the Governor, to his wife, and finally to Miss Flora. She thought perhaps God Himself might answer the architect, but instead Miss Flora tittered, then spoke.

"Oh surely you can't expect this colored girl to understand architecture. Why she's as dull as a box of rocks."

Anger rose in Sheba. Wright had asked her a question and she owed him an answer. She was afraid to contradict this famous man, but she didn't think this house was like a church at all, if that was what he was asking. She looked at Mrs. Dana for some reassurance, but her mistress' eyes were riveted on the architect, who had had seemingly lost interest and waved his hand dismissively.

Sheba was startled from her momentary paralysis by a direct command from Miss Flora. "Just finish clearing and bring the dessert." She grabbed the rest of the plates from the sideboard and backed into the butler's pantry, eager for escape.

Hattie was busy plating up the dessert course. "Well, I s'pose that crazy man off on 'nother rant, like he do. I guess Miz Dana be happy tho'." Hattie had worked for the family through the planning and construction of this house and recounted many tales of the architect's egotism and arrogance. She winked at Sheba, who, subdued and resentful, answered her in half sentences, dreading the time when she would have to take in dessert.

As she began scraping the plates into the trash, the bell sounded for the dessert course to be served. But something must be wrong with the button that activated the bell. It was placed on the floor so that Mrs. Dana could tap it with her foot, and it must have gotten stuck, because the bell kept on jangling long after it should have stopped.

"You check it, Sheba, when you go in. That ringing's like to drive me batty," Maud said. She opened the butler's pantry door to let Sheba carry in the quivering bowls of chocolate mousse garnished with raspberries, a delicacy that made Sheba's mouth water. As Sheba came through the swinging door, she glanced under the table by Mrs. Dana's chair. In the shadows she saw Mrs. Dana's foot in its satin slipper squarely on the call button, with Wright's boot resting on top of it, his leg firmly against hers.

She had never seen this kind of play before, though she guessed it was forbidden. So she averted her eyes and served the mousse. Meanwhile, Wright was expounding his architectural theories to the Governor and his wife. "This house is an example of my Prairie House, but on a grander scale." Mrs. Dana's chiseled features had assumed a glazed look, while Miss Flora was nowhere to be seen — she had apparently excused herself, as was her custom, after the main course.

A nod from Maud as Sheba passed through the butler's pantry assured her that someone, either Wright or Mrs. Dana, had finally moved a foot and the bell was free. Perhaps this was the end of the pair's shenanigans, Sheba thought, but as she poured coffee, she could see that Mrs. Dana was not ready to surrender her revered architect's real or imagined affections so quickly.

Mrs. Dana had revived her senses enough to turn to the governor's wife. "Have you heard of the new fashion, slate writing? It is used by many trusted spirit guides in contacting the dead. You see, I'm quite sure that the spirits of our dear departed can visit us and advise us." She took a dainty bite of mousse and looked at Wright, who yawned.

After a pause, Mrs. Deneen responded. "I would love to believe that spirits can come back to comfort us, but my faith does not hold with such superstitions." At this last word, she stopped herself and flushed red with embarrassment.

Mrs. Dana responded indignantly to the supposed insult. "I can prove to you that this is not just some silly 'superstition' as you put it. I have been practicing slate writing and I can contact Mama in her bedroom tonight. This will prove beyond any doubt that spirits do exist – indeed they are part of our everyday life." Her eyes sparkled in the candlelight, as she looked first at the Governor and his wife, then at Wright.

The married couple exchanged a guardedly horrified glance, then Mrs. Deneen responded. "While we would love to take part, my children await at home. Please forgive us our early departure, Susan. We have had a delightful evening." She rose to leave, although coffee had just been served. The Governor had no recourse but to rise and bid his farewells, begging the children as an excuse to depart at the early hour of ten. Sheba hurried to retrieve Mrs. Deneen's fur wrap from the huge downstairs coatroom. She watched as the couple's stylish backs retreated down the street to the Governor's Mansion, vaguely comforted that she shared a common faith with this prestigious couple.

Realizing that she would be needed in the kitchen, Sheba hurried up the steps and through the sitting room, glancing into the now empty dining room as she passed. Before she had a chance to form a theory of the whereabouts of the two remaining diners – Wright and Mrs. Dana -- Sheba saw candlelight flickering from the vacant bedroom belonging to her mistress' dead mother. Stopping to listen, she heard the scrape of chalk on a slate. Through the partially opened door she saw the architect seated in a chair with his back to the door, facing the windows, while Mrs. Dana sat on the narrow single bed, writing on a slate with her eyes closed.

"Mama, will I find my diamond brooch?" Her voice was soft and unnaturally high. Her hand began to form words on the slate. Wright looked up from his contemplation of something on the street outside. He moved from the chair to sit next to Mrs. Dana on the bed, staring at the slate. "What does it say? Who's really writing this Susan?" With these last words he grasped Mrs. Dana's hand as she held the chalk. She looked up into his face, then Sheba heard the chalk drop to the floor as she turned and fled into the kitchen.

After waiting until midnight, Sheba and the other servants retired. It appeared that Wright and Mrs. Dana had no need of their attentions, Hattie had observed wryly to Sheba as they mounted the back stairs toward their bedrooms. "I reckon they kin take care o' what crops up," she muttered as she went through the door of her room.

Next day, the architect stayed until evening. Before rushing off to catch the last train to Chicago, he recommended installing some additional lights that would make the dark house brighter. Mrs. Dana acquiesced without argument to his every suggestion and disappeared into her bedroom after he left.

Wright had designated that screens be placed in some of the windows, and Mrs. Dana arranged to have these installed that spring just as the heat began in late May. By mid June, Wright's visit seemed a part of the distant past, and even the well-shaded house was insufferably hot. Each night, Hattie and Sheba took their mattresses out to the sleeping porch, hoping to catch a cool breeze.

June 1907. The Band Concert

As he strolled across the street behind the Illinois Watch Factory, Elliott scanned Reservoir Park. All morning long, he hunched over miniscule, sparkling jewels, carefully placing them with tweezers on steel plates. When he looked up to rest his eyes, he would gaze out the long window at the waving leaves and anticipate his lunch break, at noon, sharp. Most days, Elliott grabbed his lunch pail from under his work table and lit off down the hall, eager to meet Hazel and her friends in the park, if it was sunny, or in the lunchroom, if it wasn't.

Their usual lunch spot on the south bank of the reservoir was already occupied by five men in shirt-sleeves and suspenders, rough types, maybe loading dock workers. Elliott turned away to walk across the park in search of the women when he heard a yell.

"Hey you, ain't you Elliott Loper?" The voice was deep and carried a strong Irish accent. Turning, Elliott saw one of the men, a young man with a ruddy complexion, had risen from the grass and was headed his way. Resisting the irrational desire to turn and run, Elliott forced a smile.

"Why yes, that's me. And you are?" He stuck out his hand, and the man thrust his large, calloused one into it.

"Garvey's the name, Matthew Garvey. We been hearin' a lot about you at family picnics and such. I be Hazel's cousin and it appears she's taken a shine to ye." The man narrowed his eyes, but smiled at Elliott. He wondered what had been said about him at these gatherings, which he pictured as large, rather raucous affairs fuel by Irish whiskey

"It's a pleasure to meet you. Indeed, I have squired Hazel on a few occasions to social events, with the permission of her father of course." Elliott didn't feel it was necessary to share the details of these occasions, which numbered only two, a tea dance put on by one of the ladies' social clubs and a roller-skating outing sponsored by the factory. At both affairs, he had met Hazel, who was constantly surrounded by her group of women friends. He eyed the cousin, who looked at him. He wanted to find Hazel, but this young man seemed to expect conversation. "So I assume you work here, Mr. Garvey. I myself work in the jewelling department. Whereabouts are you employed?"

The man seemed pleased to be asked about his work. "I been workin' these nine years in shippin' and receivin'." He waved toward the group near the reservoir, busily devouring their sandwiches, shiny lunch pails scattered around them on the green, well-tended bank. In the middle of the lake, a fountain shot jets of water skyward. "Those the fellas I work with. Won't find a better bunch." He turned back to Elliott. "I heard up in jewelin' you got some kikes workin' with you. That true?"

Elliott had been scanning the park, but the racial slur brought his attention back with a start. "Why a Hebrew gentleman joined us last week, Reuben Fishman. Father owns a pawn shop downtown. Seems like a nice sort, and a hard worker." The new man was quiet, but kept regular hours and asked Elliott frequently for help with the finer points of jewelling.

"Well I hate to see it. This fine company hirin' kikes." There was that word again. "They must be hard up. But if they start makin' me work with niggers, well, that's the last straw." Unaccountably, Garvey grinned, then nodded at Elliott. "I do think better of the management here though. I'd best be gettin' back, lunch break'll be over. You tell Hazel we talked and that I said you're all right."

It registered with Elliott suddenly that the only Negro he had seen in the whole of his time at the watch factory was Jones, the sad-faced janitor. The colored man worked nights with the other maintenance help, so Elliott had only seen him once. The image of Sheba passed briefly though his mind and he wondered if she was still at the Lawrence House, but the urging of his stomach brought him back to the current situation. He decided to give up on finding Hazel and stepped off the curb to head back to the factory's lunchroom.

"Elliott?" He felt a light touch on his elbow and recognized the soft Irish tones of Hazel's voice.

He turned from the street. Behind Hazel, sun shining on her brown-gold hair, stood three young women who watched her intently. She smiled demurely, but met his eyes. "We couldn't get our usual spot so we went 'round the reservoir to the north bank. I saw you talking with my cousin and I was hoping you'd spot us." She glanced back at her friends. "We've already eaten though. It's almost one now."

Elliott smiled, pleased that she'd taken the trouble to hunt him down. She was so reserved that he hadn't gotten a read on her exact feelings for him during their outings. She seemed to enjoy herself, smiling and nodding to the music and asking polite questions, but she didn't volunteer information about herself and her family. She was beguiling, with her full bosom, tiny waist, and small, pointed features. He longed to grab her hands and pull her to him, crushing the lace in her blouse to his chest. But instead he waved at her entourage. "Oh that's all right, I'll eat real quick in the lunchroom." He directed his attention to her upturned face. "Say, I didn't know your cousin worked here. He's quite a fellow." He didn't want to say much more.

"Oh, Matthew, why yes he's worked here forever. It was through him I got my position in the timing room. His father's my mother's brother."

Elliott didn't press her for the reason why she had never mentioned this. Before she departed, he seized the opportunity to see her again. "Hazel, the Watch Company band is performing this evening at seven o'clock at Washington Park. It would be a pleasure if you would accompany me to the concert."

She looked at her friends, who were departing, then reached out to squeeze his hand. Her grasp was light and cool, the flesh of her hand supple. "I'd be delighted. Come by at half-past six and we'll take the streetcar." She let go of his hand and hastened after her friends as the whistle blew summoning the watch factory employees back to work.

The promise of parting Hazel from her group of friends made the rest of the workday speed by, despite the fact that Elliott had missed his lunch. So that evening when he saw Matthew Garvey standing next to Hazel at the streetcar stop near the Garvey's north-end home, he winced, then turned to see if anyone had noticed.

"Mr. Loper, so we meet again." Matthew swung onto the streetcar then extended his hand for his cousin, who stepped daintily onto the crowded car. "We couldn't very well have Hazel here gallavantin' round town by her lonesome, now could we?" His eyes twinkled, but he didn't smile. Hazel gave the conductor two nickels, one for her cousin and one for herself, then grasped the railing that connected the first seat, which was occupied, to the ceiling as the car lurched forward.

By the time they reached the hilly, tree-filled Washington Park, Hazel had still not addressed Elliott. She directed her remarks at her cousin, who stood next to her, and she stole an occasional glance toward Elliott. He was encouraged: perhaps they could lose the boisterous Matthew at the concert. Surely there was some quiet place in the woods where they could be alone.

"Well, here we are," Matthew shouted as the passengers streamed off the streetcar, up the hill toward the gazebo, where the concert was to be held. Elliott could see the band members, small figures clad in navy blue inside the structure, instruments catching the summer evening light with brilliant flashes.

Matthew bounded ahead, and Elliott fell into step next to Hazel. She was dressed becomingly in a grey shirtwaist with a watch pinned to the bodice. A large white hat sporting furls of grey fabric nested in her soft brown hair. "I expect you've heard the band perform before. They're quite good, if I remember correctly."

"Oh yes, quite good," she replied, smiling at Elliott. They continued up the hill, Elliott feeling increasingly hopeful. When they reached the top of the hill, Matthew was nowhere to be seen. Elliott found a spot and flapped open the blanket that he had been carrying. Hazel caught the other end, and together they settled it on the grass, a little ways back from the gazebo. She was about to seat herself, when a man's shouting caught her attention and she froze.

Following her gaze, Elliott spotted Matthew, a few yards ahead of them, arguing loudly with a group of Negroes who were attempting to arrange their camp chairs and blankets. "Excuse me," he said to the motionless Hazel, and strode forward with as much quickness as he could muster and a good deal of trepidation.

A colored man in a derby hat stood at arm's length from Matthew, who had seized one of the camp chairs and holding it by the seat in a rather threatening manner. A few white men clustered behind Matthew with an air of expectancy. Elliott had a brief out-of-body vision in which he hovered above the gazebo watching himself, a slight, fair-haired man approaching a swirling caldron of Negroes and whites.

"What seems to be the problem Mr. Garvey?" Elliott stood a safe distance from Matthew, whose face was red, sweat dripping from his temples. Matthew didn't take his eyes from the Negro.

"I got this handled, Elliott. See these here niggers they be tryin' to block everybody's view of this concert by settin' up their chairs up front. They better move back there." He pointed to the bottom of the hill, near a pond.

The Negro interjected. "You cain't see nothin' from way back there. We gotta right to be here and we gonna' set our stuff down." Nodding to the women in the group, the man turned and began to spread a blanket out, but Matthew advanced and tore it from his hands.

"You ain't settin' up here. Now move back." The white men in back of Matthew moved forward as if on command. The group had swollen to at least twenty menacing men in shirt sleeves. The Negro surveyed his group, which included only one other man, an elderly gentleman who had already collapsed in a camp chair, then he turned to Matthew.

"All right, we movin', but it ain't right. Mr. Lincoln never woulda allowed it."

The colored people gathered their gear and the white men went back to their groups. "I can't stand it when those niggers play that card. Like good old Honest Abe would come to their rescue." Matthew watched the Negroes closely.

Elliott decided it was pointless to mention that the city's favorite son had penned the Emancipation Proclamation, giving these very people the same rights as Matthew, who just happened to be born white. He wouldn't be able to change Matthew's mind or the minds of the other white concertgoers. He sighed.

When the pair returned, Hazel was seated on the blanket, clutching her knees. "What did those awful niggers say to you? Low down dirty scum. I don't know why they don't just stay on the east side, where they belong." Her eyes searched Matthew's face and he flopped down next to her while Elliott stared at the object of his affections, all desire for her draining from him. Her face seemed pinched and her green eyes wicked. She looked more like a harlot sitting there on the blanket than a fine Springfield lady. He turned away, as the group of Negroes filed past, camp chairs under their arms, down the hill towards the lake.

August 1907. The Amusement Park

That summer, through the endless hot nights on the Lawrence House sleeping porch, Sheba thought of Thomas, in his airless room above the stables. The pale image of Elliott Loper lingered in the back of her consciousness, ethereal, like a spirit from another world. Sheba tossed on her mattress and shook him out of her mind. She knew better than to believe that he would ever reappear.

In the year since she had started work at the Lawrence House, Sheba had never had a gentleman friend, so the fact that Thomas had taken notice of her was flattering. He loved to tease her at meals, mostly about her manners and her rules for behavior. "Sheba such a fine lady," he would say, rolling his eyes as Sheba cut up her food into small pieces. She didn't explain that she did this out of necessity rather than preference. A number of her teeth had become decayed and had to be pulled while she was at the orphanage. Thank goodness they were in the back so they didn't affect her looks.

She admired Thomas' quick wit, his ability to appear noiselessly when he was needed, and his narrow, glinting eyes. And she sensed he liked her too. So it didn't surprise her much when, one Tuesday in August, he came round the kitchen at breakfast time and sat at the end of the table while she drank her tea, looking at her and making her too nervous to finish. Picking up her cup and saucer from the table, Sheba stepped to the sink, then felt a tug at one of her apron ties.

"Sheba, how's 'bout doin' somethin' excitin' tomorry, 'stead o' jus' watchin' that ol' Donnegan fella nod off." Thomas laughed at her shocked expression. "How's 'bout we go on down to Mildred Park and ride that Ferris Wheel?"

Sheba considered a moment. "Them Ferris Wheels, they big and scary."

"C'mon, ain't nobody 'round here done nothin' like it." He seemed almost to be begging in his excitement.

Sheba couldn't resist his enthusiasm, secretly pleased that he had asked her to go. "Well, all right. I guess so."

"Oh bless me, I's glad you say 'yes.' We have a big time. You be talkin' 'bout this 'for a good long while." He jumped up and bounded out the back door, into the searing summer sunlight.

So Sheba agreed to walk out with Thomas on an excursion to Mildred Park, a big amusement area at the southeast corner of the city. She had made a new pinstriped dress in between her projects for Mrs. Dana. Carrying a small handbag and walking side-by-side with Thomas the next day as they stepped out the servants' doorway in the back garden wall, Sheba was sure that she was the envy of Hattie, who stood watching from the kitchen porch, and Maud too, gazing, unseen—or so she thought—from the kitchen window. "Now you be back 'for dark," Hattie had cautioned. "Them streetcars ain't safe." Then she had rested her eyes on Thomas, adding, "You in good hands with Tommy."

The afternoon was fine, not too hot, as they made their way to the streetcar which ran down Fifth Street. They joined the small group of colored people also waiting there, while the white riders waited on the opposite side of the tracks under a small shelter. The clanging, open-sided streetcar arrived and they pushed their way on, grabbing two of the few vacant seats. They sat in silence, side by side on the wooden bench, holding tight to the arms and watching as the houses got progressively smaller and closer together as the streetcar headed south, and then swung east towards Mildred Park.

Sheba was excited – she had never been to an amusement park before. At the orphanage they played in the yard or the street and at the Burtons they had gone to relatives' homes for amusement. She turned to Thomas, who was watching three small white girls attempt to roll a hoop down the sidewalk as the streetcar clattered by. "So what goes on at this here park?"

Thomas pushed his hat back on his head and looked seriously at Sheba. "Oh, lots o' things. A duck pond, a merry-go-round. And gamin' too. Maybe I can win you somethin'."

"Gamin', oh land, I ain't gonna do no gamin'." Sheba had the vague suspicion that these games involved cards and dice and would not be permitted by Pastor Ball.

"Well, ain't nobody gonna make you do no games." Thomas was laughing at her again. As the streetcar swung into view of Mildred Park, Sheba caught her breath. The sheer size of it amazed her. What looked like miles of odd structures filled the horizon: long roller coasters, pony rides, a carousel, and large tents. But dominating the scene, which swarmed with people of every hue, was a huge wheel, piercing the air, higher than the trees on either side of the park, and festooned with swinging seats. In every seat sat a couple or a single person, some waving, some swinging the seats, one couple even kissing.

Thomas looked at Sheba with satisfaction as she beheld a sight like none she had encountered before. "That be Mildred Park all right. 'Somethin' ain't it?" They got off the streetcar and walked to the park entrance. "Colored only" said the sign to the right. As Thomas paid the five-cent admission fee, Sheba watched as white people in cool summer outfits swarmed through the main entrance.

Once through the gate, Sheba headed straight for the huge Ferris wheel. "I wanna ride that big wheel. Why Lord a'mighty, it be taller than them trees." She pointed with excitement at the top of the ride, but Thomas pulled her back.

"That ain't for us'ns. Look here." He directed Sheba to a part of the park down the hill, where a smaller wheel stood among other amusements. "This here's rides for us coloreds." Disappointed, Sheba looked at the four rides in the valley below. A small Ferris wheel, some bedraggled ponies, a sliding board, and swings that swung out from a central pole. She turned and looked one last time at the large Ferris wheel, then followed Thomas down to the rides.

After enjoying each ride twice, she was perspiring, and a food stand caught her eye. "Ice Cream Cones, as offered at the St. Louis World's Fair," called out the woman behind the counter, beckoning to the pair. Sheba had stolen a taste of ice cream after one of Mrs. Dana's story hours, but didn't have the vaguest notion of what a cone might be. After confiding her ignorance to Thomas, he went to the stand, returning with a waffle cone holding a scoop of strawberry ice cream. She took it in her hand then looked up at Thomas in consternation. "I 'preciate it, but I ain't sure I kin eat it."

He smiled, his white teeth flashing. "Just lick it, but you better be quick. It's meltin'." Sheba stuck her tongue in a dribble that was running down her hand. The fruity taste was so smooth, she licked the ice cream on the top, but the whole mound flew off the other side of the cone and into the dirt.

Well, at least she had a taste, she thought as she watched as the pink scoop of coolness melting in the dust. And she still had the cone, which she munched while Thomas told her of his life. "I come from Alabamy. Come north with pa, then he up and left, so's I had to find a livin'. I got work downtown, haulin' ice for the ice company but lawd it was hard. So's when I heerd 'bout Miz Dana's stable job, I near jumped at that. I been there five years, since I done turned fifteen. Workin' for Miz Dana's real good, 'specially compared to my friends." Sheba looked at Thomas' cheerful face and wondered what other hardships he had seen.

After they finished their ice cream, they took a stroll in the shade around the park's small lake, watching children throw bread to the ducks. Thomas walked close and tried to take her hand, but Sheba shooed him away. "What's you think, you somebody special?" Somewhat put off, Thomas said, "Well I's hopin' I be a little bit special t'you."

Sheba looked ahead down the shady path, wishing she had been brave enough to risk holding his hand. "First you gotta show you got somethin' special, somethin' better than folks might think." She glanced up at Thomas, who was walking by her side with his hands in the pockets of his checkered pants, staring hard at the distance.

"I got better things comin', just wait 'n see. I won't be horse tendin' too much longer. Maybe I be gettin' one o' them minin' jobs." He looked over at her, narrowing his eyes under his bowler hat. "Or maybe that ain't good enuff. Maybe you set your cap for some white boy, like that newsman, that Loper feller." He stopped and stared at Sheba while some children ran by, then spat out, "Guess you figure he gonna take you somewhere better. Well you kin jus' forget that notion. He ain't no fancy writer no more. He quit that newspaper and got a job at the watch factory." Sheba gasped. She had not been thinking of Elliott, in fact he hadn't crossed her mind in some time, but she was brought up short by Thomas' remark that he had left the newspaper. She felt a sinking in her stomach and realized that she had still hoped to see Elliott again someday. Now she doubted that would happen.

She looked over at Thomas, who, despite his sneering, seemed fearful she might walk away. She reached for his hand, which he begrudgingly let her take. "I don care one whit. I never had no dealin's with him, none 'tall." She smiled and after a moment, he grinned back. They walked on together, hand in hand. She suddenly wanted to tell him everything, even ideas that had been roaming through her mind for months. "I got plans 'o my own. Gonna set up a dressmakin' shop downtown, be in business, like Mr. Scott Burton." She hadn't confided this scheme to anyone, though she had spent long hours concocting how she could reach her goal as she pinned and cut and sewed the many gowns required by Mrs. Dana. Her mistress lavished praise on Sheba for her work, which she said was more precise and careful than that of her predecessor. But Mrs. Dana said that Sheba's real strength was in her ability to take a basic dress pattern and add small features that set the garment apart, a ruffle, a bit of embroidery, an unusual turn to a sleeve.

"When I am entertaining, I like to know that the same dress will not be worn by anyone else in the room, or even in Springfield," Mrs. Dana had said. Standing in the sewing room, Mrs. Dana had given final approval to Sheba's latest creation, a glimmering evening dress, embellished with seed pearls and a train. She used a hand-held mirror to admire the back of the skirt in the full-length mirror of the small room. "You are a treasure, Sheba. Just see how this back falls so nicely into the train." Sheba sat on the low stool admiring her handiwork, which indeed showed her creativity well on this impressive woman who would be seen by many in Springfield society. She squeezed her knees, thinking of how her mistress would respond to compliments. "Yes this dress, it is a creation of my maid, Sheba. She has quite a hand for dressmaking." Sheba could see these important society women lining up at her own shop door, her first patrons, someday in the future.

Thomas' relieved laugh brought Sheba back to the present, as they sat side-by-side on a bench to wait for the streetcar that would take them home. "I say them are some big plans, but anythin' kin happen. Maybe you get that shop, yessir. Why Springfield, it be home of Mr. Lincoln. 'Cordin' to him even folks like us kin make some big plans." Sheba looked into Thomas' brown eyes and felt, irrationally, that perhaps it was possible for her to have a shop. After all, God had brought her this far, had shown her His favor and she was only seventeen. Anything might happen if He willed it. She started as the streetcar approached, clanging and blowing up dust from Eleventh Street and they both stood up to leave.

73

The Moonlight Gardens

Work at the watch factory was decidedly less interesting without Hazel for diversion, Elliott thought to himself as he sat at his table in the jewelling room, placing minute gems strategically onto a watch plate. Further down the line, another employee, his shirt-sleeves nipped back with twin black bands around his biceps, burnished the jewels into a settings – circular rims of brass. It was Elliott's job to insert the jewel and setting into a little depression of the watch-plate. The jewels were held in place by deep blue screws of steel. He could do three or four of these before his head began to ache, which it had now.

He looked up and caught the eye of Abe, the dark-haired slender fellow who sat next to him. Abe glanced his way and winked. "Just you wait 'till tonight. You'll love the Moonlight Gardens." Then he bent his head and went back to setting the small jewels.

Elliott smiled in anticipation of the evening's imagined delights. Over coffee, Abe had hinted at the luscious young women who apparently flocked to the dance hall on Saturday evenings. "Why half the girls 'at work here go there, and after they've had a drink or two... well, look out."

He couldn't imagine Hazel drinking: the dance hall seemed too plebian for her tastes and that was fine with him. The drudgery of squinting for ten hours a day, then going back to his cramped sleeping room for a night of solitary and uncomfortable rest on his cot had primed Elliott for diversion, the livelier the better. He had never been to the Gardens, eschewing it as a working class diversion. But after seven months at the watch factory, he realized that this was what he was, and he'd best begin to enjoy a lower brow sort of entertainment. The idea of putting his arms around the waist of a youngish female didn't repel him either.

As he followed Abe into the dance hall on the outskirts of town that evening, he realized that the Moonlight Gardens weren't gardens at all. Globes holding gaslights hung between long windows that encircled the enormous, polished dance floor. In the balcony above, a band played. Although it was only eight o'clock, the floor was packed with dancers hopping about to an infectious rag. As his eyes grew used to the light, Elliott noticed that Negro waiters were circulating among the dancers, bringing mugs of beer and glasses of wine to those seated at tables around the hall.

He followed Abe around the edge of the floor and leaned next to him at the tall oak bar in the rear of the room. "Two beers," Abe shouted at the bartender, holding up two fingers to support the request. Elliott nursed his beer—he would have preferred sarsaparilla—and observed the young women who smiled at him from the nearest corner. They were middling attractive, dressed in dark or striped low-cut dresses. He was wondering what the protocol was regarding asking one of these lovelies to dance, when Abe touched his arm.

"I want you to meet a friend of mine," Abe shouted above the music.

Elliott lowered his gaze to the flushed face of a diminutive young woman with orangey red hair swept up under a broad-brimmed straw hat. Her blue eyes sparkled and she smiled at Elliott.

"Pleased to meet you, I'm sure. Mabel Hallam. My husband Earl's a friend of Abe's from way back." Introductions dispensed with, she looked Elliott up and down. He straightened and wondered if the ladies in the corner were doing the same. "Wanna dance?"

Before he could decide if he would accept this very forward invitation, a man appeared behind Mabel. Dressed in a dark-pinstriped coat and sporting a conductor's boxy hat, the man stood behind Mabel and placed his hands on her shoulders. "How's it goin' sweetie? Talkin' to Abe and his friend here?" Facing away from the man, Mabel winced and rolled her blue eyes at Elliott. He swore she winked at him before turning to look up into the man's face.

"Why Earl, Abe here has just the nicest friend... Mr. Mr..." she faced Elliott. "Wha'd you say your name was?"

Realizing after a moment that she was addressing him, Elliott looked at the man with sympathy. "Loper, Elliott Loper. I work at the watch factory with Abe, Mr. Hallam." He extended his hand toward the man. Giving up on Elliott, Mabel wandered away and began talking with the ladies in the corner.

Abe had struck up a serious conversation with a girl in frills near a window, so Elliott was left to entertain the earnest Mr. Hallam, who continued to glance at his wife every so often.

"So what is your employment, if I may ask?" Elliott was at a loss to find something about which to converse with this man.

"Oh, I'm a motorman for the streetcars – work late shift most nights, but I can't complain. See I married Mabel there a year ago and I wanted to provide for her." He was interrupted by a peal of shrill laughter from his wife. Two men had joined the group of women and Mabel was clinging to the sleeve of one of them, doubled over with glee. Hallam excused himself and rushed over to the group. Elliott shook his head and turned away. He'd seen women like Mabel before -- his father called them "fast" -- and he felt sorry for Hallam, working nights on the streetcar, while Mabel danced at the Moonlight Gardens.

He rejoined Abe, who was now engrossed in conversation with another young man near the back of the dance hall. It was quieter here and there was no need to shout to be heard. As he approached, the stranger looked up at him with recognition. "Hey, ain't you Elliott Loper? Used to work on the *Record?*" The clean-shaven man had a shock of brown hair that reached almost to his blue eyes. "Remember me? Alvin Mallory, I work for the *Register*. We ran into each other a few times, but I guess I haven't seen you lately." He looked at Elliott, who felt unaccountably embarrassed by his current job.

Abe jumped in. "Elliott here works with me at the watch factory. Has since the beginning of the year. I guess he musta' got tired of that newspaper job."

Ignoring Alvin's scrutiny, Elliott said, "Yes, I was pretty tired of that obituary writing. Wanted something new and figured the watch factory might give me a fresh start." He glanced down at his shoes and muttered "Course it is pretty tedious work sometimes."

Abe said nothing. Elliott looked back up at the newsman, who hesitated, then put his hand on Elliott's shoulder. "Well, as I recall, you were a pretty decent reporter. Ought to stick with it, if you ask me. Times like these, 'specially. This city's growin' like cats and dogs and so's the bosses and the saloons and the political types." He nodded at the colored waiter headed their way. "Negroes and immigrants, they're comin' here fightin' for jobs. There ain't enough to go 'round."

The waiter bowed politely. "Can I get a drink for you gentlemen?"

Abe looked at Elliott, who shook his head. His beer was less than half gone and was warm in the heavy mug. The lights seemed too bright and the music was making his head hurt. The women seemed tawdry and faded: Mabel's laugh trilled again. Looking back at the waiter's dark face, he thought of Sheba, picturing her sewing silently in the Lawrence House kitchen, graceful neck bent over tiny stitches. "None for me thanks."

As he moved to leave, the newsman caught his elbow. "Look me up if you care to. If you ever want to get back into the newspaper business, I mean. I remember those stories you did about the Levee. That was some good reporting."

Elliott gazed into the man's eyes. He seemed sincere. "Well, perhaps I acted hastily when I quit the *Record*, but I don't see how I could go back. Not after quitting."

Mallory smiled. "Well, this town's got five dailies – don't you suppose there's a place for a good newsman on one of them? I'll do some checking around, see if there's any openings."

"I'm much obliged to you. I would be interested. You can get ahold of me through Abe, if you need to of course. I do appreciate it." Saluting Mallory, Elliott strode to the curb outside the Moonlight Gardens to wait for the streetcar. Looking back at the long building, light pouring from the windows, the melody of a rag drifting among spurts of laughter, he realized that he hadn't danced at all.

76

February 1908. The Governor's Mansion

"You'll need something to occupy you when I'm traveling," Mrs. Dana observed one evening as Sheba helped pack her trunk for an extended stay in Chicago. Mrs. Dana had seemed uncharacteristically bored since the holidays, and she was often without a dinner companion. Dr. Potter had ceased his frequent visits some time ago and had not been replaced. Sheba wondered if Mrs. Dana was lonely.

Her mistress had not been overly concerned with Sheba's lack of work during her travels last winter, so Sheba wondered what had caused this sudden anxiety with her supposed inactivity. However, she said nothing as Mrs. Dana continued pulling clothes from drawers and talking as she packed. "Mrs. Deneen has been so complimentary about my clothes and I finally did let on that you had made most of them." It had taken Mrs. Dana only a week to forgive the Governor's wife her obvious mistakes in judgment regarding spiritualism after the dinner party with Wright. Mrs. Dana stopped and sat down on the edge of the bed. "Sheba, I have informed Mrs. Deneen that you would call on her to take measurements for a touring outfit for her next campaign trip with her husband. You do have such a way with a garment." A hint of question came into her voice, as if she had just realized that Sheba might be entitled to an opinion about the use of her time and talents.

Sheba looked up at her mistress. Of course she would make the dress – she would do anything for Mrs. Dana. But before she could answer, Mrs. Dana rose and walked back to her dressing table, changing the subject.

"Let's see, I'll want several evening dresses for dinner parties." She began to search through her vanity drawers for the appropriate gloves and fans for these occasions. "Sheba, I imagine that even you have heard of Hull House and Miss Jane Addams, the woman that runs it. Miss Flora and I have been invited to stay there as Miss Addams' guests."

Sheba felt her mistress was waiting for a response, so she blurted out, "Why I guess ever'body heard of Hull House. Why it's done world's o' good, bein' in the worst part of Chicago 'n all. You right blessed t'have Miss Addams for a friend."

Mrs. Dana nodded vigorously. "Oh my dear, you have no idea what an inspiration she is to me. Why, she has created a haven for the poor immigrants in that hideous area, and she is at the center, the very hub, of influential thinkers on women's suffrage and social reform. Mr. Wright and his wife are part of that group, you know." She paused, and then continued, "Miss Addams is very proactive regarding equal rights for colored people like yourself."

Sheba looked at Mrs. Dana. "What you say 'bout equal rights? They keep me safe from bad folks?" A slight shudder ran through Sheba as she remembered the continued disdain of Miss Flora. Mrs. Dana dropped the fan she was holding and went over to the girl, her blue eyes softening with compassion. "You should never fear while you're in this house. Nothing will harm you here." Then she turned away. "Now hurry, we need to finish all this and get to bed."

After only a few hours of sleep, Sheba rose early to help tie up the trunks and hampers that accompanied Mrs. Dana and her cousin as they embarked the northbound train. On the way home, the servants walked next to the sooty railroad tracks toward the door in the fence that led to the courtyard.

Thomas dropped back and fell into step with Sheba. "I hear her Ladyship done called for you and you be headed over to the Governor's Mansion." He bowed low before her. "I b'lieve little ole' Sheba's becomin' a dressmaker for royalty."

Sheba continued to walk without acknowledging Thomas' mock show of fealty. "You ain't got call knowin' 'bout that." She was flattered that Mrs. Dana had recommended her to Mrs. Deneen, but Thomas really had no right to have an opinion on it.

Thomas ran to catch up with her as she mounted the steps. "Word just gets 'round. You be too good for us po' folk."

He was embarrassing her now, though she couldn't fathom why. From the kitchen porch, Sheba looked down at Thomas. "No, I ain't too good, but you better watch what you do say 'round folks."

Hattie was following and turned in the kitchen door. "Don't be goin' out by your lonesome, girl. You take Thomas with you, keep you safe." Sheba resolved at that moment to have nothing to do with the teasing stablehand.

But the Hattie didn't forget her charge when, a few days later, Sheba put on her hat and coat to walk the block down the street to the grand house belonging to whoever happened to be governor of Illinois that year. The Deneens had lived there since Charles Deneen's election in 1904. Both the Deneens and Mrs. Dana were good Republicans and it wasn't long before the society lady and the gubernatorial pair became fast friends. Now, in 1908, the Governor was up for re-election so his wife had to be well turned out, even if she was only campaigning in Springfield.

Thomas met Sheba at the kitchen door, with Hattie close on her heels, dispelling any notion she might have had for venturing out alone. "Now mind, you ain't goin' nowhere by y'self today. Thomas here'll carry you to the Deneens, and then he gonna wait for you till you come back."

Sheba threw up her hands in exasperation. "Hattie, it safe as can be. I's only goin' a block." But Hattie would have none of it and in the end, Thomas and Sheba walked side-by-side down Fourth Street towards the Governor's Mansion. The yards were empty as were the wide sidewalks. Sheba glanced sideways at Thomas: despite her irritation, more than a little relieved that he had come. It struck her odd that the street was so empty, and she peered at the large, curtained windows of the houses they passed, hoping to see signs of life. But nothing moved.

As they turned in the drive to the mansion, a large colored man wearing overalls and a flannel shirt put down the bale of hay he was carrying and sat down wearily next to the carriage house at the end of the drive. "Hey Thomas, this ain't your place."

Thomas sat down next to the man. "Sheba here goin' t'make a dress for the Govn'rs lady." The rest of the conversation was lost as Sheba strode up the curving drive towards the servants' entrance of the house. As she mounted the porch steps, she saw a woman standing in the kitchen, a colored woman who struck her as vaguely familiar.

Sheba pushed the kitchen door open and stood face-to-face with a slender woman who she recognized from some dark corner of her past. "Mama," Sheba cried in disbelief. The woman stood within breath's distance of her, then her mother's face exploded in a smile. She grabbed Sheba in a hug.

"Well I be blessed. My little girl – I never did 'spect t'see you 'gin. You such a sweet thing." Her mother squeezed her tight against her bony breast, then pulled back.

Once over her surprise, Sheba felt a little irritated. Here her own mama worked so close and she never even paid her a call. "Mama, you know I work up to the Lawrence House, right close. How come you never tol' me you workin' here?"

Calmer now, her mother, sat down and absentmindedly began folding handkerchiefs. "Oh land, my little girl, I never been so s'prised gettin' a job as this here one. I guess I jus' forgot to come find you." She stopped folding and stared at Sheba. "That nice Mr. Loper, well, he wrote some kinda' story for the paper about the plight of us women workin' down to the Levee and the story musta tol' about me." None of her mother's friends could read, so Sheba knew she would have to hear secondhand about the article's contents.

Now it was Sheba's turn to be confused. "What 'd you mean? That man get you this job?" She sat down across from her mother at the kitchen table, where the older woman had evidently been ironing. A stack of handkerchiefs lay neatly to her right while a crumpled pile of nightclothes lay to her left. Several irons lay heating on the stove, ready to be attached to a wooden handle and used to press the clothes.

Her mother shook her head. "Yes chil'. See Miz Deneen she read that story and say she gonna rescue me from the gutter. So's she done asked Mr. Loper 'bout me and he found me at the Leland and she give me this job." A smile brightened her mother's thin face. "And I been doin' laundry here for 'bout a year now." She lowered her voice and leaned toward Sheba. "And it ain't none too soon t'get off the Levee. What I hear, they's some bad blood and there gonna be some big trouble."

Astonished, Sheba could say nothing. Her own mother, whom she'd given up for lost. Now here she was again, rescued from a life of degradation by Elliott Loper, a man to whom she had felt a begrudging attraction, though it didn't matter since she had no idea if she would ever see him again. And now, to top it all off, her mother worked only a block from the Lawrence House.

She decided to let sleeping dogs lie. After all, the important thing was that her mother was safe, working a good job for a prestigious family. "My soul a'mighty, what a blessin'. Now don't be a stranger no more, Mama. Come 'n see me ever' once in a while." Overwhelmed with the joy of the moment, she rushed around the table to embrace her mother again. The woman stared straight ahead, her eyes filled with tears. Then Sheba glanced at the stairs leading to the second floor.

"Well, I best be goin'. I got to get Miz Deneen's measurements today so's I kin make her tourin' outfit. See I been thinkin' 'bout tryin' to start a dressmakin' business of my own -- Miz Dana says I got a real knack for it." Sheba turned to go up the back stairs to the hallway. "Now don't you go nowheres. When I's back, we kin figure out how t'get together." She climbed the winding back stairs, trying to remember where they terminated. As she reached the second floor hallway, a small, dark-haired toddler streaked by, shrieking at the top of her lungs, her fat legs garbed in white pantaloons, chubby arms flailing. Sheba watched as the baby careened down the hall, then turned as the panting Mrs. Deneen came to a halt inches from her face.

"Oh Sheba, please catch her. She's sure to topple down those stairs." Her dark hair mussed, Mrs. Deneen pointed to the end of the hallway, towards the top of the grand staircase that descended to the reception area twenty feet below. Without a word, Sheba dropped the sewing bag she was carrying, picked up her skirts and sprinted down the shiny wood floor after the little girl. The toddler paused at the top of the stairway, apparently amazed at the sheer height of the entry way, then turned and began to wail. Sheba stooped and picked up the child, who wrestled to get free.

"What you doin' runnin' away from your mama?" Sheba hugged the squirming child, as Mrs. Deneen came up from behind.

Mrs. Deneen patted the baby's dark curls as the little girl peered at her, then held out her arms. "Come to mama, little one." Holding her daughter close, Mrs. Deneen looked at Sheba through her wire-rimmed spectacles, the corners of her dark eyes crinkling in delight. "It's providential that you happened to come up then. I was just taking little Bina to the nursery from my bedroom and she, well, she broke away." She shook her head in disbelief. "Honestly, I don't know where she gets her cussedness from. I know she's my namesake, but her pa and I are the models of propriety." The irony of this statement made her laugh as she led Sheba back down the hall toward the sewing room, while the little girl sucked her thumb and watched her carefully.

Once in the sewing room, they shut the door securely to keep little Bina safely inside. Her erstwhile child now occupied with some wooden blocks, Mrs. Deneen stood on the slightly raised platform in front of an oval wooden mirror in the center of the room. "Now, what measurements do you need?" She twirled ever so slightly, and Sheba remembered this same woman dancing a lively two-step in the Lawrence House gallery. Sheba measured Mrs. Deneen as she stood on the platform glancing over occasionally to check on the baby. She talked non-stop, and Sheba thought that the newspapers had labeled her correctly as "the vivacious governor's lady."

"I worry some about you coming down here, Sheba. There's so much trouble in this town. Why, hardly a day goes by you don't hear about some murder or drunken brawl." Mrs. Deneen paused, then pulled away from Sheba's measuring tape to lean down and swat at the baby. "Bina, you naughty girl. You leave your sweater on now," and she put the little girl's arm back into the blue woolen sweater. Remounting the platform, Mrs. Deneen turned slowly. "I hope you met Mae, our laundress. She's a woman of the streets you know. Almost right off the Levee. I like to think we gave her a second chance." She looked approvingly at her tidy reflection in the mirror, while Sheba's dark shape crouched in the background. Sheba looked up from where she knelt on the floor and met the woman's dark eyes in the mirror.

"She's my mama, Miz Deneen. Your laundry girl." She straightened to face Mrs. Deneen's reflection and continued, undaunted by Mrs. Deneen's shocked expression. "She been down a bit in life, but she good. She do good work for you." She looked down, pretending to be studying the measuring tape, feeling ashamed of her mother, but grateful to Mrs. Deneen.

The Governor's wife turned around, then stooped and pulled Sheba to a stand with her hands. "Why Sheba, your mother, how grand. It's too wonderful that we have been able to help her in this way." Before Sheba could thank Mrs. Deneen, the door creaked open, as was typical of doors in these old houses, and the Governor himself stepped into the room. Sheba remembered him from the dinner party with Wright. Dark-haired like his wife, he was an impressive man with determined, set features and the air of confidence that a man earns after winning the governorship. He came from a long line of Abolitionists and was squarely in support of equal rights for Negroes, at least that is what Sheba had read in many newspaper articles covering his intense campaign for governor.

He swooped over to the little girl, who, oblivious of his entry, was concentrating diligently on placing a fourth block on top of a pile of three. Her father tried without success to catch his daughter's attention, then gave up, shrugged his shoulders, and addressed his wife.

Mrs. Deneen had stepped down from the platform and moved to grasp his waistcoat pocket, then kissed his cheek. "Why Charles, what a nice surprise to have a visit from you during the day." In response he pulled her by her black-sashed waist and kissed her on the mouth. Sheba wished she could retreat somewhere at this juncture, and glanced around, but could see nowhere to go, so instead fixed her gaze on the still-absorbed little girl. Disengaging herself,

81

Mrs. Deneen nodded at Sheba. "Charles, you'll never guess who that girl from the Levee is that we hired as laundress. Sheba's mother. It's too wonderful."

Before the Governor could reply, a young white woman entered the room. Large and plain-featured, the woman ignored everyone in the room and made a beeline for little Bina, who acknowledged her presence with a high-pitched shriek, something she seemed to do with some regularity. "Its baby's nap time. Time to go nighty-nighty." The young woman grasped little Bina firmly by her balled-up fist and pulled her from her nest of blocks.

"Mama," screamed Bina, and Mrs. Deneen turned from her husband's attentions to stare at her offspring.

The woman collected the toddler, who was still screaming. "Mrs. Deneen, I had no idea she was in here. Why when I stepped out, she was in the nursery."

Mrs. Deneen's cheeks were red with embarrassment and she protested. "Oh Fanny, I'm afraid I took her from the nursery. I did miss her so and thought perhaps she might enjoy some playtime while Sheba measured me for this new outfit." Sheba moved to collect her measuring tape.

Still flustered, the Governor's wife made an attempt to distract attention from her error. "Fanny, this is Sheba. She just told me that our laundress is her mama." She looked from the nursery maid's face to Sheba's, but Fanny refused to even look at the colored woman, fixing her attention instead on Bina, who was trying in vain to regain the floor and freedom.

Fanny responded to Mrs. Deneen. "Oh, those coloreds. I don't have much use for the lot of them."

Scowling, the Governor whipped around, facing Fanny. "What do you mean, you don't have much use for them? I won't have that kind of talk in this house."

"As you wish sir," Fanny responded, then turned on her heel and lumbered from the room, a screaming Bina in tow. Sheba's last sight of the toddler was of a small, curly head bobbing over Fanny's white-bloused shoulder. Realizing her daughter was gone, Mrs. Deneen rushed down the hallway after them, following her wailing child. Alone in the room with the Governor, Sheba stooped to gather up the rest of her sewing materials, all the while feeling him watching her from the corner of the room.

After what seemed like an hour but was only a few seconds, he broke the silence. "Sheba, what Fanny said was uncalled-for and I hope you will accept my apologies. You have done nothing to deserve that kind of treatment." Sheba looked into his honest dark eyes and saw both compassion and frustration.

She pulled the drawstring of her sewing bag closed. "Well G'vnor, if she hates me, then she hates me. Ain't nothin' nobody kin do 'bout that. But sir, I do thank you for givin' my mama an honest job."

Leaving the Governor standing in the middle of the empty room, Sheba opened the door and walked slowly down the hall toward the stairwell that led to the kitchen. Give me patience, she prayed, and love for my enemies, and thank you God for Governor Deneen.

A Fresh Start

Leaving as he had in something of a huff had made going for his old job back at the *Record* distasteful and downright impossible for Elliott, but landing a position on the news desk of the rival *Register* had been surprisingly easy. Alvin Mallory had been true to his word and put in a solid recommendation for Elliott. This recommendation, coupled with his experience as copywriter, had gained him reentry into the newspaper world. He hated to disappoint Mr. Maisenbacher by quitting the watch factory after less than a year, but his conscience was salved somewhat by the knowledge that there was no shortage of applicants for work at the well-regarded plant.

His headaches disappeared and he woke each day excited to go to his new job. As he picked his way down the icy pavement of Seventh Street toward the Home for the Friendless, he wished, despite his gratitude at having a newspaper job, that his position had a bit more prestige. Elliott had been assigned the society news and spent his days reporting on teas, bazaars, the coming out parties of young women, and various fundraisers by the well-meaning ladies of Springfield.

The February sun shone brightly over the tower of the old mansion that had housed orphans since after the Civil War. Elliott trudged up the front steps and rang the bell of the weathered front door, pondering the injustice of the staffing at the newspaper. The *Register* boasted a female reporter, as did most of the newspapers these days. Tillie Agnew, a tall blonde woman who bore an unmistakable resemblance to a prize filly, drew front page bylines daily as a high-profile reporter on the news desk. He was all for women's rights, but it seemed a little unfair to Elliott that the paper was waving the flag of its female writer so prominently while he, the more experienced reporter, was relegated to the society pages.

He didn't have time to lick his wounds. "Yes sir, you're from the paper I see." A short woman with a pince-nez pinned to her high-collared bodice took note of the "Press" card stuck in the brim of Elliott's derby, then swung open the door and ushered him inside. "Please step right this way. We've just begun our meeting."

Elliott followed the woman down the front hall to a spacious drawing room dominated by a wooden table surrounded by six matrons, some of whom looked vaguely familiar. "Well, we're pleased you could join us." The speaker, a thin woman garbed in black bombazine, made no effort to hide her derision of his late arrival. He had hoped to slip in unnoticed, but no such luck was available today as he recognized the woman, head of the board and fixture of Springfield society, Mrs. Caroline Brown.

A dewy woman to the speaker's right smiled at Elliott. "Oh Mama, see the newspaper's sent this nice man to cover our board meeting. Do sit down Mister...?"

"Loper, Elliott Loper. Much obliged." Relieved at being saved from Mrs. Brown's chastisement, Elliott found a chair at the perimeter of the room near one of the long windows. There was something about this daughter that was unusual, but he couldn't quite define what the quality was that she possessed. The daughter glanced his way occasionally as the meeting proceeded, so he whipped out his notepad and scribbled furiously.

The board was planning its annual festival, a fundraiser for the orphanage and the reason for Elliott's attendance of the meeting. One of the members had called the *Register* yesterday and somehow convinced his boss, Mr. Sheets, that greater Springfield must be aware of the plans for this auspicious event. It was to be held at on the grounds of the State Fair, north of the city, and would revolve around a Japanese theme. Elliott stifled a yawn. With the success of Gilbert and Sullivan's *Mikado*, every women's club seemed eager to feature their members garbed in kimonos and fluttering fans. To Elliott, whose mother had been active in these fundraisers for years, it was merely a new face for the regular activities of this earnest bunch of do-gooders.

After an hour, the meeting drew to a close and Elliott was escorted down the front hallway by the young woman who had come to his rescue. Wife of businessman Francis Ide, the woman, Elizabeth, was the secretary for the orphanage. "Mr. Loper, it would mean so much to the Home if we could count on the support of your father for our fund drive. Perhaps you might be able to arrange a meeting?" She beamed, and Elliott smiled.

"Perhaps, perhaps." He said, remembering his last encounter with his mother and sisters, a mid-morning visit to the house on South Fourth. He had stopped by to pick up his ice skates, hoping for a turn on the rink downtown, but they were nowhere to be found. As he searched for the missing skates, his mother followed him from room to room.

"Elliott, you need to mend things with your dad. He's pining for you, I can feel it. We can't see why." His mother's rant was interrupted as she ran straight into his back after he stopped to open a drawer. Seated at the table, his sisters had been observing them with fascination. Now they collapsed into giggles.

"Mother, I wish you'd stop insisting that we patch things up. It's not seemly," he dodged the toast crust that Stella shot toward him. He did miss his sisters, and they were growing up fast.

Minnie looked up from her toast. "You oughta get back in Dad's good graces, Elliott. We're gonna be laughing at you when we drive by in Dad's new motor car." Minnie's chattering was cut short by his mother, who pulled him from the dining room.

"That true Mother, a motor car?" Elliott could barely contain his excitement. Motor cars were all the reporters talked about as they ate their lunches at their desks, but so far, he had seen none in Springfield. Maybe his father would let him drive it. That would show those show-offs at the *Record* and roughnecks like Hazel's brother. The sting of the memory of the night at Dandy Jim's a year ago was considerably diminished as Elliott imagined himself behind the wheel of one of the city's only motor cars. He had departed the Loper residence with a new resolve, to make amends with his father.

So when young Mrs. Ide suggested that he arrange a meeting, ordinarily a request he would have spurned, he accepted graciously. After all, it was a perfect excuse and saved him from the vaguely embarrassing encounter he had anticipated.

"I can speak with my father and see what might be arranged. He is a very generous man, but of course many charities have requested his support." He didn't want to mislead the young woman and he had first-hand experience of the rash of callers that inundated Harry Loper's office, especially around the holidays. As he took his leave, unaccountably the Lincoln Colored Home's Eva Carroll Monroe flashed through Elliott's mind. The orphanages were just blocks apart, yet there were no Negro children at the Home for the Friendless. Somehow this seemed odd to Elliott, who suspected that orphans of any color were equally friendless.

"Say, d'you know Mrs. Monroe who heads up the Lincoln Colored Home? You seem to be doing very similar work."

Mrs. Ide's smile was immobilized on her polished features. "Well, I do know of Mrs. Monroe, of course. She has done a wonderful service to those colored children and old ladies." She paused, then nodded brightly at Elliott. "We do so hope that you will be able to arrange a get-together with your father. Thank you so much for covering our board meeting. I'm sure we'll see you again." She dismissed him with a wave and he picked his way carefully down the steep front steps of the ramshackle mansion, musing on the orphanages in Lincoln's home town.

An Unexpected Return

A mere two weeks after Mrs. Dana and her cousin had departed Springfield for the bright lights of Chicago, they were back, or so it appeared from the blaze of light that greeted Sheba as she and Hattie returned one Thursday evening from a visit to Will Donnegan.

Maud greeted them as they came in the kitchen door, then hurried back to the stove to stir several pots that simmered there. "Oh law, Sheba, it's about time you came. They're both back, Miss Flora and the mistress. You got to go directly up to Mrs. Dana's room."

Rushing upstairs, Sheba threw her hat on her bed then hastened down the upstairs back hall towards Mrs. Dana's room, her mind clouded with questions. She couldn't imagine what could have brought the two ladies back after only two weeks, when usually they were gone for at least a month.

Tapping on the glass door to Mrs. Dana's room and hearing no answer, Sheba entered the bedroom quietly. As she pulled the door shut, a sob reached her ears. Her mistress lay on her back on the bed, staring at the ceiling. Every light in this room was on, as if Mrs. Dana was fighting back the misery darkness would bring. She moved closer to her mistress' bed then stood respectfully to the side. Mrs. Dana's head rested on the embroidered pillow case, her fair complexion blotchy and red; her pale eyes pink and watery.

She turned her head and moaned, and Sheba was afraid at first that she hadn't seen her. But then she spoke, a quiet lament. "Oh Sheba, I don't know what I thought I would find, I really don't." There was none of the usual light in her face today. Looking up at Sheba's face, Mrs. Dana held out her hand and Sheba, forgetting her place, moved closer and grasped it.

Mrs. Dana pulled her hand to her face, and she could feel the damp tears. "I thought I had reason to believe that someone cared for me, but I know now that I was wrong, deeply wrong. He doesn't care for me. In fact I doubt he ever did. He's in love with someone else," she sighed, staring up at the ceiling, as though it might comfort her.

The man was unnamed, but Sheba knew it was Wright who had reduced her mistress to this pitiful mess. She squeezed Mrs. Dana's hand and, since there was no sign that the hand would be released, she took a chance that she would not be reprimanded and sat down on the bed. Tears spilled out of the sides of Mrs. Dana's eyes and trickled over her cheekbones toward her small pearl earrings. "You see, I saw him, out driving, with...with her." Mrs. Dana choked as she spoke. Sheba pulled her hand gently from her mistress' grip and got up to fetch a handkerchief from the dressing table.

Mrs. Dana grasped the handkerchief and dabbed the tears from her cheeks. "I believe he will leave his family for her. There's no doubt in my mind." She paused, sobbing. "You should see them together. They're so in love, although their stars are crossed. She's the wife of one of his clients. Mamah they say her name is. Mamah." She lay silent.

More than anything, Sheba wanted to comfort her, but she didn't know how, so she blurted out the first thing that crossed her mind. "That's a funny name ma'am." Then the injustice of the situation struck her. This man intended to leave his family, and she didn't see how that could be right. "It ain't God's way, leavin' your wife and little uns," she offered. She doubted that Mrs. Dana believed in God, but it seemed so unfair that He would allow this woman to be brought so low, this woman who had so many resources, so much money, so much power. Brought down by a man Sheba judged as a callow showman, full of egotistical pride.

. But perhaps she had underestimated Mrs. Dana, who had been tested by the loss of her children, her husband, and her parents in quick succession. She rose to a sitting position on the bed, then swung her legs over the side. Pulling the handkerchief from her sleeve, she blew her nose with a rattle, then smiled as though she were very tired, looking up at Sheba. "It doesn't matter if it's God's will or not. He'll do whatever he pleases, always has, always will. True artists are that way Sheba, they make their own rules." Mrs. Dana dabbed again at her eyes, then rose and moved towards the bathroom. The weak, vulnerable woman was gone, replaced with the mistress Sheba knew, aloof yet kind. "Lay out a fresh dress for me for dinner and start unpacking my trunk." As she passed through the bathroom door she called, seeming almost normal again, "Miss Flora and I are having a guest to dinner -- Miss Pickens."

Miss Mary Pickens was a Springfield medium whom Mrs. Dana called upon when her friend Celia was not in town. According to Mrs. Dana, Miss Pickens failed to possess the heightened spiritual sensitivity of Celia, but she was acceptable. She was also talkative: when under the influence of her spirit "control," Blossom, Miss Pickens was transformed from a quiet woman to a loquacious belle.

Given an hour or so, Mrs. Dana had recovered enough of her good humor to recount details of the brief Chicago sojourn for Miss Pickens. "Mary, do have some more roast," Mrs. Dana urged, bobbing her head at Sheba, who hurried to serve up more meat to Miss Pickens.

The medium nodded and smiled, concentrating on ingesting more of the pork and mashed potatoes. "Thank you, Susan, don't mind if I do," she said. Miss Pickens depended on the generosity of others for meals, and Mrs. Dana was one of her most avid patrons.

"We were able to visit Miss Addams at Hull House," Miss Flora interjected, eager to make her contribution. "Such a great lady doing such admirable work in the slums with the poor." Miss Flora appeared to be good friends with Miss Pickens, who nodded approvingly.

Miss Pickens paused to dab gravy from her chin. "Speaking of poor folk, I have it on the best authority that the coloreds here in Springfield are getting ready for an uprising." Sheba stopped serving and Mrs. Dana put down her fork and looked pointedly at Miss Pickens.

"Whatever do you mean? An uprising – that's ridiculous. Why would there be an uprising in Springfield?"

Miss Pickens looked from Mrs. Dana to Miss Flora for signs of agreement. "Why everybody knows they're not keeping their place. They think they're better than us. Why they've come up from the South and took all the jobs." Miss Pickens began speaking more quickly. "And they're bringin' bad blood with 'em. Like the Levee, that horrible place. Those coloreds are the main reason there's all those awful saloons and brothels down there."

It was hard for Sheba to remain in the room, as if she was invisible, and Mrs. Dana seemed to sense this. Nodding at her, Mrs. Dana said, "Sheba, more water for Miss Pickens. Mary, how you do run on. Why the coloreds aren't a threat to us. I daresay there's just as many whites running businesses down on the Levee as Negroes."

Miss Pickens shook her head violently. "It's true and you know it. If you want, you can just hide your head in the sand, but I'm going to be ready when those niggers start raiding decent peoples' homes."

Mrs. Dana gave a quick nod to dismiss her and Sheba headed back into the butler's pantry, praying that the subject of conversation would change while she was gone. She was in luck and when she returned with the lemon ices, it had, and the three women were discussing the marriage of Mrs. Dana's former suitor Dr. Potter to a Miss Sweeney.

Mrs. Dana had pushed back her plate and stared at the shadows of the butterflies cast by the chandeliers, shadows that forever fled across the prairie flowers in the mural but never escaped the confines of the room.

The scene in the bedroom of a few hours ago was forgotten, or so it seemed. "And to think I could have had him. Dr. Potter, you know. Because you realize I could have. He begged me to marry him, but I don't think he cared for me. I think he was interested in my money and my house." Miss Pickens and Miss Flora were silent. Their spoons clinked as they devoured the lemon ices. "When I do marry again, it will be for love." Her ice was melting into a lemon-colored pool on the pink glass dessert plate. She directed her gaze at Miss Pickens. "And I shall be quite sure the man is free to love me in return."

Miss Flora rose from the table. "Let's retire to the library. It's quite cool there and perhaps Miss Pickens will favor us with a spirit contact."

Miss Pickens also stood. "Why yes, I do feel that Blossom may speak with us tonight." Together, the three ladies moved from the dining room through the sitting room. Sheba watched as their shadows flickered through the line of windows of the conservatory hallway towards the library.

Back in the kitchen helping Hattie and Maud do the dishes, Sheba recounted the conversation at the dinner table while Albert and Thomas listened. She wanted to see what the others thought of the startling remarks of Miss Pickens. "And the medium, she said there was goin' to be an uprising of us colored folks."

This last remark set Hattie off. She stopped drying dishes and faced the servants. "You mark my words, there's bad days a'comin'. See here, this white lady she's sayin' such cruel things, like we would hurt white folks like Mrs. Dana."

It seemed to Sheba that somewhere between Hattie's fear and Miss Pickens hatred lay the tricky reality of the situation. Finishing the dishes, she flicked her dish towel at Thomas, trying to wake the young man who had leaned back in his chair and appeared to be asleep. But Thomas kept his eyes resolutely shut, whether in teasing or tiredness, she couldn't tell.

The intercom, a new-fangled contraption on the kitchen wall, buzzed. The intercom enabled Mrs. Dana to summon servants from many points in the house, though Sheba viewed it mainly as an instrument of annoyance used by Miss Flora to interrupt her work. She picked up the receiver and heard Miss Flora's nasal voice. "We'll require some coffee in the library. Mind you don't disturb Miss Pickens when you come." Sheba had hoped they wouldn't ask for anything: she found the séances disturbing although she didn't believe that spirits were ever raised, except perhaps in the mind of Mrs. Dana.

"Yes ma'am. Right away ma'am." Soon the coffee was ready and Maud loaded a tray for Sheba to take into the library. With a quick backward glance over her shoulder, Sheba took the tray and departed.

As she carried the tray down the steps into the darkened room, she noted the three ladies were seated on low chairs around a square table. A flame flickered in the night air from the candle in the center of the table. The windows to the library on the north were flung wide open in the unseasonable mildness of early spring, and darkness flooded in from the outside.

Miss Pickens' face was pale in the candlelight, but her voice rang in the silent room. "Blossom, you seem troubled tonight."

The ladies grasped hands and Miss Pickens squeezed her eyes shut. Miss Flora's back was to Sheba, but the girl could see Mrs. Dana, who scanned the medium's face. After a moment, Mrs. Dana spoke. "Blossom, tell me what my future holds."

Sheba set the tray down on the window seat. No one acknowledged her presence, so she stood for a minute. Suddenly she heard gentle tapping which gradually increased in volume, first at the table, then at different points in the room. As she looked around for the source of the noise, the small hairs on the back of her neck began to stand on end. Then Miss Pickens let out a horrible laugh, sounding oddly unlike the mousey woman from dinner. "Ah, ha ha! There is no future here. Only horror. Horror!"

Miss Pickens stood straight up while Mrs. Dana gasped and pulled at her arm. Staring up at the sightless face of Miss Pickens, Mrs. Dana cried, "What do you mean Blossom? What kind of horror?"

"An unholy attack. A fowl black fiend has unnatural relations with a lily-white maiden." The medium screamed, her body shaking. Sheba could see that now Miss Pickens eyes were open, but turned up so that only the whites showed. A kind of foamy substance was seeping from the sides of her mouth. Sheba felt sick. Miss Pickens was writhing in quite an unnatural way in front of the small table. "I see a black man swinging by his neck from a tree. You must leave. There is nothing for you here – only horror."

Miss Pickens collapsed into her chair and Miss Flora rushed to her side, kneeling on the floor in front of her, while Mrs. Dana gazed out the open windows into the soft night of the courtyard. She was speaking "...disturbing, very disturbing. Now we must decide what to do." Her normally placid features registered concern and she appeared to have forgotten her private sorrows. "Oh Sheba, this certainly underscores the need for caution. We must heed what Miss Pickens said of course." She nodded to Sheba, then added as an afterthought, "Why improper relations between a colored man and white woman, how appalling!"

As Sheba looked into her mistress' worried face, the images of Mr. Donnegan and his small, white wife flashed through her mind. She had tutored the aged colored man almost every week. But since the Donnegans were legally man and wife and had been for longer than Sheba had been alive, she couldn't believe that they were having 'improper' relations. Since she could remember no Bible passages condemning the marriage of colored and white folk, she decided that Miss Pickens had made the story up out of her hateful, prejudiced imagination.

Miss Pickens had been listening to Mrs. Dana and offered an explanation of the spirit's utterances. "Blossom may be speaking of the future. Doubtless something like that could happen. Just look at the inhabitants of Springfield. It's overrun with colored people." She began to wave the handkerchief in a vain attempt to cool her face.

Eager to be back in the kitchen, Sheba stooped to retrieve the coffee tray. "If that's all ma'am, I'll just take these things." As she moved to go, Mrs. Dana crossed the room to grasp the medium's hand. "Mary, that must have been a particularly troubling session for you. I daresay you ought to stay here tonight."

Sheba flinched as Miss Pickens looked up at Mrs. Dana, her gray eyes brimming with grateful tears. "Oh, Mrs. Dana, you are so kind. Yes, I would love to stay. I do believe I am too exhausted to brave the trek home."

It was a long walk home for Miss Pickens to the ramshackle room where she lived, Sheba admitted as she walked up the stairs to tell Hattie to get the guest room ready. She looked out the door onto the darkened porch and started when she saw Thomas sitting in a wicker chair, rocking silently. He waved one finger in salutation, and then rose to walk with her back to the bright, noisy kitchen.

April 1908. The Studebaker

The Studebaker sat in front of the Loper house, its black sides gleaming in the midday sun. His father hopped down from the open vehicle and waved at Elliott, who stood on the porch, silently thankful that he had the wisdom to suck up his pride. It hadn't been particularly easy to push open the door to Loper's Restaurant that morning shortly after his visit to the Home for the Friendless. He had wandered through the restaurant, empty at mid-afternoon, towards his father's office at the rear, not sure what kind of reception was waiting for him. He actually started when Harry had burst from his office, arms spread, running toward him. Elliott was shocked that his patrician father would make a spectacle of himself in front of the white-aproned waiters.

"My boy, my boy," was all his father had said as he threw his arms around his astonished son. "I'm so glad you've come back."

Unable and unwilling to resist the force of his father's emotions, Elliott felt tears start to his eyes as he returned his father's embrace, memories of the long winter afternoons spent together assembling tiny ships at the dining room table.

"I've missed you, Dad," Elliott choked out. Aware of the veiled stares of the help, he composed himself and drew back. Harry gazed at him, then motioned him into his office.

The unexpectedly joyous reunion between father and son had not produced a meeting with the Home for the Friendless, although Molly had agreed to furnish the dainties for the orphanage's upcoming bazaar. But it had resulted in something even better: the promise of a ride around Springfield in the talk of the town—Harry's new Studebaker.

Elliott bounded down the steps of his parents' home toward the car. It was a beaut. The white tires encircling the spoked wheels contrasted with the black sides and the rich upholstery of the front and back seats. The driver's and passenger sides of the car were open since it was a touring car, and a steering wheel poked up behind the dashboard. The back seat sat high in the rear, and Elliott could imagine the delight of his sisters as they waved at their friends during the inaugural drive the day before. Headlights stood out like field glasses from the front of the car, where Harry stood, cranking the engine, which sputtered then started. "Hop in, let's take it for a spin."

He didn't need to be urged. Clambering into the passenger seat next to his father, who was garbed in a long driving coat and goggles, Elliott could barely contain his exhilaration. Neighbors gaped from their porches as Harry put the vehicle in gear and cruised down Second Street, passing carriages with skittish horses whose blinders prevented them from being frightened by the first and only -- for the moment -- motor car in Springfield.

They made a good trip of it, heading down South Grand past the looming Home for the Friendless and out all the way west to the woods of Washington Park, then turning back towards town. They puttered through Downtown, circling the square and stopping gawkers in their tracks. "Lookie there, what's that?" Children pointed and dragged at their parents' arms. They avoided the Levee and drove east, crossing the railroad tracks into the dusty streets of the Badlands. Harry pulled the vehicle to the side of the road and turned to Elliott.

"Want to take the wheel, son? Nothing to it. You'll enjoy driving this modern miracle."

Elliott's fingers yearned for the smooth feel of the steering wheel, but he stopped and looked at his father. "Are you sure, Dad? I bet this cost a pretty penny and I'd hate to wreck it."

"Oh pshaw. It did cost me, but I've worked hard for it. We got that restaurant, it's turning a nice profit, but it took years of buildin' it up. We ain't doin' so bad and this here's one of the rewards." Harry pulled off his goggles and handed them to Elliott.

After a few instructions, Elliott released the brake and the car took off down Eleventh Street. The few colored residents of the Badlands in evidence on this Saturday morning rushed into their front yards and gaped. Elliott's breast puffed out under his coat as he turned the car back toward the west.

As they glided by the mansions of Aristocracy Hill, Elliott had an idea. The Lawrence House was right down the street and he couldn't resist the idea of driving by. Perhaps Sheba would be on the porch or looking out a window.

The Lawrence House sprawled over the lot at the corner of Fourth and Lawrence Avenue, a beige brick masterpiece or monstrosity, depending on who you talked to. Stopping at the intersection, Elliott realized that Sheba might not even remember him – it had been over a year since their chance meeting downtown. And even though she had made an indelible impression on him, Elliott wasn't so sure the reaction was reciprocated.

As if in answer to his thoughts, a door opened on the front porch and two colored women emerged. One was a large, older woman and the other was clearly Sheba. Before he knew what he was doing, Elliott raised his arm to wave.

He was astonished when Sheba not only returned his wave, but beckoned, gesturing towards the side gate, which opened onto Fourth Street. Then she disappeared and he turned to his father. "I know that girl and I believe she wants to speak with me. Drop me over there on the sidewalk."

His father gave him a stare, causing Elliott to feel a wave of discomfort wash over him. But he shook it off. After all, he was twenty-seven years old – he could do as he pleased and, much as he cared for his father, he owed him no explanation. Without comment, Harry pulled the Studebaker up to the curb, and Elliott jumped out, running behind the motor car across the street. He shouted back over his shoulder "I won't be but a few minutes." He knew his father was watching as he bounded up the side steps to the gate where Sheba waited.

She was as lovely as he remembered, maybe lovelier, now that she was a year older. Her full lips parted in a pleased smile and her oval eyes narrowed with delight at seeing him. His breath almost stopped. He found it impossible to imagine that she had thought of him as much as he had of her over the past year since their chance meeting downtown. During the endless days at the watch factory and the interminable nights alone in his sleeping room, Elliott had pictured her graceful neck, mysterious eyes, the impossibly long curve of her back.

Sheba broke the spell. "I want to thank you kindly for the service you done my mama, gettin' her that fine job with the g'vnor. I jus' found out about it, 'else I be thankin' you proper 'long time ago."

Elliott had completely forgotten his role in Mae Tully's redemption and for a split second he felt a pang of shame for his attempt to manipulate that good turn into a journalistic coupe for himself. But as he scanned Sheba's smooth cocoa brown skin and even features, he detected not derision, but gratitude. And maybe more. He was afraid to hope.

"Why your mama earned that job fair and square, I just greased the wheels with the Governor and his wife." Elliott attempted to sound modest. Sheba had edged closer to him and was standing against the garden wall. Flattered that she wanted to be near him, he soon realized she was attempting to hide behind him and was peering over his shoulder periodically at the dark reaches of the front porch.

Although she appeared to be nervous, Sheba insisted on making her thanks. "My mama, she off the Levee and workin' for respectable folks cause of your piece in the paper. That there is one of the nicest thin's I ever did see. Bless you for that Mr. Loper. If I ever kin, maybe when I get my own shop, I'll pay you back, God willin'." She looked up at him, her dark eyes brimming with tears, and touched the fair hair on the back of his hand with her slender fingers. As thrill of excitement went through him, a heavy thud hit his back. Reeling, he staggered to keep his balance.

Turning to face his assailant, he saw a tall young Negro, a working man from the stables by his clothes, who he recognized as the driver of the carriage that had taken Sheba home from their encounter downtown. The man's eyes were wide with agitation and his fist pounded Elliott on his chest, harder this time, nearly knocking the wind out of him. Automatically he raised his fist to strike the man, but Sheba slipped between the two.

"Hold up, hold up! He ain't hurtin' me Thomas, I swear it. This here's Mr. Loper who done got my mama that fine job at the G'nor's Mansion. I just thankin' him good and proper for helpin' her out." She cowered a little but did not back down, standing solidly between the two.

Elliott stared over her fuzzy hair into the twisted features of the Negro, who turned and spat on the ground. "I 'spect he got somthin' in mind you kin thank him wif, if you get 'lone." He pulled Sheba to his side and pushed Elliott toward the street. No match for this man, Elliott turned to go.

"You get outta here whitey and don' come back botherin' her no more. If I see you agin, I beat the tar outta you," the man called and kicked some pebbles toward Elliott.

He could see Sheba looking back over the man's shoulder and something in him snapped. "Sheba, I'm at the *Register*. Please let me know if I can ever help you." The Negro couple vanished into the courtyard and Elliott shook his head as he climbed into the waiting Studebaker, realizing that his father had watched the whole encounter. The older man sat staring at the house, then glanced at Elliott.

"So that's the maid for Mrs. Dana, the one you told me about."

"Yes sir, that's Sheba."

Harry pulled out the clutch and shifted the car into gear, easing down Fourth Street towards Downtown. "Well, son, you be careful. Ain't no time to be messin' with colored folks. Things is bad and gettin' worse with the immigrants and the unions and the drinkin' on the Levee, and the Negroes are right smack in the middle of it all. You listen to me. Stay clear and find some nice white girl." And they sped by the Governor's Mansion narrowly missing a small boy.

94

Fund Raising

Shaking rugs from the side porch the next day, Sheba was still reeling from the encounter with Elliott Loper. She had never expected to see him again, yet he had appeared, a silvery angel in a conveyance that moved without horses, and exuded the same magnetism that she remembered from their first meeting. His blue eyes fringed with blonde eyelashes swam into her memory and she leaned on the porch railing, the better to savor this vision. Then, out of the corner of her eye, she spotted a darting, dark figure approaching from the east, looking for all the world like one of those spidery bugs that skates on top of the water. Something about this woman was familiar to Sheba, and after the figure moved closer, she recognized Miss Eva, founder and driving force behind the Lincoln Colored Home. Sheba hadn't seen Miss Eva, since she left the home to find her fortune over a year ago and she immediately jumped to the conclusion that somehow Miss Eva was on her way to get her and take her back.

She turned to run inside, then stopped, remembering a long-ago afternoon at the Lincoln Colored Home, where Sheba, seated on a horsehair love seat next to Mrs. Lawrence, prattled at length about her Biblical namesake while the old lady nodded and patted her hair. She sighed. Doubtless the reason for Miss Eva's visit had something to do with the dear, departed Mary Lawrence and that was the reason she was bustling so quickly past the shady lawns of Aristocracy Hill.

Pulling the small Oriental rugs from the banisters of the porch and gathering them into her arms, Sheba glanced in the living room window and noticed Mrs. Dana seated at one end of the long table facing a slender, balding man who was at that moment pointing an elegant finger at her. "Susan it is my duty to inform you that your mother made very clear provisions for this institution and you are honor-bound to carry out her wishes."

Sheba could see Mrs. Dana's placid features clearly as she leaned across the table toward the man. "I realize Mama was very supportive of the Lincoln Colored Home. I do, Joseph. But at the same time, I cannot help but think that a bequest of seven thousand dollars is excessive. I cannot believe she would not wish for her only daughter to benefit from this generous legacy."

The gentleman crossed a lean leg with an attitude of impatience. "Regardless of what you or I may believe, this is what Mrs. Lawrence's will states. And Mrs. Eva Monroe is on her way to receive this donation as we speak." With this proclamation, the man placed some rimless spectacles on his long nose, just as Maud ushered Miss Eva herself into the sunny room.

Mrs. Dana rose and moved toward Miss Eva, who advanced with her hand extended. Miss Eva's teeth flashed white in her dark face. "Mrs. Dana. What a pleasure to see you again."

Both women turned to face the man. "You know Mr. Bunn of course," Mrs. Dana said, and the tall man nodded to Miss Eva.

Miss Eva returned his nod. "Yes, I do. Mr. Bunn is on our board of directors. Good to see you again, sir."

Mr. Bunn smiled, "I daresay you'll be even more pleased to see me in the future, since I've been appointed trustee for your institution in the interests of Mrs. Dana and Mrs. Lawrence's estate. So I will be very much involved with administering funds for the home on their behalf."

The three seated themselves around the table and Mr. Bunn directed their attention toward a large stack of papers. Sheba watched, transfixed, from the porch.

As the little group studied the legal papers on the table, Sheba shifted the rugs in her arms. Seven thousand dollars. She pondered the notion of returning to the home as Miss Eva's assistant but rejected the idea. No amount of money would make Miss Eva less temperamental. She walked by the window to take the rugs to the kitchen and as she passed, the three people at the table looked up as of one accord.

"I know that girl. Is she one of your servants Mrs. Dana?" Miss Eva gazed inquisitively through the window, meeting Sheba's eyes.

"Yes, yes. That's Sheba Tully. She's an excellent seamstress and chambermaid." Mrs. Dana raised her hand and motioned to Sheba. "Sheba, come in here."

Fearful of what the impetuous Miss Eva might say, Sheba rushed from the porch through the side door, into the living room. Mr. Bunn continued to examine the legal papers but Mrs. Dana acknowledged Sheba's arrival. "Miss Eva here says she knows you, Sheba. Didn't you tell me you lived at the Lincoln Colored Home before you came here? I supposed you knew each other well there."

Miss Eva stood up and came toward. "Why Sheba Tully, you done good, better'n I 'spected."

"Yes ma'am, I have." Shifting the rugs in her arms, Sheba felt out of place in the presences of Mrs. Dana and Mr. Bunn. Miss Eva caught her concern and motioned her back onto the porch. She closed the screen door behind them, and walked with Sheba down the steps and into the shady side yard.

"God been good to you Sheba, you better b'lieve it. There plenty other colored girls wishin' they workin' here in this fancy house for a fine rich lady like Miz Dana." As they walked together down the sidewalk, Sheba's fear

96

evaporated. She knew she was fortunate and wanted to tell Miss Eva about her new life.

"Miz Dana, she so kind and good to us. And you never saw such stuff's in this place." She stopped and turned to Miss Eva. "It's even got an indoor privy." She paused.

Miss Eva turned to study her face. "But, chil'. I hear a 'but' in your voice, though you won't say so. Is something worryin' you?"

Only concern and love emanated from Miss Eva's round eyes. And although she had been temperamental, there was never any question that Miss Eva had only the best interests of her orphanage charges at heart.

Sheba couldn't help voicing the hope that had been welling up inside her. "Miss Eva, I been thinkin' and prayin' 'bout this. Cause even tho it's nice here 'n all, I think God be askin' me to do somethin' else."

Miss Eva gave a short laugh. "What you mean? I can't think what kinda work'd be better than this."

She was sure Miss Eva would think she was crazy, but then Miss Eva had followed her own dream and now she was accepting a large donation for the Lincoln Colored Home. So it was possible for a black woman to be successful, it just took persistence and nerve, Sheba decided. And Miss Eva was the perfect model to follow, even if she didn't think so.

Miss Eva was waiting for a reply, so Sheba gathered up her courage. "Miz Eva, I got a call to start a dressmakin' shop, do sewin' for rich ladies like Miz Dana. The mistress say I got the gift for seamstressin' and I wager I could make a go of it, kinda like Scott Burton 'n his barber shop. See I think God wants me to work for myself, not for some rich white lady."

Miss Eva put her hands on Sheba's shoulders and faced the girl towards her. The smile was gone. "What makes you think God want you to go off on your own? I don't see how you gonna' do better."

Her fear of Miss Eva had evaporated and now Sheba saw only a small, determined woman in front of her, not some shrill witch who could control her fate. "You did, Miz Eva. You had a call to make that orphanage. Well, it's the same for me. I seen it, seen the signs pointin' the way. Why some of Miz Dana's friends, they been sendin' their maids 'round to ask me to make dresses and such for them. Course I have to tell 'em 'no', but I reckon I could earn a livin' wage from that work."

She hesitated, then added. "And they's goin's on here at this house that just plain evil. Spirits and séances and the like. Miz Dana, she's goin' down the Devil's path."

Miss Eva's face dissolved in a grin. "Child, these rich white ladies ain't got nothin' better to do than chase the passing craze. This year, seances, next year, somethin' else." She looked at Sheba. "But child, I b'lieve you sincere and you always was a good, church-goin' girl. So I tell you what, if you think God's tellin' you to go out on your own, you do it and I'll help you any way I can." She turned back toward the house, "Now I gotta' get back. I want that money

97

for the orphanage and I'm not leaving till I see it." She shot a confident smile back over her shoulder as she climbed the porch steps.

Sheba dropped the rugs. Tears blurred the bright sunlight. Her emotions were ragged after the charged encounter between Elliott and Thomas the day before. She hadn't realized how the conflict between these two men had upset her. She cared for both of them, and that was the problem. Miss Eva's kindness had touched a nerve and she crumpled to the grass. After ten minutes or so of sobbing on the lawn, Sheba realized the mistress might need her and tried to compose herself. She rushed to the servants' bathroom and splashed water on her face, then descended to the entryway just as the visitors were preparing to depart.

Smoothing her skirt, Sheba waited by the front door until she saw the feet and legs of Mr. Bunn, Miss Eva and Mrs. Dana as they descended from the living room. "And of course I shall be honored to attend the dedication of the Mary E. Lawrence Reading Room at the home," Mrs. Dana was saying to Miss Eva.

First into the entryway, Mr. Bunn held his briefcase close to avoid knocking into the furniture as they descended. "Susan, I know you talk with a good many people in the course of performing your social duties. Be so kind as to put the word out about a vacant building of mine down on Washington. I need a tenant, and you might mention it if you happen across somebody starting a business."

"Of course, Joseph. It would be a pleasure to help you." Mrs. Dana turned to Sheba, who had attempted to make room in the crowded entryway by backing up as far as she could go without running into the statue. "Sheba, please give Mr. Bunn his hat."

As Sheba offered the bowler to the gentleman, Miss Eva entered the conversation. "Why Mr. Bunn, I b'lieve Sheba here might be interested in that vacant shop. She's plannin' to start a dressmaking business." Dead silence reigned and Miss Eva gave Sheba a wide smile.

Mr. Bunn dusted his hat off nonchalantly, but Mrs. Dana fell into one of the low seats in front of the statue. She pressed her hands onto the skirt of her white dress and closed her eyes, as if she could block out Miss Eva's statement. Apparently unsuccessful, she sighed. "Oh Sheba, I can't imagine what I will do if you leave."

Disregarding Mrs. Dana's collapse, Mr. Bunn placed his hat on his head and opened the door to leave. "Miss Eva, good to see you." He nodded toward Mrs. Dana. "I'm afraid I can't stay. I'm devilishly late for my next appointment. But I do hope you'll recover Susan. And if you find a renter, just give me a call. We can talk."

Miss Eva followed him out the door, winking at Sheba as she passed. "Good-bye and thank you Mrs. Dana." Then, sotto voice, she whispered to Sheba. "I do b'lieve God be puttin' somethin' together, jist for sweet Sheba. An' maybe I help Him a little. You'll see." Looking like a cat that had just swallowed a bird, she flitted out the door.

Sheba turned her attention to Mrs. Dana, who remained seated in the low chair, motionless. Sheba knelt beside her and began chafing one of her hands. "Don' be riled. That dressmakin' shop, why that's just some old pipe dream Miss Eva had."

Her mistress roused and opened her eyes. Sheba saw gratitude mixed with the smallest doubt on her face. "Sheba, what a good girl you are. I knew you couldn't leave us." Mrs. Dana gave a weak smile, and Sheba nodded, content that her mistress' fears had been put to rest. She was easily convinced to believe what she was inclined to believe anyway, Sheba surmised.

God's Direction

S heba was in a state after Miss Eva and Mr. Bunn had departed from the
Lawrence House. "I can't hardly b'lieve Miss Eva say that to those folks,"
she told Hattie as she paced, exasperated, in front of the kitchen sink that
evening. Hattie observed her from the table, leaning on her arms in exhaustion.
"If I didn't know better, I be thinkin' she was puttin' on airs," Sheba exclaimed.
She swung to face Hattie and waved the dishtowel at her. "She always sayin'
'Look how good my chillen done.' Now she up and say 'Sheba goin' t'start a
dressmakin' business.' Now what call she got to say that?"

Hattie shook her head and gazed down at the red-checked table cloth. "I
dunno. Alls I know is Miz Dana ain't happy. No she ain't." She looked up at
Sheba, her brow deeply furrowed, as Miss Flora swished into the room,
swinging the door closed behind her. With an effort, Hattie rose from her
comfortable chair.

Miss Flora waved dismissively at Hattie. "Sheba, I desire a word with you.
Hattie, please leave us." Miss Flora's sharp eyes bored into Sheba, who stared
defiantly back. Mrs. Dana had departed for Galesburg where her friend, the
medium Celia Hughes, was visiting friends. In her absence, Miss Flora
apparently had nothing better to do than badger the servants. As Hattie
lumbered out the back door of the kitchen, Miss Flora fired her opening salvo.
"So I believe it is your intention to leave us and start a dressmaking business, at
least that is what Mrs. Monroe told Mrs. Dana. It quite upset her."

Sheba straightened and took a step forward, closer to Miss Flora's stiff,
black-clothed figure. "Well it ain't my purpose to upset Miz Dana, but seein' as
how Miss Eva let the cat out of the bag, I guess I better 'fess. It's true, I do
want to open a dressmakin' shop. Someday 'tis. Why Miz Deneen say she done
dream 'bout my dresses."

Miss Flora grew red with indignation, interrupting Sheba. "So this is how
you repay Mrs. Dana's kindness, by imposing on her friends, depriving us of a
housemaid." She blustered to a stop.

"Why I never thought nothin' like that. Ladies like Miz Deneen and Miz
Treadway, they asked me to do sewin', but I said 'No'm, I be Miz Dana's girl.' I
never would do such a thing. But now, well, I done got a sign, from almighty

God, that's right, from God, to go out on my own. Kinda like Mr. Scott Burton, the colored barber."

The maiden cousin had regained her breath. "A sign from God, what nonsense. Why you're nothing but an impudent colored girl, just a heartbeat away from picking cotton and living in a shanty. The very idea that you could run a business. It's appalling."

Sheba wished Miss Flora would leave. It was Mrs. Dana who had hired her and it was to Mrs. Dana that she was accountable. Yet her mistress must have said something to her cousin, because here she was, going on like the world was coming to an end.

"Well, God be my witness, I'm gonna do it. You watch." Sheba heard herself say this, then wondered who had spoken those outrageous words as she watched the color drain from Miss Flora's face. The older woman sat down with a jerk in the chair formerly occupied by Hattie.

"You forget your place, girl," she muttered as she stared at her purple-veined hands. She looked very old sitting crumpled in the kitchen chair.

It was Sheba's turn to look with scorn at her. Violating every code she had learned since entering service, Sheba turned her back and left the room, striding onto the back porch, where Hattie stood talking with Thomas in the fading light. She half expected Miss Flora to chase her; however, when no one came through the kitchen door behind her, she greeted Thomas.

He flashed his brilliant smile at her. "Evenin' Miss Sheba. What all this I hear 'bout you goin' off on your own?"

Wary of Thomas' teasing, Sheba didn't respond until she had paused to consider the answer's impact. "Well, ain't so far-fetched as all that, Mr. Know-It-All. Some ladies asked me to do some sewin' for them. An I got some money saved up. So's all I need's a machine and a place."

Thomas made himself comfortable on the porch railing. The evenings had begun to stay warm and the night air was fragrant with the lilacs that poked their heads over the back garden wall. Hattie rocked in the porch's one chair and Thomas sat quietly, possibly considering Sheba's potential future. Perhaps he was on her side. She moved to sit a few feet away from him on the porch railing.

"Well, you got you a rough road's all," Thomas remarked after a few moments of silence.

Sheba shot him a look. "You mean, cause I'm colored?"

Thomas nodded. "That and you jus' eighteen. You young to be takin' off on your own, Sheba, 'specially in this town. Ain't you heard what folks is sayin'? They blame us coloreds and anybody else who ain't like them for all that badness that goes on down at the Levee. Say that Negroes like Dandy Jim and Hebrews like Fishman, they makin' Springfield bad. So how you think people gonna' take it when some uppity young colored girl opens a dressmakin' shop?"

Sheba stood up to face Thomas, trying not to show her inner fears. "Why jus' fine. They gonna' say, 'Here be some fine dressmakin'.' 'For long my dresses be the talk of the town. You know Miz Deneen? She jus' worried 'bout makin' Miz Dana mad if she bring me work." She faced Hattie, who was dozing in the rocker. "Hattie, I wager you know 'bout stores downtown. I got me some money saved for rent."

Hattie started awake. "Well even if I did, I wouldn't want you goin' down and workin' and livin' all by your lonesome."

Exasperated, Sheba decided to let the question of where she might locate her business drop until she could pursue it further, perhaps with Miss Eva. But she felt compelled to defend her actions to Hattie and Thomas, and even to herself. "Well, all right. But God tol' me plain, so's I knows He gonna help me."

Thomas leaned back and put one foot up on the railing, clasping his knee in his hands, sizing Sheba up from this position. "How you know God be talkin,' an' not some bad collard greens or little ol' apple disagreein' with you?"

He seemed interested, but Sheba couldn't articulate the reason she felt, often during prayer, that God was directing her. "You wonderin', well you come on to church tomorrow. Get a dose of Pastor Ball's fine preachin' and meet some real good folks." She glanced sideways at him, afraid he might start to tease again.

Instead, after a moment of silence, Thomas nodded and smiled at Sheba. "Maybe I do that. Sound kinda interestin'. And I reckon Miz Flora ain't goin' nowhere she need the carriage on Sunday mornin'."

The next morning the Lawrence House was quiet. Miss Flora slept late that day, and, after taking her a breakfast tray, Sheba slipped on her blue dress, and bid goodbye to Hattie and Maud, who were doing the breakfast dishes. She ran down the back steps, hoping Thomas would be ready. As he emerged from the door of the carriage house, Sheba noted his tall, muscular build, smooth skin and narrow glinting eyes. A fine gentleman he seemed, once out of those confounded overalls and into a suit.

They hurried the half-mile along the tree-lined streets of Aristocracy Hill, then crossed the railroad tracks and went south, into the Badlands to the white frame building that was the Pleasant Grove Baptist Church. Since the service could last for two or three hours, depending on how wound-up Pastor Ball got, Sheba asked Thomas if he wanted a drink from the pump in the yard before they hurried up the dirt path to the front door of the church. She led the way into the white sanctuary and sidled into the stuffy pew midway up the aisle. The rough wooden benches could get mighty uncomfortable, but fortunately she spent much of her time in church on her feet, singing, affirming the pastor, even dancing. Well, maybe just swaying to the music, after all, she was a Baptist.

After she led Thomas to her customary seat halfway back, she grabbed the paper fan from the seat, waving it in anticipation and warmth, and looking all around her. She knew everyone and they were warm and welcoming to Thomas. For his part, Thomas seemed quite at home, but Sheba reasoned that he was already acquainted with many of the churchgoers from his time working and living in Springfield. She craned her neck to see the last pew, and caught a glimpse of Scott and Ruby Burton and their brood, latecomers who usually took up a whole pew near the front.

The piano began to pound the rousing chords of "Power in the Blood" and she pulled Thomas to his feet to sing the first of many hymns with the other worshippers, who filled the small sanctuary to the bursting point. Those who didn't know the words were led by Brother Brown, who boomed out the choruses from his place on the platform.

"Would you be free from the burden of sin?
There's power in the blood, power in the blood.
Would you o'er evil a victory win?
There's wonderful power in the blood..."

Deacon Barry stood up and read from scripture, exhorting the congregation then Pastor Ball commenced preaching. Sheba waved her fan and glanced at Thomas, who sat with his hands clasped, staring hard at the preacher. Pastor Ball's sermon was titled "God Will Take Care of You."

"Now brothers and sisters, we have trouble in this life."

"Yes, Brother, trouble," said a few voices in the congregation. Thomas looked around with anticipation.

"And Jesus never promised us a life free from trouble, did He?"

"No Brother. No he did not."

"But He did say he would protect us. Hear now the word of the Lord, Matthew chapter 10, verses 28 through 29." Pastor Ball proceeded to open the Bible and read.

"Are not two sparrows sold for a farthing?
and one of them shall not fall on the ground without your Father.
But the very hairs of your head are all numbered.
Fear ye not therefore, ye are of more value than many sparrows."

Greeted by a chorus of "Amen's" and "True Brother's," Pastor Ball closed the Bible. "What does that say? Why do you worry when God cares for you? He knows the hardships you suffer. He knows!"

Pastor Ball waved his outstretched arms and the congregation grew more lively – some of the people jumped to their feet now and then. Pastor's talk of a sword coming, in our time, carried by Jesus to avenge his beloved, this congregation, was enthralling. Jesus would avenge them, all of them who had been so wronged.

At the end of the sermon, Pastor Ball asked the congregation to join him in prayer. "Oh heavenly Father, you love us all and gave us your son Jesus as a sacrifice. Show us, your sparrows, the direction you want us to fly. We all are poor sinners, but we know that you love us and we know that you, merciful God, will take care of us." After recounting a long list of parishioners who were ill or in financial hardship, Pastor Ball ended the prayer. "We ask these things in your precious Son's name, Amen," he boomed.

Sheba could feel tears creeping from the corners of her eyes at the end of the prayer. She looked sideways at Thomas, to see if he had noticed. Without a word, he pulled his brown-embroidered pocket handkerchief from his inside coat pocket and squeezed it into her hand. She looked up at him gratefully. "God spoke to me then," she whispered. Thomas' smile lit up his whole face.

After church, Sheba beckoned Thomas to the back of the sanctuary, where the Burtons were greeting friends while Pastor Ball stood "shaking people out" as they left the church. She hailed her friends. "Scott and Ruby Burton, this here's Mr. Thomas Cartwright. He say he want to see how God talks to folks. So here he is today."

Scott clapped Thomas on the shoulder. "You be familiar to me, Mr. Cartwright. Did I cut your hair once, or am I disremembering?"

Thomas twirled his bowler hat on his index finger and laughed. "Well, I don't rightly think so, seein' as I go to Wilson Glass for my shaves and haircuts. But it be good t'know you, jus' the same."

Ruby's eyes sparkled as she pulled Sheba aside. "This Thomas, he sweet on you? He seem like such a fine man, and it be high time you get married."

Sheba looked to see if Thomas had heard. "Married. Why no ma'am, I ain't gettin' married to Thomas or nobody. I gonna get me a sewin' shop, not go have babies. Why I jus' need me a machine 'n a place, and I's ready."

Ruby shook her head and stared at Thomas, who was tossing the youngest Burton child in the air. "You missin' out, Sheba. He's a fine young man, and maybe a good Baptist some day, I reckon." She turned back to Sheba. "But you serious 'bout this other idea? You know I always said God gifted you with the sewin' talent."

This was what she had hoped to hear, and Sheba pulled Ruby down in the pew, catching Ruby's hands in hers. "I knowed you b'lieve me, even if nobody else will. See God He want me t' show them white folks that we coloreds is good for somethin' more than jus' cleanin' and cookin' and tendin' horses."

Scott had joined them now. "Sheba, you and Thomas come t'dinner. Ruby's got a chicken cooked at home and some of her fine light biscuits."

Thomas was standing near Sheba, who looked up at him, then answered Scott. "Why I do 'preciate the invite, but we better be gettin' back. That Miss Flora'll have our hides if we late with her lunch." They walked as a group back down the aisle and Sheba took Thomas' arm, then felt Ruby's tug on the sleeve of her dress.

Ruby pulled her back. "Sheba, honey, if God give you a place for your business, then I 'spect we give you that sewin' machine you so good with. It ain't got no use since you been gone." Sheba wrapped her arms around the slight figure of Ruby, who returned the embrace. "You somethin', I do b'lieve you be blessed." Sheba shook free, then the Burtons struck off for their Badlands home and dinner while Sheba and Thomas walked, arm-in-arm, home to the Lawrence House.

As luck would have it, Miss Flora was nowhere to be seen when the pair reentered the house's courtyard at half-past noon. The new green grass covered the well-manicured lawn and a red cardinal darted from a linden tree, glinting across the yard and alighting in a bush on the opposite side. Already worried about lunch preparations, Sheba turned to bid Thomas a hasty farewell. "You right nice to come." She got no further. Thomas leaned forward and kissed her on the mouth. His soft lips felt like a feather.

104

Pleased and surprised, Sheba pulled back. He had made this shocking gesture in full view of the house's many windows where any servant or mistress could be watching. But Thomas didn't seem to care. "You mighty sweet, Sheba. I reckon God got some big plans for you." And then, Thomas departed, vanishing through the door of the carriage house while Sheba stood in the courtyard, becoming aware that her back was itching with the stares of the imagined watchers behind the windows.

May 1908. The Poetry Reading

When his editor approached Elliott's desk to offer him an assignment at the Lawrence House, he could hardly believe his luck. "Loper, I want you to cover a reception Mrs. Susan Dana's hosting for the Lincoln Colored Home. Mrs. Dana's mother was a big supporter of the orphanage and apparently Mrs. Monroe has talked her into a fundraiser sort of event. It's tomorrow evening. They're having some young poet named Lindsay recite his work."

So the next evening, Elliott approached the Lawrence House, heart light, sure he would see Sheba. He was a little worried about encountering the threatening Thomas, but the need to see the lissome young black woman overcame any fears he felt. Rather than follow the swarms of well-dressed citizens down the walkway in front to the house's spacious gallery, Elliott went through the back gate and up the steps to the kitchen, knocking on the back door. "Come on in," a voice called. He went around the corner to the kitchen, where Hattie stood, every flat surface around her covered by red glass plates containing wedges of white cake. A hired girl in a black-and -white maid's uniform placed the plates on large trays, while a coffee pot boiled gently on the stove.

"Well Mr. Loper, what you doin' here?" Hattie was interrupted as Sheba came down the stairs from the servant's quarters above. Her straw hat was pinned over her hair, which she had done in two puffballs on either side of her head and she carried a cardboard suitcase. The older woman swung round to face the girl. "I know what you're doin' girl and I 'spect there's no stoppin' you." She crossed the room and gathered Sheba in a hug. "But you always be welcome here."

Sheba looked over Hattie's shoulder, noticing Elliott for the first time. She gasped.

Hattie let Sheba loose and turned to watch Elliott, who took a step toward the pair. "I'm reporting on this reception for the *Register* but I wanted to see you." He paused, then blundered on. "It looks as though you're leaving though."

106

Sheba clutched her suitcase and met his eyes. "Yessir, that's what I'm doin' alright. I'm gonna start me a dressmakin' shop. Miss Eva, she helped me rent a place and the Burtons give me a sewin' machine, and, well, it just be time." She drew in her breath and waited for Elliott to respond.

At the other end of the house, Mrs. Dana's voice could be heard, "Now everyone, please be seated. I assure you that you are in for an extraordinary evening." The muffled voices grew quiet, and Elliott knew he had to hurry to take his seat before the poet began.

But he lingered in the kitchen, unwilling to say good-bye to Sheba, not sure when they'd meet again. "Well, I expect you know what you're doing. Still, it's a big world out there and I only hope...." He wondered if she had an inkling of the challenges she faced as a young Negro woman in Springfield. "Listen, good luck. I mean if you ever need anything...anything at all, let me know."

Her brown eyes were wells of darkness and her face glistened in the light of the hallway. "I'm beholdin' to you. I don't rightly know how t' thank you for helpin' Mama like that." She reached out a hand, and, impulsively, he pulled it to his lips.

She bowed her head, then squeezed his hand, and went out the door, into the dark courtyard. As he watched her go, it dawned on Elliott that he was missing the event he had come to report on. He rushed back to the gallery and took his seat in the back row, just as the poet began.

Vachel Lindsay stood on the platform in front of the fireplace, swaying and surveying the audience who were garbed in their finest evening clothes. His short, curly hair stood out from his pale face and his eyes shone with a kind of fever. "My first piece is a work in progress in which I convey the history and the plight of the dark race, the noble Negro."

The man's thin voice rang through the night air.

"Then I saw the Congo, creeping through the black

Cutting through the jungle with a golden track

Then along that riverbank

A thousand miles

Tattooed cannibals danced in files;

Then I heard the boom of the blood-lust song

And a thigh-bone beating on a tin-pan gong.

And 'BLOOD' screamed the whistles and the fifes of the warriors,

'BLOOD' screamed the skull-faced, lean witch-doctors,

Whirl ye the deadly voo-doo rattle,

Harry the uplands,

Steal all the cattle,

Rattle-rattle, rattle-rattle,

Bing!

Boomlay, boomlay, boomlay, BOOM,"

As Lindsay recited, he became more animated, throwing his head back, his eyes rolling like those of a man in a fit. His hands shot from the cuffs of his dress suit, jabbing the air. His body rocked and shoulders weaved. The elite of Springfield sat motionless in rows of wooden chairs that filled the gallery.

Elliott craned his neck to see the face of Miss Eva, who sat in the front row, but only her back was visible, garbed in black satin, next to Mrs. Dana's curving shoulders in her wine-red gown. A few people turned away their heads to hide their embarrassment, but many more let out snorts and giggles that swelled a rising wave of laughter.

The poet seemed to feel that he might keep the crowd's attention if he raised his voice even more. "Boomlay, boomlay, boomlay, boom!" he bellowed. At that moment, Mrs. Eva Monroe of the Lincoln Colored Home rose from her seat and left the room. Elliott jumped to his feet and followed the diminutive woman as she scurried down the steps of the gallery, through the library and out the door into the darkened courtyard where he caught up with her at last.

Apparently unaware of his presence, she started when he spoke. "Ma'am, pardon me, but I couldn't help but notice that you left the recitation rather hurriedly. As a reporter for the *Register*, I have to inquire as to why you took such an action. After all, this event will benefit your orphanage."

In the darkness of the courtyard, Miss Eva's eyes flashed and she left no question as to her feelings about the poetry. "It ain't right, what he say. Why 'cordin' to that we nothin' but cannibals. Ain't nothin' more important than that orphanage, but that recitin', it ain't right." She sat down on a bench in the garden and began waving a fan rapidly in front of her face.

He wondered if he should stay with her or return to the recitation, then a movement across the courtyard caught his attention. Two dark figures crouched against the back wall murmuring and, as his eyes adjusted to the darkness, Elliott realized they were Thomas and Sheba. He made a move to approach them, but Thomas wheeled around in the dark and strode off across the courtyard. Lindsay continued to declaim violently to those still listening in the gallery.

Thomas disappeared into the carriage house, while Sheba stood rooted to the ground. Miss Eva rose from the bench and moved toward her. "Sheba, girl. You be fine. We got those 'rangements made, 'member?" Sheba looked up, noticing Miss Eva for the first time, then rushed toward the small woman and enveloped her in a hug. Miss Eva patted the girl's puff balls. "Now Sheba, you be strong an' trust God an' He watch over you. An girl, you tell me if you need anythin'."

Sheba straightened, and as she turned the light from the gallery showed her face was wet with tears. "I don' know what I'd do without you Miss Eva," she called as she grasped her suitcase and walked through the front gate into the Springfield night while behind him the crowd in the gallery delivered polite applause.

July 1908. Independence Day

It was hard at first, as she expected, to move into an empty shop and stay by herself in a sleeping room, yet in retrospect Sheba never felt alone. Each night as she fell exhausted into bed, she looked up at the picture of the blue-robed Jesus knocking at the door, and blessed the milliner who had left the picture behind.

For the first week, not a single customer came through her jingling front door. Mr. Fishman sat outside his shop next door and was polite, but that was all. She had yet to meet the old lady who owned the dry goods store on the other side. The other shopkeepers stayed away, which might have been good, all things considered, Sheba thought.

She was subsisting mostly on jelly sandwiches and an occasional meal at a diner, expecting each day to have some word from her benefactor, Miss Eva. Desperate after sitting idle for days, watching pedestrians stroll along Washington Street, Sheba decided to humble herself and pay a call on Mrs. Deneen. Her bravery was rewarded by several commissions and referrals from the kind-hearted Governor's wife. Slowly her clientele increased, but the crowning achievement came just a week prior with a visit from Hattie, bearing a note asking if Sheba might please pay Mrs. Dana a call to take measurements for a summer ball dress.

Today her heart was light as she walked along the shady streets of Aristocracy Hill. It was the Fourth of July, and she had taken the day off to watch the parade with Scott and Ruby Burton. Unfriendly stares bored at her from front porches of the houses of the "aristocrats" as the locals called them, but she smiled and put their unpleasantness down to the heavy, humid heat. After all, she was an independent businesswoman and these might be her future clients.

She smiled and waved as she passed the white gingerbread house belonging to the Taylors. Mrs. Taylor stood on the porch, fastening bunting to the railings, and waved back. A friend of a friend of Mrs. Dana's had referred Mrs. Taylor to Sheba's dressmaking business. Sheba remembered fondly the previous week when Mrs. Taylor and her daughter Lily had entered her shop. Lily was to be

110

married in September and Sheba's mind whirled with ideas for the girl's frothy wedding dress. She was to make Mrs. Taylor's mauve gown as well.

As she turned north, she noticed afresh the dramatic change from the deep, well-kept lawns of Aristocracy Hill. Here in the Badlands, crackerbox houses squatted on patches of grass, many of the houses so small they contained only one room. Children played in the dusty street, laughing and setting off firecrackers.

Even before she reached the Burtons' house, she spotted the family's children, dressed in white to ward off the day's heat, sitting on the front steps. As she approached, twelve-year-old Tilda rushed toward her, waving a small American flag. "We goin' to the parade! We goin' to the parade!" She stopped short of Sheba and began jumping up and down, waving her flag maniacally. The ruffles on her white jumper bounced along with her curly braids, tied with red and blue ribbons.

"Fo' sure we are, and we better get goin' or we be late." Sheba gave Tilda a quick hug. It was far too hot, even at nine in the morning, for a long embrace. She straightened up to see the two younger boys, both in white shorts and shirts, followed by Scott and Ruby. The family was decked out for the Independence Day parade, Scott wearing a blue seersucker suit and a straw hat and Ruby in a white, fluttery dress and huge bonnet, ornamented with American flags. She was all smiles as she greeted Sheba.

"Life treatin' you good? Miz Dana still in a snit?" She put her arm around Sheba's waist and together they began to walk down the sidewalk, followed by Ruby's family.

Sheba pulled Ruby close to whisper in her ear, under her huge flag-draped hat. "No, ma'am. Miz Dana, she so good, she never stay mad too long." She gazed at Scott, who was at least half a block in front of them. "Where yo' man takin' us? Ain't we gonna watch the parade in front a the shop?"

Ruby shook her head. "No ma'am, we gettin' us a real good spot us right front 'o Mr. Lincoln's home smack on the curb." Scott had dropped back and was holding Roscoe by the hand and moving quickly down the sidewalk in front of her.

"You right there, sweetie," he said. "We goin' early so's we sure t'get a spot. That parade gonna go right through there. It's a fittin' thing, thankin' Mr. Lincoln and the good Lord for bein' free." Scott seemed a bit dazzled by his own oratorical zeal, and he spoke not only to his family, but the fair-sized crowd of neighborhood folk who had joined the procession.

By the time they reached the street where the Great Emancipator's home stood, the little band had grown to about thirty people in all, mostly colored families from the Burtons' neighborhood. The sidewalk along the front of Lincoln's Home was vacant and the group settled there, children sitting on the curb, women on the house's lawn under the trees, in a vain attempt to stay cool.

The parade would start at eleven o'clock, in nearly an hour, and many of the women were winded from the quick-paced walk. As they rested on the grass, the remainder of the street began to fill with whites from the surrounding

111

neighborhood. The heat bore down on the group's members, making them quiet. Even the children seemed subdued.

As eleven o'clock approached, Sheba strained her ears for the sound of horses' hooves and the color guard of the Union Army, which marked the start of every parade. Many of the veterans of that long-ago war were gone now, but those few who remained were proud to wear their outgrown blue uniforms. They marched, carrying sabers, at the very beginning of the parade. Behind the first ranks of white soldiers would come the colored soldiers who had also fought in the Union Army.

But instead of the color guard with its flags and the veterans marching down the street, a group of white men and women advanced down Seventh Street. Many of the men carried flags and guns, and most also had bottles of beer to quench their thirst in the July heat. Sweat trickled between Sheba's shoulder blades, but something about the group made her shiver.

The motley group stopped squarely in front of the Lincoln Home, where not an inch of empty curb or sidewalk space remained. The Burtons and their friends had filled it all to overflowing. It was only then that Sheba noticed that they were the only colored people on the sidewalk or even on the street.

A perspiring woman wearing a yellowed shirtwaist pushed forward onto the curb, stepping on the fingers of Tilda, who yipped in pain. "Move, you little pickaninny. We're gonna watch the parade from here." She pulled a man behind her onto the curb, which by now had been vacated by the Burton children and their friends.

Scott stepped forward, overly polite, though it was apparent from the slight frown lines on his forehead that he was offended. "Ma'am, these seats are taken. We been here for least an hour. I do b'lieve they some spaces down the way there," and he pointed a half block to the south, where the crowd had thinned somewhat.

The woman turned to face Scott, and it was clear she was not about to move down the street. "We're gonna watch the parade from here, so you all better move. Can't you see there's no coloreds on this street? You niggers can watch the parade from your own neighborhood." And she elbowed her way through the crowd of colored people, then turned to beckon to her friends, a surly bunch who matched her in temperament. The men followed her, pushing Scott and his friends roughly into the street.

Dapper in his blue suit, Scott stepped forward to protest and looked as if he might do some shoving himself, but Ruby tugged at his arm. When he stopped to see what she might need, she whispered into his ear and nodded toward the children, who clustered in the street, talking among themselves. The ribbons from Tilda's pigtails had wilted with the heat and drooped sadly down her back as Scott motioned for his friends to follow him away from the curb now occupied by the woman and her friends.

As they progressed slowly across the intersection, a clod of dirt flew toward Scott. Seeing it in advance, he ducked and it shattered in the street a few feet away from him. He turned angry eyes toward the woman, while one of her friends cried, "Atta girl Kate, you show 'em. Damn niggers dirtyin' up the neighborhood."

Ruby pulled Scott around and continued down the street, as Sheba followed with her friends. Her back flinched involuntarily as she walked, and she realized that she was afraid that she'd be hit by a clod of dirt. But the group proceeded unharmed, stared at by the white folks lining the curbs, until they found a vacant spot a few blocks down the street. Sheba settled on the curb next to Ruby, then looked up, straight into the blue eyes of Elliott Loper.. His fair skin was flushed with heat and emotion.

"It's an outrage, that's what it is. Do you know that woman ? That's Kate Howard, just the most low, common boardinghouse keeper in town. And the biggest hater of colored people too. There ought to be a law against people like her." Sheba felt a glow of pride as Elliott turned to greet Scott. "Mr. Burton. I couldn't help but notice your very poor treatment by the group down the street."

Scott pulled his hat off and started fanning himself with it. "Sometimes folks, they just....well y'know... it like to make you crazy sometimes." Scott paused and tried to collect himself, glancing around nervously, as though another missile might materialize at any minute. "I tell you, I ain't never been treated so poorly as by them folks. And this here's the Land of the Free." He lowered his voice. "It jus' ain't right, the chillen seein' this. Specially in front of Mr. Lincoln's home and all. Ain't people got no shame?"

Still shaking from fear, Sheba looked with open-hearted thanks at Elliott, who seemed suddenly reticent. "Well, I'd best be off. But I do hope your business is still going well and you haven't been bothered by people of that type." He nodded toward the group lounging on the Lincoln home lawn.

Sheba looked into his sky-blue eyes, noticing how they crinkled at the edges when he smiled. "I'm doin' right well, right well indeed. Why don' you come by an' see?" Sheba looked up at him, and as he stared at her in the hot July sun with the horns ompahing "Star and Stripes Forever" she wondered what that might mean, for him to call on her shop.

"I will indeed, delighted to." Elliott touched his bowler. "Now see here, make sure you look for my article in tomorrow's paper. I'm covering the parade. Certain to be a front page piece."

He turned to leave and the color guard appeared in the distance, the horses' hooves signaled the parade's start. James rushed up to her – "C'mon back. You get runned over." And Sheba, her good humor restored, walked back to the sidewalk to take her place among the colored and white folks waiting patiently for the parade to begin.

The Murder

The biggest story of the year was on page one of the *Register* the next day - - a colored man had slashed the throat of a respected white engineer. Elliott remembered his pride at being assigned to cover the parade, a minor story now, relegated to page two. It was a consolation, albeit a small one, that he had seen Sheba Tully, the object of more of his idle imaginings than he cared to admit.

For comparison's sake, Elliott opened the *Journal* and scanned the front page of the rival paper. "Wounds inflicted by Negro Intruder Result in Death. Clergy A. Ballard, Victim of An Assassin, Dies in Hospital." In the center of the page was a large photo of a man staring in mild confusion. "Clergy A. Ballard," Elliott read the caption below the photo, and then another photo caught his eye: a pig-tailed girl clutched a doll and stared sleepily at the camera. "Little Molly Ballard," the caption said. Elliott leaned on his elbows and pulled the paper closer. Behind him another young man, a fellow reporter, began reading over his shoulder.

"Well, do you think their story's better than ours? I wrote it of course." The reporter behind Elliott sounded worried, as if Elliott's opinion meant something to him.

Elliott placed the paper next to that day's *Register* and leaned back in his chair. "Oh, I don't know. It's pretty much the same, but we didn't get this crackerjack photograph of the little girl – now that's something. From what I hear, this James character, the man's that supposed to have killed Ballard, he's still on the loose. And he's no good. Folks say he came to town a couple months ago and started living on the Levee, drinking and causing trouble. Just what this city needs, a colored man getting drunk and attacking a white man." Elliott shook his head.

The editor approached, his hands under his suspenders, from across the busy newsroom. "Just got a phone call, Potts. You need to head down to St. John's directly and talk with the coroner. Ballard's dead."

Elliott stared at the photograph of the melancholy man, Clergy Ballard. So he was dead, throat slashed by an intruder to his home in his daughter's bedroom.

114

"I'm on it sir," Potts said as he grabbed his reporter's pad and his hat from the rack by the door, then vanished.

The editor turned back to Elliott. "Damn shame, that fellow killed. Seemed like a respectable sort too. No telling what kind of reaction this will get in the community. Loper, you've been doing a good job lately, that story on the reception for the colored orphanage, that was good copy, earned us some readers, some advertisers too. You run down to the police station and see what they've got on this James fellow, if they've got a lead on his whereabouts. Poke around a little, you know, find out what you can."

Elliott leapt to his feet. This was the chance he'd been waiting for; finally, he was covering the biggest story of the day. He grabbed his notebook and his hat and was out the door before the editor could change his mind.

A crowd surrounded the door to the small police station, but, possibly because they observed the "press" card in the band of his bowler, the mass parted as Elliott made his way to the door. "What're all these folks doing here?" he asked a young man who stood next to the door.

The man pointed toward four schoolgirls who stood huddled in their pinafores, next to the front window, talking earnestly among themselves. "Them girls over there, they found him, that scoundrel James over by the railroad tracks, dead drunk. And if these damn policemen hadn't come, we woulda made short work of that dirty nigger." The man cursed again, and Elliott escaped into the stuffy police station. He looked around, remembering it vaguely from the visit when he witnessed the incident on the streetcar involving Joe Craig.

A blue-uniformed policeman, who appeared to be the chief, turned to yell directions to three other men, who were attempting to handcuff a large, unconscious Negro prostrate on the floor of a cell. He looked up at Elliott, as if seeing him for the first time. "What do you want?"

Elliott drew himself up and looked sternly at the officer. "Name's Loper and I'm a reporter for the *Register*. Here about the Ballard murder."

The police chief stared at him. "So I see, but you ain't the usual fellow. Most times it's Potts that comes here."

The other men had succeeded in cuffing the Negro and were attempting to hoist him onto the cot in the cell. Elliott realized he needed to explain Potts' absence. "Well, he's at the hospital so I'm here instead. Is that Joe James, the accused murderer? I thought he was still at large."

The police chief was staring at the men in the cell. "Get out of there and close that door," he shouted, and the three men rushed from the cell and clanged the door shut.

The policeman sat down at the desk and turned his attention to Elliott. "Now sir, what is it you need to know?"

Elliott watched to see if the man on the cot was breathing. A slight motion in his chest put his fears to rest. "Well, how was this man located? Was force necessary to subdue him?"

115

The policeman put his feet up on the desk. "We didn't need force to bring that fellow in, but we had a little trouble with the group out front." He motioned his head toward the door. "They'd like to have strung him up if we hadn't got there when we did. You see those four girls outside? They kinda' stumbled on him -- dead drunk he was – and 'for long that bunch set on him like there was no tomorrow. Course they like Ballard – he was well regarded – he was an engineer and had lots of friends."

Elliott was taking copious notes, but glanced occasionally at the Negro in the cell. "Can you summarize what occurred? The murder I mean?"

The police chief grew more expansive. "Well, night before last, that nigger there broke into Ballard's home while they were all asleep and was gettin' ready to attack his daughter when she woke up and saw him in her room. Course Ballard rushed in and started fighting with this fellow, who had a razor on him I guess, because he slit Ballard's throat. He got scared then and took off and looks like he did some drinkin' down on the Levee afterwards, because when those girls found him, he was pretty well gone. So they spread the word that the nigger who attacked Clergy Ballard was layin' on the grass, and sure enough, this big crowd of folks like to beat him senseless 'for we could get to him." He nodded at the Negro. "He's a good for nothin', but the law says everybody's entitled to a trial"

The other policemen were clustered around the window, peering anxiously at the crowd.

"What're they doin'?" Elliott asked.

The police chief peered out the window and scratched his head. "Looks like the crowd's breakin' up. Guess they're gonna have to wait to see him hanged. Hope they don't cause us no problems."

Elliott glanced up. "What do you mean 'problems'?"

The police chief pulled back from the window and retreated to his desk, the other policemen following in his wake. "Folks is fed up, fractious-like anymore. 'Specially those miners and men out of work." He lowered his voice and Elliott moved closer. "They blame them niggers, they keep comin' up from the South like this was some sort 'o promised land or somethin' and takin' jobs away from the whites." He glanced over at Joe James, who remained motionless.

A wave of concern for the colored man washed over Elliott. "Are you sure he's all right? He was pretty badly beaten from the sounds of it."

The policeman faced Elliott, staring. "Oh, he's all right. Good thing we came along when we did though, they would have had him dead and strung up." He poked the air. "You write about how we got him, how we saved him from those folks, but be careful we don't come off like a bunch of nigger lovers."

Nigger lovers -- it was a harsh label. Elliott bit back a response and stood up. "I'd best be getting this story filed. What will you do with this man?"

116

The police chief yawned. "Keep him here I guess, 'till his trial. Hope it's soon though. That's a mighty angry bunch out here tonight. They want justice served and if it don't happen soon, seems like they might do it themselves."

Elliott stepped toward the door. "I believe the law says 'innocent until proven guilty'. They can't judge this man, a judge and jury will do that. Thank you for your time, officer."

He filed the story, a straightforward rehashing of the previous day's events, with added details about the girls' discovery and the police rescue of the man. He was surprised when his editor chose to downplay the story, placing it on page two and allowing only a scant three inches of newsprint. But the editorial on the facing page offered some explanation. Entitled "Murder of a Good Man," the editorial eulogized Clergy Ballard and then referenced Joe James. "...concerning (the Negro) and the questions which arise from his presence in the community, it is well to preserve silence at this time. The state of the public mind is such that comment can only add fuel to the feeling that has burst forth with general knowledge of the crime."

Warnings

Sheba sat in the August heat in the dressmaking shop, pumping the Burtons' old sewing machine and wiping perspiration from her fingers. A feeling of apprehension hung over her and she looked up every few minutes, scrutinizing the empty street outside. As the clock struck one, she looked again through the plate-glass window, started, then stood up, the green fabric on her lap falling to the floor. A heavy woman in a blue shirtwaist advanced across Washington Street and mounted the curb, headed straight for Sheba's dressmaking shop.

She sat motionless behind the sewing machine, her stomach seizing up with fear. The woman was Kate Howard. Before she had a chance to think what she might do, the bell on the door jingled and the woman stepped into the shop, blinking a little as she advanced into the dark from the bright street outside. She looked around at the large mirror, platform, sewing machine and bolts of fabric, then noticed Sheba standing at the center of the front of the shop.

"You the girl what runs this shop?" She peered into the shadows of the back room, as if more colored people might suddenly appear.

Sheba stepped forward. "Yes, I's the shopkeeper here. What you be needin'?" She watched as Kate continued to peer about through squinting eyes still not accustomed to the gloom of the shop.

Kate smiled at Sheba, more of a sneer than a grin, and Sheba stared back. "'Pears you be operatin' a sewin' business here. I recollect you ain't been open long. We don't need no more niggers 'round here." She paused and Sheba interrupted the silence.

"I got ever' right t'be here, same's you do." She pulled the door open, but Kate Howard didn't budge. She stood, solid and defiant, in the center of the large room. "Now you listen here, you're drivin' good customers away from my boardin' house. You get out and you get out now, or we'll be makin' damn sure you go. They's plenty more think like me, and you ain't ruinin' my business, I kin tell you that." Kate walked to within inches of Sheba, and looked her up and down. Sheba backed away, but kept hold of the door. The street outside was empty and she felt suddenly very alone.

118

"You better go now." She stared at Kate Howard, who seemed for a minute as though she would strike the girl. Instead she shook her head, turned on her heel and walked past Sheba, into the street. Sheba could feel the cool breeze as she passed by and watched Kate's bulky figure recede down the sunny sidewalk.

It was all Sheba could do to keep from slamming the door, but she held herself back, remembering Pastor Ball's sermon on Sunday. Pointing into the congregation, Pastor Ball had delivered his words as if talking directly to her as he read from the book of Matthew. "But love ye your enemies, and do good, and lend, hoping for nothing again; and your reward shall be great, and ye shall be the children of the Highest: for he is kind unto the unthankful and to the evil."

Pastor Ball had gone on to exhort the congregation to love those who did evil to them. "Why it's so easy to love your mama and your friends and even nice folks who do good to you. Ain't so easy to love those folks who call you names, now is it?"

Instead of responding with the usual "Amen," the members of the congregation had been silent in the summer heat. No one moved from the pews to raise a hand in assent.

Undeterred, the pastor continued. "But that's what our Savior wants us to do. Yes brothers, it says right here in this great Sermon on the Mount. He stood on a hill and talked to folks just like you and me, folks who were getting' spit on by the Romans and forced to pay awful taxes. Did he say 'Rise up and smite those who persecute you?' Well, did he? I'm here to tell you today, he said you need to love them and he said you need to turn the other cheek."

Pastor Ball turned again to the thick Bible, which lay open on the lectern. "And as ye would that men should do to you, do ye also to them likewise. For if ye love them which love you, what thank have ye? for sinners also love those that love them."

Scott Burton, sitting quietly next to Sheba and Ruby, had slowly risen to his feet. "Amen brother," he intoned, and, a group of men around Scott also stood and shouted their assent.

Standing at her doorway remembering the scene in the church, Sheba started, as if she was seeing a ghost. Pastor Ball himself and his wife Phoebe trudged down Sixth Street. Pastor Ball's tan suit made his dark skin appear almost black and his wife, also dressed in light brown, walked like a shadow at his side. They appeared to be headed toward her shop, and Sheba glanced around the room, wishing again she had more than two chairs in which to seat company. As she watched, the forms of Pastor Ball and his wife loomed through the glass window, which proclaimed, "Dressmaking. Garments. Fine Seamstressing." The bells jingled, signaling the visitors' entry and Sheba hurried from the backroom where she had been checking her hair in the small hand mirror.

"Pastor Ball. Mrs. Ball. I'm right pleased to see you." The couple's visit was reassuring, especially on the heels of Kate Howard's castigation. She pulled the chair from the sewing table and made a move toward the other chair by the door, but Pastor Ball was quicker and grasped the back of the chair, moving it close to the other. He looked around for a third chair, but seeing none, motioned for Sheba and Mrs. Ball to sit. Sheba, realizing it was fruitless to insist on standing, collapsed into the wooden chair and gazed into Mrs. Ball's earnest face.

Without hesitating, Mrs. Ball leaned forward, searching Sheba's face. "Sheba, we so worried 'bout you, bein' down here by yourself amongst all these white folks. Lately, you know, they's so much bad blood, so much hate. We just want to make sure you safe. Ain't that so, Pastor Ball?" She leaned back in her chair and pulled a fan from her bag, waving it rapidly in front of her face, then looked up at Pastor Ball who was leaning against the window sill with his arms crossed. Sheba had long since gotten used to the fact that the eminent pastor and his wife addressed each other by their formal titles at all times, or at least in public.

Pastor Ball nodded, then placed his index finger on his lips, as if to emphasize a point. He moved his finger away, all the while keeping his eyes fixed on Sheba. "People gettin' jumpy 'round us colored folks since that white man got killed. And some colored folks been drinkin' and carousin' more than is fittin'. They's fault both ways." He moved closer to Sheba. "But Sheba, it ain't safe down here, specially for a young girl like you. I figured you were safe while you were in service up at the rich white lady's house. But here, why they's all kind of folks want to do you harm. What ever happened to that nice young man you brought with you to church that Sunday? What was his name?"

Sheba felt a flush and gazed away out the front window. Countless times had she longed for Thomas, with his teasing smile and smooth brown skin, to come and keep her safe, to protect her from people like Kate Howard. "Thomas, he gone. I ain't seed him since the Lawrence House. He jus' kinda took off."

Pastor Ball and his wife exchanged a meaningful glance, then he looked back at Sheba. "Well, ain't nothin' stoppin' you from goin' away for a spell. At least go stay with Mr. and Miz Burton, they'd be pleased to have you." He nodded emphatically.

Sheba sat still for a minute, gazing at this well-meaning couple. But as she sat, the anger that she had felt earlier returned with such force that she sprang to her feet. "What you sayin'? If you had any idea how hard it be t'get this shop, you never even think that."

Mrs. Ball jumped up and patted Sheba's shoulder in an attempt to calm her. "Now, we only want well for you. Why we proud as all get-out you got this shop and all. But girl, you don't know what it's like."

Sheba threw up her hands. "Oh land, I do know. That evil Kate Howard jus' left, after havin' the nerve t' tell me I better git. She a scary lady, that Kate Howard." With this, Sheba sat down and began to sob.

Mrs. Ball gathered the girl into her arms. "You hush now chil'. God helps the likes of you, and He's gonna keep his little lamb from harm."

120

Sheba sobbed but made no reply and Mrs. Ball continued to hold her while Pastor Ball paced up and down in front of the window, praying and waving his hands. "Oh God, protect this young woman who has made so great a sacrifice for her people. Put your loving arms around her Lord and keep her safe from harm." He stopped, and then laid his large hands, one on Sheba's head, and one on Mrs. Ball's satin-covered shoulder. "May God be with you, Sheba."

Sheba, feeling somehow comforted, raised her tear-streaked face to the pastoral couple as they prepared to depart. Mrs. Ball dabbed at her eyes with a white handkerchief embroidered with red roses and gave Sheba a parting hug. "'Member you kin come on over t' our house anytime. The Badlands ain't so awful and 'sides, it's your own folks around you."

At least an hour passed before Sheba could collect her wits enough to continue her work. She considered visiting Hattie at the Lawrence House for a bit of comfort, but one look at the bolts of fabric leaning in the corner, selected for her clients' various garments, was enough to keep her sewing until the evening shadows fell long into her work area. At last, she tidied the room, checked the lock on the door again, and then climbed the stairs next to it to her stuffy sleeping room above the shop. Although she had only a few provisions, she was too exhausted to venture out to a café or grocery for food. Instead she ate some bread and jam, drank some water, and pulled on her white cotton nightgown, and then climbed wearily into bed.

August 1908. Chautauqua at Old Salem

As the month dragged on, Elliott got the same story each time he visited the police station. The trial had been postponed again due to concerns about the safety of the prisoner. "That's what the boss says," the police chief muttered as he looked over his shoulder while Elliott pretended he hadn't heard.

That Friday, August 14, was already a hot day in a summer full of hot days when Elliott caught the 6:15 train to Petersburg. He had on a fresh shirt and tie with a red carnation in his lapel: he was going somewhere he wanted to be, to the cool banks of the Sangamon River, the Old Salem Chautauqua, to hear Mr. Billy Sunday.

Of course, he hadn't got this plumb assignment by waiting for it, Elliott reminded himself. He advanced down the sidewalk towards Union Station where an Illinois Central train was scheduled to leave for Petersburg, about 20 miles away and a short hike to the Chautauqua grounds. Ever since he learned that the great preacher was speaking, Elliott had endeavored to impress upon his boss that he would be the perfect reporter to cover the Billy Sunday lecture. "I've heard he's quite an impressive man, very anti-alcohol." He was aware of his editor's feelings on the subject of strong drink. Almost daily, Mr. Stevens could be seen shaking his head and muttering over the latest crime committed while the criminal was under the influence of alcohol.

Fortunately, the editor agreed. "You're just the man to cover his speech and there's plenty of local interest. You train out to Old Salem Friday, then catch the eight o'clock train back so you can file the story before deadline."

Elliott flushed. "Oh thank you sir. I'm sure I can capture Reverend Sunday's wonderful words for a story tomorrow."

The train ride was short and Elliott closed his eyes and felt the hot breeze beat his face without cooling him. He had been to the Chautauqua once, about five years ago, but he remembered little except huge crowds of people, tents, parasols, perspiration and a large open-air auditorium. Here speakers shouted from a stage at thousands of women in their best dresses and men in blue serge suits and straw boaters.

The train emptied out at Petersburg, a small town with dusty streets dominated by the train station, and Elliott walked a few steps to the shuttle train to the Chautauqua grounds. It was filled with families and single people wearing their Sunday best. All were in a festive mood, talking and laughing as they disembarked. Gatekeepers asked for a dime a person for admission, waving the children on through, but these day attendees were an exception rather than the rule. Most folks stayed the two weeks on the shady grounds of the Chautauqua. As Elliott trudged up the unpaved road that bisected the grounds, women rushed past him carrying slop buckets that reeked of human urine, headed for the large round latrine buildings.

The campground lots were spacious and boasted tents of varying sizes. Some of the tent fronts were rolled back, revealing families eating breakfast at large tables, probably brought from their homes for the Chautauqua. Further along, Elliott glimpsed cottages and even what appeared to be houses among the trees, even some two-storied affairs where men sat in rocking chairs awaiting the day's education and entertainments.

Elliott prowled the grounds, visiting an open air pavilion where a class in elocution met among its Grecian columns, watching a kindergarten play blind man's bluff, and sitting for a lunch of cold chicken at the Dining Tent. After lunch he climbed the steps of the Chautauqua Hotel, poking his head in the door to view its inviting lobby, Indian rugs covering the wooden floors and a ceiling fan whiffling the potted palms.

As it got closer to four o'clock, he headed toward the main tent. He wanted to arrive early, since it was bound to be crowded. He had heard that there were overflow crowds for many Chautauqua spectacles and the newspaper had been running advance stories on Reverend Sunday for weeks.

Elliott followed the crowd to a large covered building, open at all four sides. Flags decorated the tops of each bunting-wrapped post that branched out to support the huge roof that stretched high above the rows of thousands of wooden chairs. As he advanced down the aisle toward the front of the auditorium, he noticed the seats were rapidly filling with men in bowler hats, women in dresses with lacy high collars and squirming children in sailor outfits.

As he approached the wooden platform at the front of the tent, a woman in blue blocked his way. "Who are you with, young man?"

"I'm here to cover the Reverend's lecture for the *Springfield Register*." The wooden platform was topped by a wide lectern and a chair at one corner. The musicians had not yet taken their seats at the piano and music stands behind the platform.

The woman examined his "Press" card, then, handing it back to him, said, "You can sit in the front row, that's reserved for press and family." Taking this excellent seat, Elliott congratulated himself. The seats around him filled up with people and he turned to survey the crowd in back of him. Rows of chairs filled with men and women stretched almost as far as he could see. It was a veritable sea of faces; then it struck him – not one of them was black. There were no colored people at the Old Salem Chautauqua.

123

A bell rang and the audience fell into silence. He turned to face the stage as a man walked to the lectern. Dressed in a serge suite and white shirt, the man had thinning hair combed back on either side of a gleaming face. He grasped the lectern with both hands and leaned forward, booming into the silence. "Welcome to the Old Salem Chautauqua. I am honored tonight to introduce to you a man renowned for his oratorical skills, for the truth of his message. The Reverend Billy Sunday, an ordained minister in the Presbyterian Church, has brought thousands of people to Christ through his powerful speeches." The crowd exploded in applause, an almost deafening pounding that seemed to last for minutes. The man held up his hand and the clapping subsided.

A small man took the stage and the crowd seemed to simultaneously breathe inwards. He was short with razor sharp features and slicked-back hair. Not too impressive really, Elliott observed, yet something about the way he carried himself was focused and compact. There was no fear in him and he raised his hands to embrace the thousands-strong crowd.

He wasted no time and the audience hung on his every word.

"Drink, that's what I speak to you today about. Alcohol is wresting our very nation to its knees and just a few miles away from here, in the home of our Great Emancipator and most honored President, it is eating away like a canker at the very heart of the city, just as it is destroying our country." The Reverend's movements were athletic. He bent, punctuating what he said with pitching and batting motions.

"I tell you, gentlemen, the American home is the dearest heritage of the people, for the people, and by the people, and when a man can go from home in the morning with the kisses of wife and children on his lips, and come back at night with an empty dinner bucket to a happy home, that man is a better man, whether white or black. Whatever takes away the comforts of home, whatever degrades that man or woman, whatever invades the sanctity of the home, is the deadliest foe to the home, to church, to state and school, and the saloon is the deadliest foe to the home, the church and the state, on top of God Almighty's dirt."

The man pointed directly at Elliott, who shrank into his seat. "Do you know the ravages of drink, the havoc it can wreak in your lives? Do you? Because I tell you now that if all the combined forces of hell should assemble in conclave, and with them all the men on earth that hate and despise God, and purity, and virtue, if all the scum of the earth could mingle with the denizens of hell to try to think of the deadliest institution to home, to church and state, I tell you, the combined hellish intelligence could not conceive of or bring an institution that could touch the hem of the garment of the open licensed saloon to damn the home and manhood, and womanhood, and business and every other good thing on God's earth."

A tug on his elbow brought Elliott back to his senses. A little boy of about eight stood facing him, his hair wet with sweat. "You Mr. Loper from the *Register?*"

He guessed the boy had been sent and saw his "press" card on his hat.

"Why yes, why? Is something wrong?"

"You gotta' go back right away. There's a riot in Springfield and you're to catch the six o'clock train. The man at the paper telephoned the train station and pa tol' me t' come here ' fetch you." The boy waited and Elliott pulled a dime from his pocket.

"Thanks. I'm on it." The audience rose to its feet as Elliott dashed down the aisle behind the boy. He blinked as he came into the sunshine outside the building where overflow crowds stood, hoping to hear the famous Reverend Sunday. "Excuse me," he tried to avoid the people who were pressed forward, as he wended his way through the shady yard toward the road that led down the hill to the gate. He was running now, aware he had only minutes to catch the train. He followed the boy, who stopped and waited for Elliott to catch up.

"I'll show you a short cut," the boy shot back, gesturing for Elliott to follow him up a path through the trees which opened across the railroad track from the station.

"I'm obliged to you," Elliott shouted as he hopped aboard the train, which was just pulling out from the station. He lowered himself into his seat and waited for the conductor, who would sell him a ticket home. A riot, a riot in Springfield. He thought about Joe James in the county jail and the crowd that gathered there most days. But something else must have happened. Something really awful. And he'd wager everything he had that this was a riot between Negroes and whites, a final boiling over of the stew that had been simmering for as long as he could remember.

He gazed at the woman's hat in front of him and wondered what might become of Sheba, sitting alone in a shop in the midst of a white business district. He remembered Kate Howard and her crowd on the Fourth of July, the clod of dirt thrown in anger or something worse at Scott Burton and feared the worst. As the train cut through the August landscape, green fields of corn and soybeans, Elliott fanned himself with his notepad. He'd find out soon what awaited in the dusty streets of Springfield.

The Riot

It was Elliott's misfortune that he had not read the newspaper that day. The front pages of every paper in Springfield sported similar headlines, all reporting the alleged rape of Mabel Hallam. "Dragged from her bed and outraged by Negro" shouted the story that ran on page one of the *Journal.* "No effort should be spared to find the black viper and to force appropriate punishment," the newspaper proclaimed.

And it was this lack of information that made it so hard for Elliott to understand what he saw happening as he stood on Fifth Street in front of his father's restaurant about seven that night. Unable to move, Elliott watched as a seething mob of angry men rocked his father's prized new 1908 Studebaker back and forth, then, with one all-out heave, went wild as the vehicle rolled onto its side. Encouraged by the spectators, the group of men grew larger as they pushed even harder and with more urgency. The car was soon toppled to its hood, to the increasing delight of the cheering crowd.

Almost instantly, someone produced a can of gasoline and doused what had been Elliott's father's pride and joy. A match was tossed onto the flammable heap and the automobile was instantly enveloped in flames. The fire gave the streets an eerie yellow glow that made the shadows dance in celebration as the flames reached skyward.

Elliott was frozen with horror as he stood on the curb in front of his father's restaurant, staring as the shiny automobile was slowly reduced to a metal skeleton. Collecting his wits, he pulled the pencil from behind his ear and began to scribble on his reporter's pad, glancing around him to see if any of the crowd recognized him.

"Abe Lincoln brought 'em to Springfield and we'll run 'em out of town!" shouted a heavy-set white woman, appearing almost out of nowhere at the front of the crowd that had worked its way to Loper's Restaurant, growing larger each block it traversed. The woman shook her fist skyward, her brown hair straggling from under her straw hat and her bosom sagging in her faded blue dress. In the torchlight she turned to face Elliott, and he saw it was Kate Howard. "What the hell are you fellows afraid of?" she bellowed, standing in the street in front of the restaurant. Then she pried up a loose brick from the pavement, turned and

126

hurled it through the plate glass window. The brick landed in the middle of the empty dining room, where just a few minutes before Harry had stood at the door with a shotgun, before turning to flee. "Women need protection and this seems the only way to get it," Kate Howard screamed as she turned and marched through the door, into the now-empty restaurant.

"We're right behind you Kate," yelled a man in the crowd that swarmed over the interior of the restaurant like ants, demolishing the gleaming oak bar, large gilt-framed mirror and cloth-covered tables in a matter of minutes.

While the crazed men broke mirrors, tables, pitchers, and goblets, glass shattering around them as they advanced, Elliott crept through the alley at the back of the restaurant just in time to see his father striding from the back door still holding his shotgun. "Dad, Dad!" Elliott called, then he turned to see if any of the men had followed him down the alley. No one was in sight and his father shook his head in disbelief.

"I can't believe they're doing this. All my years of work to build this restaurant into something we could be proud of -- something successful. But the Studebaker, oh." Harry momentarily covered his face with his hands as if to erase the memory of the tangle of metal and wheels that had been the source of so much pride. "I guess I never knew they hated me, at least not so much. But earlier today Sheriff Werner asked me if they could use my automobile to get those two colored prisoners out of town, take 'em to Bloomington where they'd be safe. He knew there was trouble brewing, what with that white woman accusing that colored fellow of violating her. So of course I said 'yes.' And now look at what they've done. My fine restaurant ruined."

Elliott reached out to touch his father's shoulder, but Harry had no time for sympathy. "Come on, we've got to get out of here. God knows what they'll do next." He turned Elliott around and began to run down the darkened alley. They didn't stop until they reached safety, several blocks south of downtown.

Elliott stopped, winded but determined to face his father, who was clearly exhausted with the heat and the devastation. "I have to go back, Dad. It's my job to cover this...this riot." Elliott realized at that moment that this was no mere disturbance, no small ruckus. This was a race riot and, as he listened to the shouts and gunfire, he knew it was just getting started.

Harry looked toward his welcoming two-story house, light flooding through the front windows. "I'm going up to Michigan with your ma and sisters. Those men downtown, they know where we live. They might come lookin' for me." His gray eyes peered at Elliott from under his bushy eyebrows. "They might come lookin' for you too, son. I don't want you goin' back down there." For a second, Elliott thought his father might grab him by the shoulders, like when he was little, and pull him inside. But instead, the older man bent his head and muttered. "Oh, I know I can't stop you from goin'. I just hope I'll see you again. You're the best son I got." He looked up, his sharp grey eyes full of tears.

"Don't worry old man, I'll be fine. And the restaurant, it can be rebuilt, you'll see. It's just that this awful night..." Elliott embraced his father, then

127

turned and did not look back as he sprinted toward downtown. Reaching his father's restaurant, still alive with the crowd's destructive activity, he peered cautiously inside. No one seemed to notice him, and Elliott was relieved. This was looking like the biggest story of 1908, maybe the biggest story since Lincoln's departure from Springfield for Washington to begin his first presidential term fifty years earlier.

He didn't have time to ponder the irony of the situation. The mob was heading north toward the Levee. He followed the torches and gunfire from the crowd at a safe distance.

Walking and writing at the same time in the dim light, Elliott took notes. "Eleven o'clock at night, Friday, August 14, 1908. Crowd at least a thousand strong completely wrecks Loper establishment and moves to Levee." For an instant the enormity of his father's loss, and what it meant to the city, stopped him in his tracks. But he turned the page of his notepad and walked on: he had a job to do. He watched as only the businesses owned by colored people were sacked. When the crowd looted taverns they also swilled the contents of the bottles behind the bar. Chester Johnson's saloon, Dandy Jim's, where he had watched Mae Tully quaff beer, the Star Theater – the crowd shattered windows and splintered furniture as it made its way inexorably through the Levee.

Around him angry, shouting men ran past carrying guns, stones and pitchforks. Elliott's ears were assailed with the sound of shattering glass. He heard a voice, "Let's find 'em and get rid of 'em."

The crowd was turning north now, towards the Badlands, home to hundreds of colored Springfield residents and the location of Scott Burton's Tonsorial Parlor. Stumbling down the Madison Street railroad tracks in the wake of the crowd, Elliott noticed a red glow in the sky above a warehouse. His stomach sank as he saw the tips of flames over the top of the massive, dark building. They were torching the Badlands.

Fighting the urge to turn and run, Elliott headed down Madison Street as fast as he could. A fire engine caught up with him and passed him on the right. "Thank God" he muttered, running now, and clutching his bowler hat to keep it from blowing off in the hot night air.

The horses that drew the fire wagon were frightened by the flames and reared as the wagon approached what seemed to Elliott to be blocks of burning residences. He stopped and gazed in terror and awe as the small shanties erupted in flames. The firemen hurriedly unrolled a length of wide rubber hose attached to a large tank on the wagon. One of them fastened blinders to the horses so they could not see the flames.

As he watched the firemen, Elliott glimpsed a dark shape of the corner of his eye. Turning to see what was slinking through the yard across the street, he was just in time to see a Negro woman and three children hurrying into the alley. The children were wearing what appeared to be light cotton pajamas and were barefoot in the summer night. They disappeared down the alley, followed by other colored neighborhood residents, furtively rushing away from their homes. Some carried baskets or cardboard suitcases, while others, like the first family he saw, had apparently escaped with the clothes on their backs. He wondered where they would go.

Pulling his pencil from behind his ear to write some notes, Elliott glanced back at the fire wagon where two men where training the hose on a small house that was engulfed in flames. Suddenly, a group of about ten men, dirty and raucous, surrounded the wagon and one man grabbed an axe from the vehicle, waving it above his head. "You won't undo what we done," he yelled. Then, with one well-aimed swipe, he cut through the fire hose, spraying the crowd with water. At the other end of the useless hose, the firemen watched the house and its neighboring homes as the rampaging fire destroyed them.

"One o'clock, Badlands. Whole blocks of homes in flames. Crowd cuts through firemen's hoses." Elliott backed away from the heat, then noticed that the houses across the street, identical to those in flames, had not been touched. He walked cautiously across the street and noticed something white stuck to the top of the porch entryway. A white towel was wedged in the fancywork of the porch, large enough to be seen from the street. As he stared at the front window, a curtain moved almost imperceptibly. The face of a white man with a beard peered out. Elliott scribbled, "Houses owned by whites marked by cloths and spared by the mob."

Elliott walked down Ninth Street toward the newspaper office, fighting a rising tide of white men rushing north to see the spectacle. But he hadn't seen the worst. To his dismay, Elliott saw that the crowd, not content with destroying the homes of hundreds of Springfield Negroes, was assailing Scott Burton's business, where his family lived on the building's top floor. His heart sank as he saw the mob, several hundred strong, surrounding the barbershop's front door. Over their heads he spied the round, genial face of Scott Burton, and directly beneath it, a shotgun aimed at the crowd.

"Scott," Elliott cried, rushing forward. But before he could part the crowd, Scott had fired and one man fell to the ground, wounded in the upper arm. This was the excuse they had been waiting for, and four shots rang out. Burton slumped to the floor in the doorway of his shop.

"My God, what are you doing?" Elliott screamed, but no one seemed to hear. Two men at the front of the crowd grabbed Burton's lifeless body and pulled it into the street, then raised the gray-suited Scott aloft, his head lolling frighteningly backward. The burly miner pushed the body into the air. "We got a nigger! Let's string him up!"

Sweat streaming down the back of his neck, Elliott searched the windows of the residence above the barbershop for a sign of Ruby and the children, but no light or movement came from the upper story.

After dragging the body a few blocks north, the mob used a short rope to string up Scott's body from a tree in front of a saloon and then began to pepper it with shotgun rounds. After each round, the body swung madly from the tree trunk, a mangled black man in a grey suit, bearing no resemblance to Elliott's friend.

As Elliott watched the body recoil from shotgun fire, he remembered the last time he had seen Scott Burton, shaving a customer in his barbershop, and irrational fear for his own safety gripped him. He ran fast through the hot, dusty night, away from the reports of gunshots and duller thuds of rocks. Turning down an alley, Elliott stopped, pulled off his hat, and stooped with his hands on his knees, panting. It was so blessed hot, he thought, then he started, unable to breath, as he felt a hand touch his back.

He swung around, his fists raised in the only gesture of defense he could summon, but what he saw were not the rough faces of miners or laborers. Instead, he saw three colored children huddled together behind their mother, who was crouched under a ragged shawl. As she pulled it down, he saw the thin face of Ruby Burton. She was almost too afraid to choke out the words, and the sky in back of her grew red with flames.

"Mr. Loper? I reck'nized you from your hair." She beckoned the children closer and grasped the hand of the youngest. "We friend 'a Sheba's. 'Member us from the parade?"

Suddenly overcome, she pulled the shawl over her head and sobbed. "You gotta help us. If they find us..." The children crowded around her. The oldest girl looked up at Elliott with eyes as deep as two holes in the ground. "We gotta go somewheres safe, Daddy say so."

Elliott hadn't the faintest idea where to take them. Ruby stood and glanced over her shoulder. "We better go. No tellin' what they do if'n they sees us." Her voice trailed off

He put his arm around the woman's thin shoulders. "Come with me." An idea had appeared, seemingly out of nowhere. He would appeal to the charity of Mrs. Dana. Surely she would not turn away this poor mother and her children. They started down the alley toward downtown. "Come on. We're going to the Lawrence House."

As he followed the little family down the dark streets of Springfield in silence, Ruby chastised her oldest daughter "Tilda, mind you keep up." He watched a shadow moving across the lawn of the Governor's Mansion, looming to their left. He started when a tiger-striped cat darted from the bush and streaked down the street ahead of them and into the darkness. Elliott peered at the impressive bulk of the mansion, but though the shouts and gunfire of the mob could be heard to the north in the Badlands, no light pierced the windows of the home of the Governor of Illinois.

He walked behind Ruby and the children to be sure that they were not accosted. The mob appeared to be contained to the Badlands, at least for now, but he was worried about the Burtons; the children seemed especially pitiful to him. Tilda seemed determined to assure herself that Scott would join them. "Pa'll come too, won't he? You find him and bring him too."

Her mother stopped and put her arm around the girl's shoulders. "I guess he'll do best he kin to tell your pa where we be." She stopped and waited for Elliott to catch up with their small group. Her tattered shawl was around her shoulders now, and she gripped it tightly, even though the night was stiflingly hot. Elliott realized it was almost two o'clock and wondered who, if anyone, would answer the door at the Lawrence House.

"That rich lady, she hide us, won't she?" Ruby grasped the hand of the little boy to help him catch up with Tilda and the middle boy who were walking ahead. In front of the little band, across Fourth Street, loomed the long, low roof of their hoped-for refuge, the Lawrence House.

"Oh yes, of course," Elliott responded, trying to make his voice deep and commanding. The summer night was hazy and no light emanated from the interior of the huge house, but Elliott remembered how it looked with sunlight gleaming from the red tile roof, playing on the upturned tips of the eaves making the house look faintly Japanese. Rather than risk discovery by ringing the bell at the arched front door, he led the Burtons along Lawrence Avenue.

As they skirted the house, it crossed his mind for the first time that the house might be empty or worse, they might be turned away. As he headed down the alley, flanked by the house's garden wall on the right and the Union Pacific Railroad tracks to the left, he considered the alternatives. There was always the train, he supposed. Possibly he could slip the little family on the southbound as it passed the house. But first, he'd try to appeal to Mrs. Dana's sympathies.

"Come on. We need to stay together." Elliott beckoned to the straggling children, then summoned his courage and knocked on the worn wooden door to the carriage house, which stood across the garden and to the rear of the house. Elliott was counting on Thomas hearing the knock. Immediately the window on the floor above them squeaked open.

"Who's there?" It was Thomas, his voice wavering with fear.

"It's Elliott Loper and Scott Burton's wife and children. Please let us in. They're in danger." Elliott craned his neck to see if Thomas had leaned out the window, but could see nothing in the darkness.

"Daddy's comin' too," Roscoe chimed in from behind Ruby, who hurriedly shushed him.

There was no sound from the window above and Elliott stopped breathing to listen. Then, before he had time to panic, the wooden door scraped open and he stood face-to-face with Thomas.

"Thank God," Elliott exclaimed as he pushed Ruby and the children inside, then stepped into the close, horse-scented carriage house. Two horses stood, swishing their tails in stalls to the rear of the building, while a four-seated carriage and smaller buggy dominated the floor in the center of the large room. A ladder to the left led up to an open hole in the ceiling where Thomas had his sleeping quarters.

Once inside, Elliott turned to face Thomas, who clearly had not been asleep. Fear showed on his regular features, but he crossed his arms and spoke belligerently to Elliott. "What you want? Ain't you got some big story t'write? Guess a swell reporter like you don't have time for these po'folk." He glared at Elliott.

131

There were bigger things at stake here than the unstated rivalry between them for Sheba's affections. Elliott knew Thomas thought he was taking unfair advantage of his friendship with Sheba. After all, he was a white man and she was a Negro whom he had helped. He could see how that must look to Thomas, to the rest of the world. But that situation had nothing do with tonight's dilemma, Elliott reasoned. "You need to hide these folks. They'll never think to look here." He found himself pleading with Thomas, who walked across the room to the door that led to the enclosed garden, motioning for the group to follow.

As he led them away, Thomas remarked over his shoulder. "Oh, they be lookin' all right. They know'd I live here, least I used to." He beckoned to Ruby and the children. "But I come back t'night. I ain't never seen the like a what's goin' on downtown. But they be all right in the big house."

So they could stay at the Lawrence House, that was a relief, but even as he sighed, Elliott realized with a start that he had missed his deadline and the opportunity for a front page story on the riot. Maybe there was still time to file a story for a later edition. He turned to Thomas. They faced each other in the dark carriage house, while the Burtons waited in the courtyard beyond. "I have to get back to the paper. You'll see that they're safe. I trust Mrs. Dana will let them stay."

Thomas turned through the door, motioning the little group into the courtyard. "Well, she ain't here right now. She's travelin' with Miss Flora. But I guess they can stay here a spell." Then he turned and muttered "But don' you come 'round here 'gin." He fixed Elliott with his dark eyes.

Elliott stared back at Thomas, unafraid. "Just make sure that the Burtons are safe. And don't let them find out that Scott's been lynched. It's too awful – they can't hear it now."

Thomas' jaw dropped and he stared in disbelief. "Wha' you say, that Mr. Scott Burton's dead? It ain't true." He grasped Elliott by his sleeve, but the young man shook him free. He had to get back and the sad truth was that no amount of conversation with Thomas would bring Scott back.

"He's dead all right, the mob, they shot him in his own barbershop, then they dragged him down the street and hung him," Elliott said, shaking his head to rid it of the persistent vision of Scott Burton's body thudding against the tree. "Now, I have to go," he shouted, and turning on his heel, he began running down the alley towards the offices of the *Register*.

132

Refuge

Awakened by the shattering window of her dressmaking shop, Sheba was momentarily confused. Then her mind sped back to the events of the day before – Kate Howard's threat, the cautionary visit from Pastor and Mrs. Ball, the oppressive silence of the airless streets of downtown. She was not sure exactly what had happened, but sure, from the menacing shouts of the crowd, that she was in danger. She paused and listened before descending the steps from her darkened sleeping room, but she could hear the crowd only faintly in the distance. Shots were still being fired, so she wrapped a few belongings in a shawl and fled to the Lawrence House. Her journey through the murderous streets of downtown Springfield was mercifully brief as she scurried down murky alleys and across shadowy yards, away from the torchlight, the sounds of gunfire.

At last she reached the long expanse of Fourth Street and the spacious lawns of Aristocracy Hill. There were lights in some of the houses and she glimpsed figures at the upstairs windows. Behind her, she heard footsteps on the grass, and she instinctively jumped for a nearby clump of bushes, cowering as the dark group of people, some women and children carrying parcels passed. Although the group was a colored family and posed no threat to Sheba, she waited until they were gone before leaving the shelter of the bushes. She couldn't take any chances – not this close to possible safety. The Lawrence House loomed dark against the black sky. It must be after midnight, she guessed.

As she walked toward the arched door, she saw light streaming through the windows above, windows she had cleaned many times. She gathered her courage and thought of a scripture often quoted by Pastor Ball: "Take unto you the whole armor of God, that ye may be able to withstand in the evil day, and having done all, to stand."

She knocked, then, hearing no response, began pounding on the heavy wooden door with her fists. "Please, lemme in. Please help me." She looked over her shoulder. Perhaps the rioters would find her and would see that she was colored. At that moment, her only hope of survival seemed to be attaining the safety of the Lawrence House.

Wondering if anyone could see her, she stepped back from the doorway arch, glimpsing movement above through the elongated windows that opened onto one of the musicians' balconies. "Who's that?" A woman's voice called down softly.

"Sheba. It Sheba. 'member me? Please lemme in." She whimpered, cowering in the bushes next to the long walkway that led to the gallery.

The figure in the window disappeared. Sheba looked northward, the sky still crimson from the burning buildings in the Badlands. Then she noticed an odd phenomenon: instead of colored people fleeing downtown and the Badlands, she saw white men and boys, even some women, making their way in groups toward downtown.

"Mind you hurry, Jimmy. We don't want to miss the hangin'. And they said there's lots of houses still burning." A man urged his young son to a trot along Fourth Street as Maud peered out the front door of the Lawrence House. Sheba rushed to the door, and the cook opened it just wide enough to admit her slender frame. Sheba slid through and the heavy door slammed shut behind her. Feeling that she had been saved, she flung her arms around the startled older woman.

"God bless you, Maud, I never was so 'fraid in all my life. They drivin' all us colored folks out and burnin' ever'thin'." Quickly, Maud hurried her up the steps toward the safety and obscurity of the kitchen. The rest of the house, with its many windows facing the streets, might exhibit too much to the angry city.

When they reached the kitchen, Maud broke her silence and began to question Sheba. "So there's a big riot goin' on. It figures. We seen all these folks comin' by and then saw the sky get all red, so's there's a fire somewhere. But with the missus' gone and only Albert here to protect us, we none of us wanted to get out and see what was goin' on."

In the light of the kitchen, Hattie dozed at the table. Sheba shook her shoulder and she started awake, yelped in surprise, then enclosed Sheba in a hug. "Oh child, it good you come here. We so scared you was run out of town or strung up somewhere." She stopped, looking at Maud with suspicion, as if she couldn't trust any white person, then continued. "Child, you gonna be so pleased when you see that boy Thomas done come back too. Yes, he did, and now he's hidin' out to the carriage house." Hattie glanced around the bright kitchen, then listened in silence to the gunshots outside. "We gotta get you hid, girl. I ain't so worried 'bout me, but you, they might be lookin' for you, cause you're a shopkeeper and all." She grasped Sheba by her shoulders and marched her toward the cellar door. "You go on down there and stay hid till we say it's safe," Hattie ordered.

"Well, alright, but only till it safe," she said, obediently descending the wooden plank stairs into the cool depths of the cellar. The cellar was one room stretching the length of the kitchen. In the gloom, sheets hung like ghosts from clotheslines that spanned the far end of the room. Beneath the room's one window, a narrow opening near the ceiling, the ceramic basin of a white wringer washer shone. Lit by the eerie glow of the Badlands fire, the room bore little resemblance to the laundry room she remembered. She knew this room well after spending hours washing, bleaching, rinsing, wringing and hanging out Mrs. Dana's sheets, pillowcases, and undergarments.

She knew that the best place to hide was in back of the washer, since she had done so frequently when Hattie came looking for help with the dusting, a chore she despised. So she crawled into this snug enclosure, remembering that Hattie could never find her there, as the upstairs door closed and the room was blanketed in silence. Seated cross-legged on the floor, Sheba thought the cries of the rioters were moving closer, and she crouched lower. She was comforted by the realization that the spot was directly under the window, impossible to see from the outside. She leaned against the cellar wall, aching for some of its coolness to penetrate her skin and felt a sob working its way up from deep inside her. She swallowed and summoned up the familiar words of the Twenty-Third Psalm: "Yea, though I walk through the valley of the shadow of death, I will fear no evil, for thou art with me."

The sheets on the line seemed to move in a nonexistent breeze, and Sheba looked away. If she couldn't pray for herself, perhaps someone else could use her prayers. Eva Monroe, Scott and Lydia Burton, Pastor and Mrs. Ball... they were all the wrong color for this night in the city of Lincoln. "God, protect them with your mighty hand..." Pressing her face against the back of the washer's cool ceramic basin, the girl started as she heard boots on the floor overhead and voices. She made herself small, curled in a ball against the wall and stopped breathing as light slashed through the darkness from the doorway at the top of the stairs.

A man's voice pierced the silence. "Sheba, you down there?" She froze. It was too risky to cry out, although she was uncertain whether she was more afraid to be discovered or stay hidden. If only she knew to whom the voice belonged.

Boots clomped down the stairs and Sheba curled lower behind the washer. It was possible that the man would spot her.

"Come on girl, Hattie say you down here. I don't mean you no harm." The voice came nearer and narrow brown eyes peered into her hiding place. Thomas.

"Com'n up, you all right. I brung Scott Burton's family here and they need to see you real bad," Thomas said as he pulled Sheba to her feet. She stretched her length, feeling her flexibility return and overjoyed that Ruby and Scott were safe. She rushed past Thomas and up the steps, taking them two at a time.

There in the bright kitchen with Hattie stood Ruby Burton, her head draped in a blue shawl, which she pulled from her matted hair. The children huddled around their mother, silent and watchful.

"Ruby, you are a sight for sore eyes." Sheba cried as she pulled Ruby to her, examining her haggard face.

Ruby leaned her head against Sheba's shoulder and sighed, "I like t'never thought I see you here. It an awful night for colored folks."

From the corner of the kitchen came Hattie's voice. "Where your man, Ruby?"

Ruby looked up from Sheba's shoulder. "He stay back, wasn't gonna leave the house. I jus' hope he's all right." Ruby patted her little boy, who was now asleep in her arms. The two older children were quiet; it had been a long night and was nearing dawn.

Hattie shook her head. "I wishin' he be here too. It a bad, bad night for us'n." She moaned and sat down.

Meanwhile, Thomas had followed Sheba up the stairs and was regarding her warily. "What you doin' here, anyways? I thought you had a fine business downtown."

Sheba turned from Ruby. Thomas was thinner, but seemed older. His eyes contemplated her calmly and she noticed a new definition to his arms and shoulders, as if he had been doing heavy work.

"I got my own shop, or leastways I did. 'Member I tol' you I was gonna? But it got ruined, got a brick thru the front winda," she said, glaring at Thomas. "If you don' know, they burnin' the Levee an' they after us coloreds. This the only place they might not look."

Thomas sat down on the kitchen table and avoided meeting Sheba's eyes, then began to explain. "Well, I come here t'night too. I been workin' back t'the ice house. They give me a job 'cause I worked there before, even though it a long time ago. But when they starts burnin' houses where I'm livin' in the Badlands, well, I figured I better high tail it outta' there. So I come here." He sighed, and turned toward Maud. "This ol' lady here, she let me in." Maud looked fondly at Thomas, then regained her frosty demeanor.

Sheba still couldn't see how Thomas had ended up with the Burtons. "But how you come to be findin' Miz Burton and the children? They just turn up by the traintracks?"

Thomas looked at Sheba with resignation. "Not 'xactly. See your friend, that Mr. High 'n Mighty Loper, he come by and they with him. He done asked real nice like if they could come in. Don' have no idea how he got 'em."

Ruby and Hattie began herding the children to the cellar where it was hoped they would be safe. Sheba could hear commotion as beds were made up near the stairs. Thomas' mention of Elliott Loper brought back pleasant memories to Sheba, exhausted as she was. He was somethin', that man. Look at what he'd done for Ruby Burton and her children. But she had to wonder about Scott.

"Where those chillen's daddy go?" Sheba touched Thomas' hand as it lay on the table and he looked into her eyes. Maud had left the kitchen and they were alone. He glanced toward the basement door then whispered, "He dead. They done hung him dead, that's what Loper said. Mr. Scott Burton, he gone." Thomas choked, then was silent.

Sheba closed her eyes. Scott Burton, the brave and good soul who she had held up as an example of a successful colored businessman. Scott, whose wife

136

and children, unknowing, slept in the cellar of this house, under their feet. Scott, dead, dead in a manner she was afraid to picture in her mind.

The comment of the father to the boy from earlier that evening came back to her. "Mind you hurry, Jimmy. We don't want to miss the hangin'..." It all made sense now. It was Scott Burton's hanging they didn't want to miss.

She wasn't sure how long they sat at the kitchen table, but it suddenly seemed right to her to ask for help, to pray. She reached out and grasped Thomas' sinewy hand and began to whisper, over and over, "Protect us sweet Jesus, protect us sweet Jesus." Slowly, imperceptibly, the tensions of the day drained from her. She opened her eyes: Thomas was watching her, questioning, admiring, doubting -- she wasn't sure which.

As morning came and the sky began to lighten, he rose from his seat. "I gonna' get some rest. You better too. I'm goin' on out t'th carriage house."

As she walked with Thomas to the kitchen door, the rosy dawn light picked out the leaves on the hollyhocks along the courtyard walls. A long, low whistle sounded in the distance, then the train tracks on the other side of the garden wall began to rumble ever slightly. As the train drew near, the tracks shook and clatter, then, with a rush, the coal-belching mountain of steel engine surged past, a line of cars in its wake. Both Sheba and Thomas stood silently as the train passed, snorting smoke and bellowing, the whistle sounding again and again. As they stood so, inches apart in the courtyard, Sheba could feel Thomas' labored, hot breath on her face and see the whites of his eyes in the dawn.

Thomas grasped her hand and she did not withdraw it. He bowed his head. "My friend Jack, he on that train, ridin' a box car to St. Louie."

Sheba's eyes widened. He could have gone south too, but he chose to stay in Springfield, where danger floated in the air if you were a Negro. Then she realized that somehow, she cared about what happened to Thomas. She reached up to touch his cheek and he closed his eyes and kissed the palm of her hand.

She knew he would follow Jack to St. Louis, it was just a matter of time, and she wanted more than anything for him to stay. "Listen Thomas, don' go. Maybe we be all right. Maybe all this killin' and hurtin' is over."

He shook his head. "I don't think so. It ain't over by a far piece. It probly never gonna be over." He had dropped her hand and started across the yard toward the carriage house. "I gotta get me some sleep."

She let him go and turned to mount the porch steps. The newsboys were out, hawking papers on the corner of Lawrence and Fourth Streets.

"Extra, extra. State Militia Called to End Reign of Terror in Springfield. Loper's Restaurant Destroyed. The Dead, The Dying, The Injured. Read all about it," the newsboys shouted. Sheba listened for a minute until Thomas disappeared inside the carriage house, then turned and went inside.

Secrets

Sheba awoke the next morning to sunlight flooding in the west window of the bedroom where she had slept so often. She realized it must be late, but didn't want to bother wondering why she'd been allowed to lie abed. Instead she rolled over onto her side, away from the window. Staring at the closet door through half open eyes, she began to feel that something was wrong. She didn't belong here. Her place to sleep was in the room above her shop. Her bed had a blue bedspread and there was a picture of Jesus knocking at a door hanging above it. Her shop had gilt lettering on the glass and a bell on the door that rang when someone came in, as Hattie did now.

"Sheba, you 'wake?" Hattie called. She sat straight up in bed as Hattie peered through the doorway. At the sight of Hattie, downcast and somber, Sheba sat up reluctantly. The sheet fell to the bed and she looked down, noticing for the first time that she was still wearing the calico dress she had pulled on in her sleeping room. It seemed to have happened to someone else, the wrecked shop, the flight through the nighttime streets, the flames rising into the night sky.

"They askin' for you, them Burtons. Think you kin tell 'em what to do, 'n where their pa is. You better come on down." Hattie vanished, and Sheba tried to make herself presentable. She had no idea what to tell the Burtons, but she knew Elliott had not wanted them to know about Scott's murder at the hands of the mob. Of course, they would find out soon enough, probably it was all over the newspapers. It was only because the ladies of the house were gone that there was no newspaper on the kitchen table already.

The ladies of the house. The thought that they might be returning, especially when they heard about the turmoil in Springfield, was enough to strike fear into Sheba's heart. Not that she was concerned about Mrs. Dana's reaction to her presence – she knew her former mistress well enough to be sure she was welcome. Her main worry was for Ruby Burton and her children. She was certain that they were not safe anywhere in Springfield. The rioters knew Scott was a successful Negro businessman and that was enough to place his family in peril. Someone would discover their whereabouts and string them up, just as Scott had been strung up the night before.

As she descended the stairs into the kitchen, Sheba pasted a smile on her face and summoned up the most cheerful tone she could. "Well, how you sleep?" she asked the Burton children, who were perched on chairs around the kitchen table. Tilda leaned her head on her hands as she picked at some eggs. Roscoe had given up any attempt at eating and pushed back his plate untouched, closed his eyes, and collapsed onto his folded arms. Urging James to have yet another slice of toast, Sheba met Ruby's worried eyes.

"I shoul'a let 'em sleep, but blamed if I kin. I gotta see what's goin' on," Ruby explained, nodding towards the Fourth Street side of the house. In response, Sheba walked out the door of the butler's pantry, through the empty dining room and onto the side porch, which afforded a view of Fourth Street, as well as the neighbor's yard. It must have been getting on towards noon, and the trees cast short shadows on the green lawns. Sheba almost ducked down below the walls of the porch when she saw what was going on. There in the middle of Fourth Street was a file of uniformed men wearing khaki and badges. Men carrying guns. The men marched in lock step down the center of the vacant street towards downtown. A small boy on the porch of the gabled house across the street jumped up and down and cried, "Hey Mr. Soldier, can you guard my house?" The soldiers ignored the child and continued their progress down the street.

Mystified, Sheba returned to the kitchen. Ruby pulled Sheba out the door through which she had come, into the half-dark coolness of the dining room, with its long, shining table and tall, slate-backed chairs.

Ruby didn't let go of her arm and Sheba winced with the pain of her grip. "You see them soldiers? Somethin' real bad happen last night an' it ain't over yet," Ruby muttered, pulling Sheba close, searching her features. She breathed a question. "Tell me straight. Is Scott comin'? I b'lieve you know." She released Sheba, who, suddenly weary, pulled back a dining room chair and sat down. As she sank into its upholstered seat, her senses registered slight discomfort: it was the first time she had sat in a dining room chair.

"I tellin' you true 'coos you my friend. I don' wanna hurt you, but you better know the truth," Sheba said, looking at Ruby, who had leaned to grasp the table for support. Sheba breathed in, then continued, "They kilt Scott, hung him dead. He ain't comin' back. That what Mr. Loper tol' Thomas, so's it mus' be true. I so sorry Ruby. Scott was suc' a good man."

Wordless, Ruby dropped to the red Oriental carpeting. Curled on the floor with her head cradled in her folded arms, she seemed impossibly small and defenseless. "No, no, no," she moaned, rocking back and forth, a tiny mound of sorrow on the rich carpet. Sheba grasped her small, boney shoulders as Ruby continued her moans. "Oh Scott, you can' be dead," she cried and raised her wet face to implore Sheba. "Why ever'body liked Scott. Nobody want to kill him. That Mr. Loper, he done made a mistake."

Sheba wished there was a shadow of a doubt, but she knew in her heart that Scott was gone. Elliott would never risk this heartbreak on a guess. "Oh, I wis't were't, but Mr. Loper, he a newsman. He don' get things wrong," she cried and stroked Ruby's hair. "An' this here's the truth, those hateful white folks kilt Scott. For nothin', for no reason than he's colored," she exclaimed. It was as if Sheba had slapped Ruby on the face. The small woman recoiled, then fell back onto the carpet, wailing.

It tore at Sheba's heart to see Ruby so devastated by the reality of Scott's death -- or murder, or lynching. Sheba's stomach turned over and she retched, leaning over in the chair. Then she noticed the swinging door to the dining room crack a bit. Fearful that the children would see their mother prostrate with grief, Sheba jumped to her feet, then spied Maud's haggard face peering through the crack.

"Don' let them chillen in," she said, rushing over to the door. "They caint see they mama like this."

Maud surveyed Ruby with disdain. "What's the matter with her? Those little darkies in the kitchen are askin' for her," she sneered, then turned to Sheba, her hands on her hips. "And I ain't watchin' them. Not with all this commotion outside. Fact I don't reckon you all niggers should be up where folks can see you," she finished, staring at Sheba with open resentment.

Sheba turned to glare into Maud's faded eyes but stopped herself short. She needed this white woman now and had to retain her goodwill, even at the cost of her pride. Sheba glanced out the window, toward the street where she knew the soldiers patrolled. She hazarded a question. "What all them soldiers here for?"

Maud seemed pleased that she had more knowledge of current events than Sheba. "There was a big riot last night – guess you knew that. Well, the governor called out the National Guard to stop it. That's them, marching up and down the streets."

Sheba reached down to caress Ruby as her shoulders shook, then asked Maud a question. "The National Guard. They here to keep us colored folks safe?"

Maud laughed, "Not likely. They're here to keep order. You niggers is supposed to go to the Arsenal if you wanna be safe." She nodded at Ruby, who finally had fallen silent, her face still pressed into the carpet. "The Governor's got the militia guardin' there. That girl, she oughta' go there and take those little pickaninnies with her," Maud said, shooting Sheba a menacing look and retreating to the kitchen.

Ruby climbed to her feet, grasping the seat of one of the angular chairs for support. Sheba leaned over to help her friend and found her as light as a bird. Ruby gazed at her. Sheba knew she was in shock. It might be days before she could function again. In the face of Maud's animosity, she could hardly offer them refuge here, where she herself was an outsider now.

Sheba sat wearily in the fine chair and watched the sunlight dance through the amber sumac art glass windows. Though it was midday, no children's voices sounded from the neighboring lawns. In the distance she heard the sharp report of hammers, and the voices of men shouting orders. As she sat, praying for strength, a faint whistle sounded, and then the racket of the train approached. A roar rose, such a familiar sound after living for years next to the railroad tracks. But now, as the clatter grew louder, Sheba jumped to her feet.

"The train, Ruby, that's where you kin go. You kin take the train to St. Louie," she exclaimed. She turned, face aglow, to the tiny woman beside her, staring into space. Hoping to rouse her, she grasped Ruby by the shoulders and pulled her close. Sheba continued, "Ruby, you understan'? You all'd be safe in St. Louie. You got any kin there? Friends? Church folk?"

Ruby seemed to waken from the spell. "Well, my ol' aunt Jane be there – she my mama's sister. I reckon she could put us up, till, till..." she faltered, then broke down again, bending her head over the shining table. Ruby looked nothing like the fine lady she had been, only a month ago, when they had turned out in style for the Independence Day parade.

"Oh child, you ain't goin' no place yet. You stay here jus' now," Sheba said soothingly. But she knew that time was short. After what she had seen and heard last night, after Scott's horrific murder, she doubted they could be safe anywhere in Springfield. Then an image of Miss Eva, smiling, came unbidden into her mind. She could see the small woman's dark-brown face and flashing white smile. "But if you think God's tellin' you to go out on your own, you do it. I'll help you any way I can," Miss Eva had said that sunny day that seemed so long ago now. Miss Eva would never leave this city, where so many children needed her, where the spirit of Lincoln still walked.

While she was pondering her next step, Thomas came into the room, unnoticed by either woman, both lost in grief and fear. He placed his hand on Ruby's gingham-clad shoulder. "Miz Burton, your little ones be needin' you," he said. Ruby looked up into the young man's solemn features, rose without a word, and went noiselessly through the swinging door. Thomas addressed Sheba, voice full of concern. "How you farin'?" he asked, his voice almost a whisper. Thomas opened his arms and Sheba went into them, leaning on his broad chest. She shut her eyes and felt, for a moment, safe. "It alright," he murmured and his lips brushed her hair. Then Sheba pushed herself free and Thomas, startled, stepped back.

"It ain't though. It ain't ever gonna be right neither. Scott Burton's dead, strung up by folks like we see ever' day. Ain't no tellin' what they gonna do tonight, ma'be after they get some lickker in 'em." Sheba began pacing the room between Thomas and the breakfast nook.

Thomas watched her pace, then answered, "Sheba, you best watch yo'self. If a body had a mind, why they'd look right in that window and see a colored woman, out in broad daylight."

She whirled on him and shouted, "What's wrong wit'a colored woman out in th'light? I don't see that we any dif'rent from those folks walkin' down that street." She pointed to a group of white men and women with a few children in tow, walking down Fourth Street toward downtown. They were dressed for a holiday and a couple of the men carried Brownie cameras. Sheba wondered what they were going to see this summer Saturday.

Thomas shifted from foot to foot, staring at his boots. "You right Sheba, but that don' change what happen last night," he muttered. She took his hand and walked with him back across the dining room and into the kitchen, where the Burtons huddled around the table.

Smiling, Sheba addressed the group. "You all, tomorrow you goin' on a train trip. How 'bout that?" She rubbed James' close-cut hair, then sat down at the table to plot their trip south. Tilda listened, rapt, but Roscoe spoke up.

"Don' forget Pa. We gotta make sure he kin find us if we go to St. Louie? He be here by tomorrow when we go?" Roscoe asked, his face full of questions.

Sheba avoided Ruby's eyes as she answered. "Don' worry 'bout yo' pa. He'll know where you go and he be so glad you safe."

The child accepted the explanation without question, then jumped from his chair. "Kin we go 'side 'nd play? Ain't no fun settin' in here all day like an ol' lady."

Thomas shot to his feet and grabbed the boy. "You lookin' fo' some fun, Mr. Roscoe? I show you some. You kin come wit' me, we gonna' groom us some horses." Thomas crowed as he guided Roscoe out the back door. He shot back over his shoulder to Sheba. "Don' you worry none, we be in the carriage house." As Thomas departed, she remembered the warmth and comfort of his embrace in the dining room. If only she could always feel that safe.

Hattie blustered into the room, full of noise. "What we gonna do, tha's what I wanna know. You oughta' hear what they sayin' on the streets, what those white folks is up to next. This ain't over, not by a long shot."

Sheba looked at the young Burton girl, Tilda, who was staring at Hattie, "Little pitchers got big ears," she said, but Hattie continued as if Tilda was invisible.

"Albert, he come from the hardware store and don' he have a tale to tell. Oh land. He say they out to get Mr. Donnegan -- that kind ol' man. He say they done bought some clothesline rope and be talkin' 'bout stringin' him up," Hattie blustered.

At this moment, Albert himself entered the room. Usually taciturn, Maud's husband seemed distraught. He blurted out, "You all'd better not be found here, or we'll all be hangin'. That crowd at Payne's Hardware, they're out for blood. You niggers better get out of here." Albert shared his wife's scorn of Negroes, Sheba knew. But she also was aware of Albert's status as a hired man and not a particular favorite of Mrs. Dana. So she gambled, hoping that if confronted he would back down, as most cowards do.

"You got no cause to say that," she cried, then turned and pushed Tilda and James through the cellar door. "You chillin go down there whiles we talk," Sheba said, slamming the door shut on the two children, while their mother continued in her catatonic state at the kitchen table.

"I got every cause to say it," Albert said, looking hard at Sheba, his narrow blue eyes boring into her face.

"I don' think you do. If Miz Dana was here, she'd never turn us out. And if she find out you did, you 'n yo' cold wife be gone," she snarled. The image of

142

Albert, standing in the kitchen in his blue work shirt, doubled and she grasped the table for support.

He hadn't noticed her momentary weakness and sneered, "But she ain't here. She's over in Europe or some such place and won't be back for months. You and this colored family just drawin' that crowd on. If they goin' for Will Donnegan, they likely come right by here. He don't live but a couple blocks away. I say you're out, and the sooner the better."

At the table, Ruby moaned. Her head wavered, then she put her hand to her face and looked around as if waking from a long nap. She addressed Albert sharply. "Why you wicked man. You givin' three fatherless chillen to a lynch mob?"

A shriek erupted from behind the cellar door and Sheba realized that Tilda had heard every word of their argument. It was pointless to keep them out, so she swung the heavy door open and Tilda fell into the room. Behind her, oblivious to the drama unfolding in the kitchen, two-year-old James was occupied with rolling pebbles down the basement steps.

Tilda rushed to her mother, braids flying behind her. "Mama! Mama! What you call us 'fatherless' chillin?"

Ruby enveloped her daughter in a hug. "Your pa's gone, darlin'. He gone to heaven wit' God. But he watchin' over us 'n won' let his darlin' get hurt."

James clamored around his mother, with little reaction to the news that he had only one parent. Tilda sobbed incessantly into her mother's skirt.

Albert stood in center of the room, speechless, as Maud entered from the dining room with an envelope in her hand. She stared at it with consternation. "A delivery boy just brought this here telegram." Maud looked up at Sheba and she remembered that Maud could not read.

Sheba held out her hand and Maud surrendered the envelope without protest. Sheba sat down at the kitchen table and slit the top of the envelope open, then unfolded the paper inside. Maud moved to stand behind her. As she squinted at the paper, trying to piece together the words typed on it, she recalled an afternoon in July when she had paid a visit on the Donnegans. The old man had sat, much in the same position as she sat now, squinting at a child's primer while his wife stood behind him, encouraging. Mr. Donnegan had not made much progress with the reading in the time she had been working with him, but she enjoyed seeing his pride with each mastered word and phrase.

The telegram swam into focus and she paused after each word as she read aloud. "Have news of riot. Protect Lawrence House at all costs. Will return post-haste from Boston. Susan Lawrence Dana."

Mrs. Dana was coming back, and she had not left the country yet. Sheba knew she had friends that she stayed with in Boston and it was a bit of fortune that she sojourned with them a few days before her voyage to Europe. All would be safe then, Sheba was sure. Not even a rioting mob would dare enter the home of Mrs. Dana with the great lady in residence. She raised her eyes to meet Albert's and gave him a hint of a smile. "She be home soon, so's you better not put us out."

Unable to think of a retort, Albert left the room, almost bumping into Thomas as he sauntered in the back door with Roscoe on his heels. He called out, "What the matter wit the ol' man? Gone loony?" Thomas laughed, then noticed the solemn faces around the room.

Tilda, silent until now, began to tremble as she spoke. "Pa, he got killed 'n he gone with God. An' that mean ol' man gonna' put us out on the streets." Exhausted at this long litany, she jumped up from the table and ran down the cellar stairs.

The late afternoon sun slanted into the kitchen, and Sheba closed her eyes to block it out. She could hear Maud telling Thomas what her husband had heard at the hardware store. "They say they're goin' to the Arsenal to get all the colored folks, then they're goin' to string up Will Donnegan. That's what Albert said he heard at Payne's," Maud explained.

Thomas replied, "That jus' plain foolish. Nobody in they right mind be doin' crazy things like that wit' all them soldiers ever'where." Sheba opened her eyes to see Thomas smiling at her. She smiled back, before she remembered the danger they all were in, especially with darkness coming in a few hours.

Far away, at the front of the house, a doorbell rang. Grasping Sheba's hand, Thomas pulled her to her feet, then pushed at Ruby's arm. "Cm'on. We gotta' go t' th' cellar." Snatching up James from the floor, Sheba followed Thomas, Roscoe and Ruby to the cellar. She wasn't sure where Hattie was, but since she belonged with the house, perhaps she was safe.

Downstairs, Tilda whimpered facedown on the makeshift bed in the half-darkness of the laundry room while the rest of the group huddled in the darkness. She had to do something to dispel the fear that pervaded the room. "I think we need to ask God for His protection," she said, as she felt Thomas' hand coming to rest gently in the small of her back. "Oh God, we are sore afraid, but we know you love us and you will protect us. Cast your loving arms around us, oh Lord. Clasp us to your bosom. Sweet Jesus, keep us safe. Have mercy, have mercy."

The cellar door squeaked open and Maud called down. "You all can come up. It's only that fella from the newspaper. He's been here before. That Mr. Loper."

Sheba sprang to her feet and raced up the steps, overcome with an unaccountable feeling of relief. Bursting from the darkness of the cellar, she stopped short. Elliott Loper stood in the center of the kitchen. He stammered, "Thank God you're all right. I thought... I thought..." The unflappable reporter was at a complete loss for words. He stood motionless in the slanting sunlight next to the old oak kitchen table with its red checked tablecloth and stared at Sheba.

Without turning, Sheba could feel Thomas' warm breath and solid presence inches from her back. He spoke. "What you doin' here?"

Elliott hurried to answer Thomas. "I came to see that all of you were all right. You colored folks I mean," he said, grasping his bowler hat by the brim and squeezing it. "See, there's a mob goin' to the Arsenal and then they're going to Donnegan's. I heard them talking, the mob I mean. It's far from over and you mustn't go out. It's too dangerous," he added.

Thomas stepped in front of Sheba, who stood at the top of the cellar stairs, unsure whether to advance or retreat. "We ain't goin' out. Fact is, we hidin' here in the cellar till we kin go back where we b'long," he said solidly.

Elliott took a step toward the couple on the stairs, but looked only at Sheba. "I saw your shop last night and it's ruined. You can't go back. They knew it was a colored business," he said, his eyes locked on hers.

Thomas answered before Sheba could. "She ain't goin' back there. Miz Dana's comin' back quick's she kin. She let us stay here as long as we want."

Sheba pushed Thomas aside and stood face-to-face with the perspiring Elliott. "That ain't right," she said, contradicting Thomas. "I be goin' back soon's it safe. But I reckon that won't be for awhile, judgin' from the news," she added, looking down and feeling suddenly shy.

Meanwhile, Ruby had crept up the stairs. Holding a whimpering James, with Tilda and Roscoe hanging onto her torn skirt, she glanced at Elliott Loper, then a look of recognition came into her face and she flung herself, toddler and all, at the reporter.

"Oh, Mr. Loper, we be so thankful to you. Why, if you hain't been so kind, we all be dead, jus' like, jus' like…" she stopped. "Did you see my po' Scott when they strung him up?" Ruby asked, searching Elliott's face.

Elliott nodded. "Ma'am, I did see the murder, yes, though I wish to God I'd never witnessed it. It will forever be burned in my mind." He continued telling her the story she seemed to yearn to hear. "He was brutally murdered by that crowd of thieves, for no reason other than he was colored. Nobody respected your husband more than I did. Believe me, his death at the hands of that mob will be avenged." As the setting sun hit Elliott's pale blue eyes, he squinted, temporarily blinded, then seemed to come back to himself. He looked at the little family, clustered around Ruby's wan figure, and said, "Look here, you've got to go down to the cellar right away. They're coming, they're coming."

As if in reply, sounds of cries a few blocks away rent the air and, as of one accord, the Negroes rushed down the cellar stairs. Sheba held back, and as Elliott turned to leave the kitchen, she spoke. "Where you goin'? Your pa's restaurant and car, they ruined. You ain't safe," she said.

Elliott moved closer. "I'm going to Donnegans. I have to see if I can make things right, or at least warn them. Old Man Donnegan's married to a white woman and he's well-off. Those two things make him a sure target. And they're out for blood, Negro blood," he whispered.

A shudder ran through Sheba and she went cold with fear in the ninety-degree heat. A mob a hundred-strong that would go after a harmless old man seemed hopelessly evil. "You a good man. God keep you safe," she said, and looked into his eyes.

He reached out, as if to touch her hand.

"Sheba, come quick," Thomas shouted from the top of the cellar steps.

Elliott snatched his hand back. "Yes, go where you're safe, with Thomas." He pulled his notebook from the pocket of his suit jacket, and clutching his hat under his arm, left the room.

With a sigh, Sheba allowed Thomas to put his arm around her shoulder as they both descended into the gloom of the cellar.

Will Donnegan

To avoid being spied by passersby, Elliott departed the Lawrence House through a side door. Clapping his hat on his head to hide his springy hair, he glanced left and right down Lawrence Avenue in the failing light. No one was in sight, but now that he was outside, he could hear voices a few blocks to the north. Yelps assaulted his ears, but he could make out no words, so he began to sprint up Fourth Street in the direction of the noise.

Soldiers milled about on the curbs and lawns of the houses. He waved at one who was close to him, a khaki-uniformed fellow leaning on a white picket fence in the fading light. "They're gathering again, that mob, like last night. Come with me and I'll show you where they are." But the man's eyes glazed over and turned his head and began talking with the other soldiers who were lolling on the steps of the white house. Elliott, feeling spurned and ignored, resumed his hurried flight down Fourth Street.

As he ran toward the voices, he thought of Sheba, slim and somehow full of silent strength, crouched in the cellar of the Lawrence House, listening for shouts and gunfire. He slowed as he remembered Thomas, with his burly arms and narrow eyes, watching Sheba from the cellar doorway. But he couldn't worry about Thomas now. As he approached downtown, he spied the assembling crowd, rough laborers and working class men, outside Payne's Hardware. The men were already making their way down Adams Street. He drew up short, a block shy of the steadily growing mass and looked around for signs of National Guardsmen. They would surely move to break up the mob, and Elliott knew that Governor Deneen had ordered more than fourteen hundred troops from all over Illinois to come guard the city after the chaos of the previous night.

Curious as to the crowd's destination, Elliott slipped closer, although he was loathe to join the mob. "Let's finish what we began last night," one swarthy miner urged as he and his compatriots moved, almost at a march, behind a slight young boy waving, of all things, an American flag.

Shaking his head in disgust, Elliott hurried down the wide, clean streets of downtown Springfield. The mob was moving in a deliberate fashion toward the State Arsenal, a massive, turreted stone building. As the crowd rounded the corner and headed south toward the Arsenal, it slowed and Elliott, a few steps to the rear, saw the reason why. Bristling all along the gray walls of the Arsenal and five deep at its central doors were the spikes of bayonets, held high by militia men. Rifles were ready to stop any rioter who dared try to breach the line of khaki.

He knew from the morning's paper that more than three hundred colored men, women and children huddled within the Arsenal's thick walls. Three hundred souls burnt and beaten out of their homes the night before.

Elliott himself had written the short item near the bottom of the *Register's* front page that very day. "To Care for the Homeless" read the headline. The article continued, "Plans were made by Governor Deneen for caring for the negroes of the city whose homes were destroyed. The State Arsenal has been designated as a haven for those negroes who desire to use it as a refuge. Tents will also be available at Camp Lincoln for colored people who have been driven from their homes. Armed military guards will assure the safety of colored individuals and families who come to these locations."

Armed guards indeed. Undeterred, the mob surged onto the lines of militia and the soldiers retaliated by charging, rifles pointed and bayonets waving. As he stood watching near the Episcopal Church, Elliott saw the panic on the faces of the rioters who had turned to run shouting away from the Arsenal.

He stopped and slipped behind a tree. While some of the rioters dispersed to the north, a small crowd had reformed south of the Arsenal and was winding its way across the manicured green lawns bordering the domed State Capitol. Dashing down the hill through the thinning ranks of the retreating rioters, Elliott followed the group across the Capitol grounds, keeping a distance of several hundred feet. He had been worried that someone in the crowd might recognize him as Harry Loper's son, but this fear was soon allayed. The crowd was bent on one purpose and was advancing, almost marching, single-mindedly toward it. "Let's get Donnegan," cried one man. "Yeah, we'll get that nigger," responded the mob.

Elliott waited while the mob made its way down Spring Street towards Donnegan's house. An interracial relationship, a mixed marriage – these were anathema in Springfield. Maybe everywhere, but he wasn't sure, having never traveled further than Chicago in his twenty-six years on earth. Here though, interracial couples were simply not "seen." Even his father, the estimable Harry, who had raised Elliott and his sisters to be open-minded adults—even he would not forgive Elliott for loving a colored woman.

Realization dawned on him like a rush of heat in the night and Elliott stood still in the shadows. Sheba—he loved her. He had discovered the name for the feelings he had in her presence and apart from her. Her bravery, her sweetness, her beauty, they provoked a feeling he could not name, until now, as he followed the rioters through Springfield. Sheba, who hid in the cellar of the house, not more than four blocks away. He loved her.

Shouts from the crowd drew his attention as the mob stopped in the center of Spring Street and began to circle the white, two-story house that belonged to

Will Donnegan. The sight of the schoolyard of Edwards School, swings hanging limp in the summer twilight, made Elliott uneasy. His palms were damp and he realized his notebook was wet with sweat. Raising his hand, Elliott could see the evenly curling blue letters imprinted on his palm. "Donneg" he could make out, backwards on the center of his right hand.

A large man wielding a hoe emerged from the front of the crowd and, urged on by friends, climbed the steps to the porch. At the same time a middle-aged white woman appeared at the front door. "Come on Abe, get the nigger out here," someone in the crowd yelled. The man towered over the tiny woman who stood at the door. "Are they white folks or niggers here?" he demanded.

"There are none but white folks here," the woman spoke with a trace of an accent and stared straight into his eyes. For a moment, no one said a word, then the silence was broken.

"There he is, back of that curtain," a man shouted. Elliott looked just in time to see a front curtain fall across the window. The crowd surged forward past the powerless woman and into the front room of the house. A few minutes later, two men emerged bearing an old black man between them. Though he had never met Will Donnegan, Elliott knew instinctively that this was the man Sheba spoke of with respect, the man who had brought many slaves north to jobs in Springfield. Without warning, a young man in overalls slammed a brick down on the old man's skull, and he crumpled like a sand castle stepped on by a malevolent child.

Elliott slipped behind the fence as he watched the crowd drag Donnegan across the street towards the schoolyard. "A tree. A nice strong tree," chanted two or three men in the crowd as another whirled a rope like a lariat. Elliott could see that they would stop short at nothing but lynching and he was gripped with a need to do something. He expected the militia or the police to appear. Surely someone would come, they could not all be guarding the Arsenal.

"Hang 'im up! Hang 'im up." A chant rose from the end of the yard, and he gasped, almost choking in horror as the white-haired figure was hung from a sapling maple, legs dragging on the ground.

Rushing forward, Elliott cried, "Cut him down! Now, I say!" The man closest to the tree was attempting to hoist Donnegan higher off the ground by means of what appeared to be a clothesline around his neck. Blood gushed from the old man's neck and his head flopped back as the rope jerked his body. They'd slashed his throat to make quite sure he died. His white shirt and black pants dripped with the thick blood. The sight diverted Elliott's attention too long. As he stared, he felt an axe handle come down on his shoulder. "Ugh," he cried involuntarily, then turned to see what manner of person had attacked him in such a cowardly fashion.

A dishwater-blonde, heavy-set woman with a flushed face and hate in her eyes swung at Elliott a second time. Elliott ducked, but not before he saw that the woman carried a curiously familiar-looking gun in her other hand, a pearl handled revolver with the initials "KH" scratched above the "Colt" insignia.

Kate Howard. She pointed the gun at his chest. "You gonna' die, you no-count nigger lover," she spat. Elliott stared at her, a question on his lips. She fired.

The impact of the lead bullet entering his body at such close range knocked Elliott off his feet, then pain tore through his shoulder and he fell into the dirt of the schoolyard. "Atta' girl, Kate. Get that no good pond scum," he heard as Kate Howard's heavy shoe plowed into his stomach. "You're dirt," her coarse voice muttered and a slimy glob of spittle hit on Elliott's forehead as he lost consciousness.

Mrs. Dana

The high-pitched voice of Mrs. Dana woke Sheba who was curled on a mat in the Lawrence House cellar. "Appalled, I must say, and astonished. How could this happen?" Mrs. Dana was saying. Sheba stretched her neck from its cramped position. By the thin light of the window she could see that Ruby was still sound asleep, her arms wrapped tight around James who lay next to her with his thumb in his mouth. Thomas was nowhere to be seen.

Sheba jostled Ruby, who opened her eyes and gazed up at her. "You hear that? Sound like Miz Dana be home."

Ruby rubbed her eyes. "You go'n up," she whispered, motioning to the children who were still asleep.

Sheba smoothed her dress and patted her hair into place, then tiptoed up the stairs so as not to disturb the sleepers. She paused before opening the door. She could hear no noise from the outside and only muffled voices in the kitchen. She wondered if the riot was over or just interrupted by daylight, only to resume this evening. She didn't know how much longer they could cower in this cellar, away from the light and freedom of their individual lives. Then she thought of Elliott Loper, striding into the thick of the riot to protect Will Donnegan, and she said a prayer for his safety. She opened the door and sunlight spilled down the stairs.

Mrs. Dana, oblivious to the sleeping family below, called out. "Sheba, please come up. There's absolutely no danger." Mrs. Dana sounded calm, almost serene. Sheba entered the kitchen and saw her former mistress, resplendent in an oversized feathered hat, a high-collared white blouse fastened with her favorite brooch, a cameo of her father's head surrounded by tiny diamonds. "Hattie said you were here. I must admit I'm a bit surprised to see you, though of course you're welcome here," she spoke, radiating goodwill.

Sheba smiled with gratitude. Mrs. Dana loved the opportunity to be generous. "I 'preciate the kindness, ma'am. It been pret' near crazy 'round here what with mobs and hangin's and fires…" she trailed off, then glanced over her shoulder as she heard muffled voices in the cellar.

Mrs. Dana had also heard the noises. "Who else is down there, Sheba? Hattie didn't mention anyone." She got her answer as Tilda came running up the steps two at a time, pigtails flying. When the girl saw Mrs. Dana, she stopped. Just then, Miss Flora, garbed in an elaborate ruffled traveling outfit of purple silk, entered the kitchen through the swinging door from the butler's pantry.

Miss Flora gaped at the refugees in the kitchen as the rest of the Burtons' faces appeared in back of Tilda. "Land sakes, Susan, we're just overrun by these Negroes. We'd better get them out of here quickly or this house will be ransacked, sure as I'm standing here," Miss Flora exclaimed.

Mrs. Dana whirled to face her cousin. "Why Flora, I'm surprised at you. Of course, we'll do no such thing. This family is seeking refuge from this…this insanity. A man was lynched last night, just a few blocks away from here, at Edwards School," she said, shaking her head with disgust. The heavy clomp of soldiers' boots down Fourth Street was the only sound in the silent room.

Sheba felt the blood drain from her head and she grasped a chair for support. "Oh Miz Dana, who was that fella, that one was lynched last night?"

Mrs. Dana turned to her in surprise. "Donovan. Donnegan. Something like that. An old colored man. He's in St. John's Hospital now, but they don't expect him to pull through."

The room began to spin, but Sheba focused on the bleary figures of Mrs. Dana and her cousin.

Out of nowhere, Ruby Burton spoke up. "Will Donnegan. He old, never did nobody no harm. I kin't fi'gre why they got 'im," she cried, seeming to forget her own husband's violent end.

In response, Mrs. Dana pulled a newspaper from under her arm and opened it to the front page, then glanced up at Ruby, acknowledging for the first time the stranger in her kitchen. "Well, it says here that this fellow was quite elderly and that he is married to a white woman," she read, then raised her eyebrows and lowered the newspaper. "But I don't believe I've made your acquaintance," she said, addressing Ruby. Her voice trailed off and she looked for help to Sheba.

Sheba started back to life. "Oh this here's Ruby Burton and her chillen. Mr. Elliott Loper brung 'em here and he say he hope you shelter 'em. See Mr. Scott Burton, he their pa and the mob, they done killed him dead, so they got nobody t'care fo' 'em." She watched Mrs. Dana for any softening in the pale blue eyes and was relieved to see her mistress move forward and address Ruby.

"Oh my dear, what you must have suffered. Of course, you and your children may stay here as long as you wish," Mrs. Dana said. The feathers in her hat shook as she reached for the newspaper. "But Sheba, I suppose you don't know – then again, how could you know? That fine young man, Mr. Elliott Loper, why he's been shot. For all we know he is near death at this moment," she announced.

Miss Flora interjected from the corner of the kitchen. "You don't say. Well, it serves him right for traipsing around town during this horrible riot."

Sheba stared at the *Journal* lying open on the kitchen table. Beneath the three-tiered headline telling of Will Donnegan's lynching was a smaller article. "Son of restaurateur Loper shot, Reporter for *Register* critically wounded at

Donnegan Lynching." There was no photo of Elliott, but Sheba had an immediate mental image of him standing in the sunlight in this very room just the day before.

Mrs. Dana turned to her cousin. "Well, since I do know Mr. Loper, I believe it would be a gesture of goodwill to visit him, especially after all his family has been through." Not waiting for Miss Flora's protests or thanks from Sheba, she rustled from the room, to make preparations to depart.

Ruby rounded up her children and seated them at the table, while Hattie, who had just entered the room, started a pot heating on the stove to prepare oatmeal for the brood. Thankful that Mrs. Dana was going to visit Elliott, Sheba continued to ponder the paper, reading it aloud as Ruby and Hattie listened. "Here the headline. 'State Protection Assured,'" she read haltingly. She continued, stumbling over some of the longer words, "Now here what Gov'nor Deneen say, 'It is as intolerable as it is inexcusable. The idea of wreaking vengeance upon a race for the crimes of one of its members is utterly repugnant to all notions of law and justice. No government can maintain its self-respect and permit it. Our state will not permit it. The entire resources of the state will be drawn upon, if necessary to protect every citizen of Springfield in his person and property, and those who violate the law must suffer the consequences.'"

Hattie looked up from the stove. "Them strong words. Now what you s'pose Mr. Gov'nor gonna' do 'bout all this?" she said, shaking her head as she sprinkled oatmeal on the boiling water.

Ruby settled a squirming James in a chair. "They best be strong. My Scott he gone and we ain't safe here." She lowered her voice. "That Miz Dana, she talk wit' her friends an' 'for you know it, she fig're out it ain't smart to be keepin' us. Then we be gone. We best be on that train. Sooner we get t' St. Louie, the better."

Sheba watched as Ruby bustled about, toasting bread and pouring glasses of milk for the children. Ruby had enough of her wits about her today to manage the three-hour train trip. And she was right, it wouldn't be long before the same men who killed Scott discovered his family's whereabouts. From the years of working and living in this house next to the train tracks, Sheba knew when every southbound train passed by. The train paused to pick up passengers at the Lawrence House because of its mistress' social prominence, although it was not a regular station stop. Ruby seemed to guess what she was thinking. "We be ready at quarter past two. We be there," she stated.

Mrs. Dana reentered the kitchen wearing a fresh lilac suit and a small, plush hat. Sheba realized her mistress had taken no rest since she arrived on the early train. Aflame with the importance of the hospital visit and aware that it was grist for the mill of the local newspapers, the queen of Springfield society wanted to look her best. Maud's husband Albert followed, garbed in his customary suspendered trousers and long-sleeved shirt. Though Mrs. Dana was a white woman, the charged atmosphere of the city and the presence of thousands of soldiers made a visit to the hospital alone impossible. Albert would accompany her and drive the rig.

"I will certainly give Mr. Loper your regards, Sheba," said Mrs. Dana as she swept through the room.

Sheba shot a request at her mistress' back. "Oh ma'am, you think you could see how po' ol' Mr. Donnegan's doin'? The paper say here his throat was cut 'fore he was hanged. He's near eighty, and I 'spect he might pass."

Mrs. Dana stopped in her tracks and turned to face Sheba, a slight frown on her fair features. "Well, he'll be in the colored ward you know. I'll just have to see," she answered, then crossed the room and went out the back door, Albert following.

Sheba sat down. "She ain't got no thought o' goin' t' see that ol' man," she sighed.

Hattie moved from the stove to rest a hand on Sheba's shoulder and said, "Now don' fret, ain't nothin' you kin do."

Sheba closed her eyes, blocking out the disturbingly bright rays of sun. Then she realized it was Sunday, a day she usually spent in at the Pleasant Grove Baptist Church, south of the Badlands. She wondered now if her beloved church had escaped destruction, if somehow it might still stand.

Departure

He thought at first that his mother sat by his side. When Elliott opened his eyes, he was confronted with the face of a fair-haired, middle-aged woman hovering near the side of his bed. His mother, bless her, back from Michigan to care for him. Elliott sank his head further into his pillow. Everything would be fine now that Mother was here.

But the voice was wrong, he realized. It wasn't his mother after all. "Mr. Loper, Mr. Loper. Can you hear me?" said the woman. His mother's voice was low and she never raised it, not even in anger. This woman, whoever she was, had a higher-pitched voice and was raising it even now in consternation.

With an effort, Elliott opened his eyes. The hospital room swam into focus, white curtained windows, white walls, and, to the right of the bed, a handsome woman in her mid-forties, well-dressed yet agitated. On the wall above her head hung a crucifix. Now he remembered, he was in St. John's Hospital and he had been shot in the riot the night before. And the woman, she did look vaguely familiar.

"Thank heavens you have returned to consciousness, Mr. Loper. We believed we had lost you," the woman said, pressing his right hand, which lay on the white blanket of the bed, as a black-coiffed nursing nun entered the room.

Elliott sputtered and tried to move, but the pain in his left side forced him back on the pillow. He looked at the woman. He still couldn't place her and couldn't think what brought her here. "Are you a friend of my mother's?" he asked.

A pleased smile brightened her chiseled, almost masculine features. "Don't you remember me? I'm Susan Lawrence Dana. We met while you were paying a call on my maid, Sheba." She lowered her voice. "She's terribly concerned for you, but, well she's colored and couldn't very well come, not under these present circumstances," she added, looking at him with fondness.

Present circumstances. The words brought back the gruesome images from the previous night. Despite the overpowering feeling of weakness and desire for sleep, Elliott forced himself to question Mrs. Dana, who he now remembered meeting sometime, long ago. "Where is Will Donnegan? Is he dead?" he asked.

155

Mrs. Dana looked down at her kid-gloved hands. "He passed away earlier today, I'm told," she said. Elliott closed his eyes. All he could think of was the awful pain coursing up and down his left side. He was flooded with shame because the helpless old man had perished at the hands of the mob, while he, Elliott, had been gunned down by, of all people, a woman.

He forced his eyes open again and saw the kind face of the tiny nun. She murmured, "Yes, it's true. He was near dead when they brought him here last night, after the soldiers broke up the riot." She moved to feel his forehead, while Mrs. Dana fanned herself with a religious tract entitled "Jesus Saves."

The nun applied a cool rag to his forehead. "You're feverish. Those soldiers brought you here and nobody expected you to live. Not and take a bullet like that at close range." She dabbed at his forehead. It didn't help ease the pain, but at least Elliott felt cared for.

So that was why it was so hard to catch his breath. That and the fact that he had been kicked in the gut by the woman who shot him, he did remember that. "Did they catch her, the woman who shot me?" he asked, looking up at the nun.

She answered, "Oh yes, they got her all right. Kate Howard. She's in the county jail." She lowered her voice and looked at Elliott. "And I say she can rot there."

Mrs. Dana started and shot a look of horror at the nun, but the little woman stared straight at Elliott. As her dark eyes bored into him, the room began to swim again and he turned his head. Blonde and aloof, Mrs. Dana gazed at him. She looked like a statue of an angel atop a headstone.

As his eyes drifted shut, he heard Mrs. Dana, and was somehow soothed by her cool hand on his arm, her gentle voice filling his thoughts. "There, there, you did what you could. No one blames you for anything that happened. You are a wonderful, brave man," she said, her gentle voice fading.

Then, faintly, he could hear a man's voice. He wondered when the man had come into the room and why he was reciting what sounded like some kind of chant. "God the Father of Mercies through the death and resurrection of his Son," the man's voice droned. I wonder what will happen now, Elliott thought.

"Don' tell me you been out. Don' you tell me that," Sheba exclaimed as she stepped through the door of the carriage house just as Thomas, dressed in a pinstriped suit, came in from the alley.

"Well, I don' see it no concern to you Miz Fine Lady," he said mockingly, then pulled off his hat.

Sheba, threw up her hands in exasperation and shot back, "It only be the wors' day of the year fo' a colored man be out by hisself. A fella could get strung up, like poor Scott Burton. What you thinkin'?"

Thomas walked up to her and smiled. "You sure are pretty when you're mad, Sheba," he said, putting his hands on her shoulders and pushing her down on a hay bale. "All them crazy rioters, they ain't 'round. Just regular folks today – it Sunday."

Sheba looked up at his strong chin, his close-cut hair, and easy smile. She was relieved that he was safe. The alleyway door to the carriage house next to the railroad tracks began to rattle and Sheba heard a familiar woman's voice. "Let a po' soul in, mercy on us," she whimpered and pounded on the door. Sheba pushed the locking bar back, swung open the door, standing face-to-face with her mother, Mae, who was carrying a satchel, a red hat far back on her head.

"Mama, what you doin' here?" she cried and flung her arms around Mae, who burst into tears.

Mae staggered in and cried, "Oh sweetie, I so glad you safe. I heard you got a shop Downtown and then, after that riotin' 'n all, I so scared fo' you."

Sheba was still shocked to see Mae. It had not crossed her mind that her mother wasn't safely holed up at the Governor's Mansion. "Mama, I 'spect you be safe with the Gov'nor," she said, a question in her voice.

Mae dropped her trunk and looked at her through large eyes that were beginning to well with tears. "They done put me out, took away my job and told me to git," she said, nodding for emphasis.

Sheba was confused. "How come you got put out like that? Why Miz Deneen, she so kind." She put her arm around Mae's shoulders, which were shaking as she sobbed.

Mae looked up at her through tears. "It weren't Miz Deneen what fired me. It was that bad ol' governess, that Miss Fanny. She say I stole baby clothes."

Sheba shook her head, as if to clear it. This just wasn't making sense. She grasped Mae by the shoulders and turned her to face her. "But you never took 'em, did you?"

Mae stopped crying and silently regarded Sheba. "Child, you hurtin' me. I never snitched nothin', but that don' matter 'gainst a white woman's word." She looked down at her hands, clad in fingerless, dirty white gloves, then glanced up at Thomas, who was staring at her. "Why, what you doin' here? I know you sweet on my girl Sheba, but I heard you left, up and quit, and was workin' at the ice house. Fact is, I seen you cartin' ice just last week up our alley," she said, knowingly.

Thomas leaned against the wall. "Yes'm, I done work for the ice house for a spell, but this here's bad riotin', it kinda swayed me to come back here to the Lawrence House, to keep safe I reckon," he explained.

Sheba's mind was running full tilt. "Mama, what you gonna' do now? You got no job. And I don't guess you can stay here."

Ruby and her three children chose this moment to parade through the door from the enclosed garden. Garbed in clean clothes, they looked almost presentable as Ruby led them toward Sheba. "It 'most two o'clock. Train to St. Louie be by here anytime. We ready, mor'en ready," she said. Tilda and Roscoe fidgeted in anticipation and James took off, running so quickly his brown

157

knickers were a blur on his chubby legs. "We goin' t' St. Louie on the train," he chanted, waving his arms in delight.

Sheba she whirled to face Mae, still collapsed on the bale of hay. "Mama, Ruby and her chillen be goin' St. Louie and that be the best place for you too. Why there ain't nothin' fo' you here, and Ruby be needin' some help with those chillens," she said, hardly aware of the words coming from her. But the truth was that her mother would be better off away from Springfield and the Levee, with Ruby, who could put her on a better path.

Her mother's face creased with resignation and Sheba realized she was too tired and defeated to protest. "Oh Sheba, I ain't never been to St. Louie, but if you and Ruby think I be a help..." she sighed.

Ruby spoke up. "I'm right beholdin' to you if you come. 'Member long time go, all us'n went t' church t'gether? You a fine friend an' I do b'live we get a new start t'gether." She knelt in front of Mae, and a faint smile lightened her narrow face. "You come 'n stay with aunt Jane. We both be startin' fresh, you and me," she said.

Mae stared at Ruby, then looked at Sheba, who nodded. She gathered her belongings and pulled herself up from the bale. A train whistle pierced the air and Sheba jumped to her feet. The children trampled after Ruby toward the back door of the carriage house. Behind them, Mae followed, carrying her satchel in both arms. The little group rushed into the alley and watched as the train crawled down the grimy tracks toward them. Sheba raised her arm and waved, signaling the engineer to stop for passengers. She glanced back at the carriage house to see Thomas in the doorway, keeping guard, watching the alley for signs of menacing rioters.

The engine rolled past, then the train ground to a halt and the conductor beckoned to the little group. "All aboard," he called. The children mounted the steps and Sheba could see dark faces pressed against the windows of the passenger car, watching as she handed Ruby coins for her fare. Mae was the last one up the steps. As she brushed by Sheba, she whispered, "Be careful girl. This ain't no kinda' town for us." And then she disappeared into the sea of faces along with Ruby's little family. The train creaked to a start again, chugging away from the town torn with strife, south to St. Louis.

Return

Miss Flora was munching her dry toast at the dining room table as Mrs. Dana entered the room, brandishing a newspaper. "What did you see at the hospital?" Miss Flora asked, looking up. Sheba paused from pouring tea to listen to Mrs. Dana's response.

Mrs. Dana took her time, seating herself and spreading the paper out on the table, then running her finger down the page. Miss Flora cleared her throat and Mrs. Dana looked up at her, then caught Sheba's look. She leaned back in her chair. "Well, I must say that there is some very bad news, bad news indeed."

Sheba knew it was inappropriate for her to speak, but she had to know. "What happened? Is they dead?" she cried, then bit her tongue for speaking.

Mrs. Dana smiled and shook her head, as if Sheba was a child. "Do calm down, Sheba. Yes, unfortunately, Will Donnegan is dead, in fact, he was killed by the mob in a rather gruesome fashion. They cut his throat and then tried to hang him, though I daresay it was the loss of blood that did him in, poor old soul."

Although deep inside she had known he was dead, the news of Donnegan's death stunned Sheba. She couldn't believe they had killed that harmless old man. Almost to herself, she muttered, "Why folks used t'say 't took all day just for him t' walk downtown." But then she remembered the other man whose life was in danger, a man who was beginning to mean more to her than old Mr. Donnegan. "What 'bout Mr. Loper?" she asked, then, stopped, afraid to say more, afraid of what the answer might be.

A faint smile crossed Mrs. Dana's face, like a cloud on a waveless lake, then she began to speak. "He was just holding onto life a few hours ago. We thought we'd lost him about noon. Why I was sitting at his bedside and they called a priest to say the last rites or some such Catholic nonsense. I do believe he stopped breathing. But something brought him back. I leaned over his poor face and said 'Mr. Loper. Mr. Loper. Are you all right?' And after a minute he opened up his eyes – he does have wonderful blue eyes – and said 'Oh sure, I guess.' And then, of course, I knew he was better and the doctor came in and said they were going to do an operation to take out the bullet and I had to leave." She tossed her head with evident pleasure at imparting such pleasant information.

Sheba stood still, aware that Miss Flora was staring at her. "I much 'bliged t'you for this news. It real sad that Mr. Donnegan's gone, but I do 'preciate that Mr. Loper is all right," she said, making a move to leave, then deciding to risk one last question. "He is all right, ain't he?" Her voice quivered with uncertainty.

Mrs. Dana had completed her pronouncement and was now eager to be on to the next item on her busy agenda. She spoke dismissively. "Yes, yes. I inquired after him before I left the hospital. He's recovering nicely. Of course, he won't be back on his beat any time soon, but I daresay there are plenty of reporters who can fill his shoes." Mrs. Dana sat down and waved at Sheba, then ordered, "Now please bring me some tea." She looked up as Sheba stood, motionless. "I assume you're staying and taking back your old job. Thomas too, of course. So please." She resumed reading her newspaper. Without a word, Sheba turned and went through the swinging door.

The kitchen seemed to be filled by the large, dark figure of Pastor Ball. The preacher was engrossed in conversation with Thomas, but he turned to face Sheba as she entered.

A smile lit up Pastor Ball's face, but Thomas spoke first. "Hey Sheba, wait'll you hear. The church, the Pleasant Grove Baptist Church, well it be safe. Yessir, church folks took turns guardin' it so's it wouldn't get burnt down. And it didn't."

Pastor Ball smiled, showing his generous white teeth. "It still standin' my chil', and good thing too, cause this here young man done got hisself baptized today, right there in that church," he said, beside himself with pride.

Thoughts of Elliott were still crowding her brain. Pastor Ball's voiced sounded faint and faraway. But she realized the men expected a reaction to this news. "Baptized? That true Thomas?" she asked.

Thomas regarded Sheba. "I think you got somethin' wrong wit' you, you don' b'lieve it," he said, planting his feet in the center of the yellow pine floor.

As if a brick had been slammed on her fingers, Sheba came abruptly back to life. Thomas regarded her while Pastor Ball backed away, coughing under his breath. It was almost too much to absorb, yet here the men were, waiting for her to acknowledge this huge commitment Thomas had made. She sputtered, "Why I guess that's pretty wonderful, I jus' had so much happen t'me I cain't quite b'lieve it." Somewhere in the back of her mind, she realized what a good decision this had been for Thomas, though she was unsure why he made it now. But she did approve, she more than approved.

Thomas nodded. "See I been watchin' you, Sheba. I seen how you be, how you pray and ask for help. And sometimes things, they don't go so good for you, like when your shop got ruined. But they's somethin' you got, somethin' strong that won't give up that keeps you goin'. That's what I want. That's why I got baptized," he said in a low voice.

Sheba looked up at him, but Thomas, seemingly uncomfortable with so much soul-baring, especially in front of a preacher, spoke to lighten the mood. He turned to Pastor Ball and said, "You did some fine preachin' today, but the congregation was pretty slim."

Pastor Ball laughed. "Well, some folks they left town. Those rioters got to 'em and they left. They won't be back. But we got some folks still here, folks that didn't get their homes burnt or run out of town on rail. They're scared, but they still come to church. And God bless 'em, it's a mighty powerful congregation we got left. Mighty powerful," he boomed, then turned to depart out the back door. "We're glad you came here, Sheba, but the riot's over now. It's safe again -- you can read it in the papers," he said reassuringly, and was gone.

As the pastor left, a "brrinng" sounded in Sheba's ears. The bell rang, summoning her to the dining room. The teakettle was just beginning its whistle and Thomas helped her prepare a tray with tea cups and toast for Mrs. Dana, talking as he helped. "You won' have to carry trays for white ladies much longer. I'll take care of you," he pronounced. Their eyes met over the tea tray and Thomas reached out to grasp Sheba's long fingers. She inhaled sharply as he touched her, feeling a kind of electricity coursing through her. He smiled, his lips parting over white teeth. His dark eyes glistened. "We'll go to St. Louis and start proper, jus' you'n'me. Let's get married," he said quickly, as the bell rang again, and Sheba pulled her hand away.

This was too sudden, and came too quickly on the heels of the news about Elliott. Sheba loaded the tray and tried to put him off. "You movin' too fast for me. I cain't think. There too much goin' on now." She turned and saw that Thomas' face bore a look of serenity. Perhaps the baptism had been prompted by a real change of heart. He continued as she headed for the dining room. "Jus' think 'bout it, all right? I be leavin' on the noon train tomorrow. If you're there too, you kin come wit me," he said, as she passed through the swinging door into the light of the dining room.

Shaking, she began unloading the tea dishes while Mrs. Dana, oblivious to her emotional state, read aloud from the newspaper to her cousin. Reading glasses perched on her nose, Mrs. Dana bent her blonde head studiously over the newspaper. "Listen to what the pastor of First Pres said in his sermon today. What courage he has. 'The so-called good citizens who stood around while the mob lynched the Negroes must bear their share of the blame.'"

Miss Flora snorted. "Well, what were they supposed to do? Help 'em?"

Mrs. Dana took off her glasses and stared at her cousin. Ignoring the now predictable remarks of Miss Flora, Sheba tried to serve her mistress tea, craning her neck to see the newspaper. A headline was emblazoned across the top of the front page: "Vigorously Denounce Mob Violence in City –Church Service was Abandoned Last Night to Promote Peace."

Mrs. Dana protested, "Flora, we cannot condone this violence, despite your personal feelings. I won't have you speaking this way, especially in front of Sheba."

161

Sheba stopped pouring tea. Mrs. Dana looked at her, and she felt afraid and oddly proud of her mistress' attention. "We have done you and your people a grievous, horrible wrong. And in the shadow of our greatest president, Mr. Lincoln. I only hope you can forgive us." Her mistress spoke to her, not as a subordinate, but as a human being.

She was tempted to salve her mistress' guilt, but images from the preceding days stopped her. She remembered the flight through the dark streets, the horror of Scott Burton's death, the line of soldiers patrolling Fourth Street, Ruby's family huddled in the dark cellar, the sky reddening slowly as the Badlands burned.

After a long silence, Mrs. Dana bowed her head and began reading aloud again. "No community is ever justified in taking the laws into its own hands. No crime, however horrible, can justify another crime. It cannot justify the destruction of property of a citizen who merely did the duty assigned to him by the sheriff when deputized for that purpose." She paused, then glanced at Flora. "That was a quote from Harry Loper, you know." She continued reading. "It certainly cannot justify riot, arson and the murder of innocent citizens, either white or colored. There are no innocent spectators of mob violence."

For a moment, Elliott had the illusion that he could see through his eyelids. They felt impossibly heavy, and whatever was on the other side was so bright, it made them seem pink and translucent. He felt light and wondered if this might be heaven. Opening his eyes, he half expected to see the chiseled features of Mrs. Dana, the marble guardian angel stationed next to his bed. But instead he saw a middle-aged, grey-haired man, handsome despite the lines of care on his face. The man was napping, his head propped against the white wall of the sunlit hospital room. Elliott moved his right arm to touch the man's knee and achieved the effect he wanted: the man opened his grey eyes and leaned forward. "Elliott, my boy, you're awake," his father said.

Despite his grogginess, tears started to Elliott's eyes. He had never been so relieved to see someone. "Dad. You're here. I must be pretty bad, I guess," he gasped. Harry Loper reached to cautiously embrace his son, who tried, unsuccessfully, to return his embrace.

"You scared us good, real good," Harry Loper said, seemingly unable to take his eyes from his only son. "Your ma and me, when we got the news that you'd been shot in this craziness, well, it seemed the last straw," he added then paused and gazed out the window. Elliott looked too and saw sun shining down on the streets of Springfield. The hospital was north of the business district, but from this room on the third floor, signs of destruction were clearly visible, even from a distance. Timbers from charred buildings pierced the clear blue sky.

Harry looked back at Elliott and said, "I came as quick as I could, after they telegraphed us. They said Kate Howard had shot you at close range, course I guess they haven't properly proved that yet, but that hag is in jail, where she belongs. And now, you got that bullet out of you, you're on the mend."

The door opened and the nun came into the room. Harry asked her, "What's the prognosis on this fellow? When can we get him out of here?"

She bowed her coiffed head and murmured, "Oh that is for Doctor Payne to say, but this young man, he is doing well. You may be able to take him home in a couple days." She tucked in the sheets around Elliott's arms, which he immediately threw off.

He was restless, eager to see what kind of damage the mob had wrought. "Why can't I go sooner, now that my dad's here? Say, I imagine the *Register* called and is needin' me back. Why there's plenty of news and, well, I do have a first-hand account."

Harry sat down in the chair, watching the nun moving about the room. "I wouldn't be in too big a hurry to go back there, Elliott. Sure the riot's over and the Governor's pushing the State's Attorney to call a special grand jury to prosecute all those rioters. But just look what they did to us, to our family, to our business, to you."

An image flashed through Elliott's mind, an image that would stay with him until he died: his father's new car being turned on its top and set aflame, the fire reflected in the shiny metal. Then another image came to him: the bulky figure of Kate Howard hurling a brick through the plate glass window, puncturing the ordered elegance of the Loper's Restaurant dining room.

"Don't get me wrong. Springfield's a fine city and I intend to hang on, to keep on doing what I can do, and that's running successful businesses. But you son, I don't think you should stay here. After all, you were almost killed." He sighed, then pulled a newspaper from his pocket and unrolled it for Elliott, who saw it was the August 14 edition of the suburban newspaper, the *Oak Park Leaves.*

"Soon's you're able, I want you to think about going to work on this paper. My sister can pave the way—she lives there you know."

He didn't seem to expect a response, and Elliott acknowledged to himself that indeed, the excitement and possibility of a big city intrigued him. But he couldn't leave Springfield, give up on his birthplace, abandon the city Lincoln called his home for so many years. And he couldn't face the thought of never seeing Sheba again.

He wasn't ready to tell his father though. "What's in the news, Dad? Has Springfield even made the Chicago papers?"

Without taking his eyes from the newspaper, Harry nodded. "Yessir, we're famous, but for all the wrong reasons. That crazy young poet Lindsay's got himself all worked up and spoke at the 'Y' last night on the topic of race." He put down the paper and stared out the window at the setting sun. "You know, I used to believe in giving every man a fair chance, but lately, well, I don't know for sure. People are bad, Elliott, and they'll act their worst if they can. And this town's got more than its share of bad ones," he said.

Hearing his father sound so cynical rallied Elliott. He felt strength beginning to ebb back into his weary body. He protested, "I don't believe it, Dad. People are good, it's just that bad element that got out of hand. There's plenty of good folks here, always have been. Just think, this is the city that spawned 'Honest Abe'." And he felt his mouth form a smile, which resulted in some pain along his jaw, but not nearly as much as he would have guessed. Encouraged, he smiled again. "You know, Dad, there's plenty of good colored folks who just want a chance and I want to give it to them. If I leave town, there's gonna be one less white person to stand up for what's right," he said, realizing that this was only part of the reason he wanted to stay.

Harry leaned over his son in consternation. "Now see here, son, where do you think most of the colored folks in Springfield are? I'll give you a hint, they're gone. They left town on trains and on foot, however they could, after the mob burnt their homes and tried to lynch 'em. And the ones that are here, they're hidin' out, hidin' in their houses and in their churches and in white folks' cellars."

Elliott left off his painful smiling. He had to get his father to understand what he felt, what he knew to be true. "It won't be forever Dad, just until its safe. You mark my words, Springfield'll be a great place for colored folks soon enough. Why this riot's just a warning, a sign to get good folks out makin' things right. And that's what I'm gonna' do."

His father leaned back in his chair as the nun began tucking in Elliott's sheets around him again. "Well, Mr. Loper, how's this young man doing?" she asked.

Harry lowered his voice and Elliott closed his eyes, but listened intently. "He's not makin' much sense, I'm afraid. Could be he's a little 'off' still. Maybe he needs some rest." His father and the nun consulted in the corner of the room away from Elliott's bed. A couple of times, the nun looked toward him and Elliott heard snatches of conversation. "Yes you can have him moved to Chicago on the train in a week maybe. When he's stronger, but I don't see why." The rest of the conversation was lost.

The surge of energy he had experienced earlier was only a memory and now his eyelids felt heavy, though he tried to open them to see his father's concerned face. His father refused to give up the idea that he would leave, and said again, "Elliott, promise me you'll think about Chicago."

It was too much trouble to argue with his father. "I'll think about it Dad, I will. Thanks for coming." Elliott closed his eyes against the setting sun and began to dream of Sheba.

August 20, 1908

The man and woman were walking in the Badlands, in the rubble of the tiny houses colored people once called homes. The man was dressed in black and walked slowly, kicking at the burnt grass, while his wife, a small, dark-haired woman wearing a scarf knotted around her head, leaned on his arm. Both were silent.

The couple had come from Will Donnegan's home, where they talked with Mrs. Donnegan about the events leading up to the Negro's murder the previous week. Sarah Donnegan had barely been able to speak to the couple, and finally they gave up. They walked across the street to Edwards School and into the schoolyard, where a child was swinging. The small tree at the center of the schoolyard was dying – it had been completely stripped of its bark. "They took bark for souvenirs," the child had said, without stopping her swinging.

The man was William English Walling, a socialist writer. He and his wife, Anna Strunsky, had come to Springfield from New York City. They were appalled as the nation was appalled by a race riot within eyeshot of Abraham Lincoln's home.

"Look William. We are not alone." Anna and her husband stopped walking. Across the street was another couple, a slender colored woman and a young man with curly blonde hair. The man halted every few steps, as though he was winded and when he stopped, the woman stopped as well. They moved in unison down the street, toward a church that stood intact on the corner.

William waved his hand in the air and the man turned, with some effort. "Hello, can you spare a minute for two strangers?" William called. The couple stopped and waited while William and Anna caught up.

"What you want?" the colored woman spoke, eying them suspiciously.

William started to explain. "I'm writing an article for a magazine on this race riot. If you witnessed it, I'd be interested to hear what you have to say."

The blonde man shot a piercing look at the writer. "What do you want to know? Can't you see what the result is?"

"Yes, yes, I see the damage. But what caused all this?" William pressed.

The colored woman spoke first. "Caused it? Why licker, fo' sho. You cain't even count all the saloons this here town has. I done hear a bunch 'o them

165

asked that fine Rev'rnd Sunday t'come 'n preach 'gainst the licker. But I don' see's that make any diff'rence."

The blonde man addressed the writer. "Well, I can tell you what I think caused the riot. I think it was human nature, plain and simple, that made those rioters do the things they did."

William tapped his pencil on his pad and Anna stared at the man. "What do you mean 'human nature'? Surely you don't believe it's human nature to destroy homes and lynch people," he protested.

The blonde man nodded emphatically. "Yes, I do and I think the same folks that did this will do it again. They want Negroes to leave town, to be gone for good, and the riot was a way to scare them out. And it worked too. No telling how many colored folks left town." He pondered his hands for a minute, then looked up. "They think that if Springfield is white, that will solve all their problems, that everyone will have well-paying jobs, that there will be no unhappiness," he said, then grimaced and took the woman's hand. "But of course it's not true. Negroes aren't the source of their problems, they're just a scapegoat," he said as they rose to go.

"So why have you stayed?" Anna spoke finally, stepping up abruptly from behind the writer. "What keeps you here?"

The blonde man looked at the colored woman, whose oval face remained impassive. He smiled. "Each other, I guess. We keep each other here."

The colored woman squeezed the man's hand and did not let go. For a moment, no one spoke, then she broke the silence. "We better go, Elliott. Pastor Ball's waitin'." Together, the couple advanced toward the church, hand in hand, through the ruins of the Badlands.

Walling and his wife returned to New York City the next day and later that month an article titled "The Race War in the North" was published in the magazine, **The Independent***. In the article, Walling concluded that it was race hatred had provoked the race riot in Springfield. After reading Walling's article, social worker Mary White Ovington urged Walling to call a meeting of likeminded individuals to discuss forming a biracial organization to correct the injustices suffered by blacks. The meeting occurred in January, 1909 in New York and led to the formation of the National Association for the Advancement of Colored People (NAACP) that year.*

About the Author

Born in Iowa, Melinda McDonald was a roving reporter and photographer for three small Iowa newspapers before starting a career in business communications. She managed publications and wrote for a variety of organizations including an insurance company, a community college and an association for funeral home directors, while keeping her hand in journalism by writing freelance articles. Since 1997, she has managed marketing communications for a beverage equipment manufacturer in Springfield, Illinois.

She has published devotionals for the book *Women at the Well,* Volume II, Judson Press (2003). Besides writing, she is fascinated with all things (Frank Lloyd) Wright. She has served as volunteer tour guide at the Dana-Thomas House in Springfield and is editor of the *Volunteer Voice,* a monthly newsletter for volunteers at the house.

Melinda lives in Rochester, Illinois with her husband, Ron. They have two grown daughters and a macaw.

981091

Made in the USA